# SATURDAY NIGHT AND SUNDAY MORNING

## THE 2001 BRADFORD RIOT AND BEYOND

JANET BUJRA AND JENNY PEARCE

# About the Authors

**Dr Janet Bujra** and **Professor Jenny Pearce** are social scientists who bring a global perspective to investigation of urban conflicts in Britain. Janet Bujra is an Honorary Reader in the Department of Peace Studies at the University of Bradford and has extensive research experience and publications on Africa. Jenny Pearce is a Professor of Latin American Politics in the Department of Peace Studies at Bradford University. She has conducted research and published widely on Latin America.

Both authors were amongst the founder members of the Programme for a Peaceful City at the University of Bradford, and have been actively engaged in the city for at least two decades. Professor Pearce is the Director and Dr Bujra is a Senior Research Associate of the International Centre for Participation Studies at the University of Bradford.

# SATURDAY NIGHT AND SUNDAY MORNING

## THE 2001 BRADFORD RIOT AND BEYOND

JANET BUJRA AND JENNY PEARCE

**VERTICAL EDITIONS**
www.verticaleditions.com

Copyright © Janet Bujra and Jenny Pearce 2011

The right of Janet Bujra and Jenny Pearce to be identified as the authors of this work has been asserted in accordance with the Copyright, Designs and Patents Act, 1988

All rights reserved. The reproduction and utilisation of this book in any form or by any electrical, mechanical or other means, now known or hereafter invented, including photocopying and recording, and in any information storage and retrieval system, is forbidden without the written permission of the publisher

First published in the United Kingdom in 2011 by Vertical Editions, Unit 4a, Snaygill Industrial Estate, Skipton, North Yorkshire BD23 2QR

www.verticaleditions.com

ISBN 978–1–904091–49–3

A CIP catalogue record for this book is available from the British Library

Cover design by HBA, York

Printed and bound by MPG Books Limited, Bodmin

# CONTENTS

Introduction ................................................................. 7

1 Reporting the Riot .................................................. 16

2 Making Sense: The Rioters Speak ........................... 29

3 Under Fire: Police Perspectives on the Riot ............ 58

4 Limits to Peacemaking .......................................... 81

5 Why Bradford? Life and Livelihoods ...................... 99

6 Why Bradford? Politics and Activism ..................... 127

7 The Aftermath ...................................................... 150

8 'The Drums Started Beating'—the EDL Comes to Bradford .... 183

9 Conclusion: Bradford Journey ................................ 202

References .............................................................. 216

# Bradford Riot Sites 2001

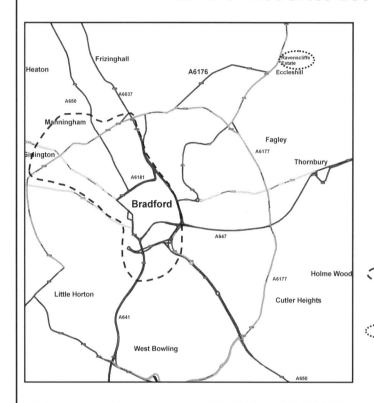

### Key

- - - Areas of Bradford affected by riot in 2001

······ Ravenscliffe Estate, scene of smaller disturbance 2001

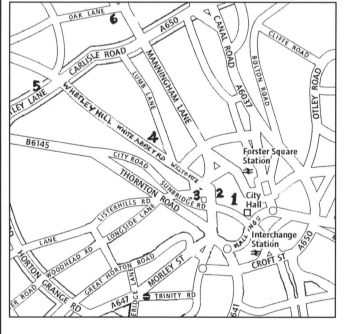

### Key

1. Centenary Square, site of initial rally
2. Ivegate, where first trigger incident took place
3. Southgate/Sunbridge Road where stabbing took place
4. Bottom of White Abbey Road where police and rioters first massed in confrontation
5. The Labour Club which was torched
6. The BMW garage which was burnt down

# INTRODUCTION

The Bradford riot of 2001 lasted from around 5.00pm on Saturday 7th July to the early hours of the next morning. It was one of the worst examples of mainland unrest in the UK for 20 years, with major physical damage and criminal acts of looting characterising the final hours. More than 320 police officers were injured as they battled rioters who hurled missiles and petrol bombs, and pushed burning cars towards them. A vivid sense of the horror of the developing situation is conveyed in this account from a woman officer on the front line:

> . . . we ran forward and we ran back and we got bricked and . . . the sound was getting louder and louder and louder as the night went on, it was just . . . constant. At that point, I thought we were dead, you know, this is it . . . there was nobody left—we were stood there and there were hardly any of us left, it felt like everybody else had gone home or was in hospital and we were it . . . But there were bricks coming and bricks coming and bricks coming and petrol bombs and it was just bang, bang, bang, bang, bang, bang, bang, bang, bang . . . I was so tired, you know, I stood there with my shield and I was falling asleep and it was the sound of the rocks hitting my shield that kept waking me up.

There have been many riots in Britain's history, when the normal rules constraining people are abandoned and there is open confrontation and violence on the streets. Bradford has its own history of riots going back at least to the social and economic upheavals of the industrial revolution. It is usual to think of 'riot' as mayhem and meaningless violence, but most of these events are triggered by feelings of injustice. Some were associated with the emergence of organised opposition to harsh conditions and gross inequality. Some marked the demands of ordinary people—for food, for a voice, for work that did not exploit and crush them, for the right to join unions, to express their political views in elections, to fight fascism or to challenge racism. Was the riot of 2001 different? One police officer expressed the view of many when he claimed that this was a riot 'without a cause'. We want to show that this is too easy a judgement. Without recognising what spurred on the rioters, the forces of law and order were unable to defuse the outpouring of rage that engulfed the city.

Our account begins with one disturbance in 2001 and ends with another in 2010 when the English Defence League arrived with a new challenge to peace in the city. We link the two disturbances by putting them in the context of a post-industrial city with a complex history of de-industrialisation, immigration and settlement. First and foremost we explore the events of that momentous Saturday and Sunday in 2001 from the diverse viewpoints of the key actors in the drama. Secondly we trace the fortunes and misfortunes of Bradford in prosperity and decline and show how its peoples have responded politically to economic expansion and opportunity, grinding hardship, fascism and racism. The 2001 riot was a culmination of rising tensions and problems which had not been addressed. It had a major and devastating impact on the city as well on the young men who rioted, the overwhelming majority of whom were young Asian Muslims from disadvantaged backgrounds. The question is, why them? Earlier generations had fought for political objectives, built organised opposition to capital and exploitation around the solidarities of working class lives. These young men thought they were defending their families, communities, and even the city, from 'fascist' threat, but they were not organised or politically aware. Unrest was not restricted to this particular ethnic group. White youth in one of Bradford's council estates responded with their own violent disturbances on the following Monday. Were they rioting for the same reason?

Subsequent events—9/11 in September of the same year, the wars with Iraq and Afghanistan in 2002 and 2003; the bombings in London on 7/7 in 2005 (the fourth anniversary of Bradford's riot)—led to other fears—of 'homegrown suicide bombers', even of a radicalised 'generation jihad'. Bradford was seen by some as a potential breeding ground for such developments, given its recent history of violent urban conflict involving Muslim young men of Pakistani origin.

Another major theme in this book is about policing in a multi-ethnic urban setting. After the police failed to quell the riot of 2001 they did some radical thinking which was put into striking effect in 2010. In 2010 the whole city pulled together to manage the EDL protest and to avert violence. Here we explore both the failures of 2001 and ask why different strategies worked in 2010.

Finally and most importantly, this is the story of Bradford: simultaneously provincial, cosmopolitan and fiercely democratic, as Priestley described it in his book, *English Journey*. Blown this way and that by the winds of global markets, Bradford continues to seek its destiny in Britain and the world. We travel with it on its journey into the 21$^{st}$ century.

# Doing the Research

In order to investigate the questions we posed, we needed to assemble evidence. There were already sources such as newspaper reports, but at the time (2003) no other in-depth research on the riots had been published. We were struck by some of the silences here—the rioters themselves had not spoken about their actions and little was known about the strategic decisions and tactics chosen by the police. Our project was set up initially to talk to rioters about their motivations, but it soon expanded to other parties—the police in all ranks, the organisers of an initial rally, people who had intervened to try to halt the violence and others who had observed events or been affected by them. This is a book of their stories. Children in Yorkshire used to be told off for 'telling stories'—it was tantamount to telling lies. We have many stories here and not all agree on what happened. Our point is that all of them represent some 'truth' as seen from contrasting perspectives and social positions. And perspectives can change—one of the aims of this book is to show how lessons were learnt from criticisms of the policing in 2001, leading to the police positioning themselves differently when it came to the challenge of the EDL incursion in 2010. Rioters also changed their perspectives—illustrated in the way a number of them worked with police to prevent their younger brothers, sons and nephews from responding to the EDL provocation.

Our first chapter, Reporting the Riots, offers an immediate take on the riots of 2001, based on contemporary media accounts, backed up by police logs of the fast unfolding events and by photographic evidence. Reliance on these sources has to be tempered by a recognition of the extent of participation and understanding of reporters. The police logs record calls into the police from both officers and the public, rather than police actions, and sometimes report rumours or opinions which cannot be verified.

Accessing first hand accounts of participation in a riot is not easy, especially one in which there were no leaders to proclaim a mission, no leaflets or banners. By the time we began our work, most of the rioters were incarcerated in jails across the country; the police have not usually been willing to offer insider accounts and other parties had not been asked for their recollections. We explain in the relevant chapters how we found ways to hear what they had to say, whether those who gave their views could be considered representative or not, and how much reliance we can put on this evidence. In total we did nearly 50 interviews on the riots of 2001 and over 50 around the time of the 2010 EDL demonstration. These were accompanied by hundreds of conversations and more importantly by living in and/or participating in the life of the city and engaging in its many struggles.

Our interviews were not conducted on the lines of a formal 'survey' with tick-box spaces for answers. We asked people to tell us in their own terms about the experience of riot and disturbance and were more confident with findings that emerged from these spontaneous accounts which could then be probed for greater understanding. What we did not want was a series simply of 'opinions' or attitudes on the riot and its participants. These are important but they have to be set against the accounts of what people actually did, their actions and behaviour—so this is where we started and this is how we have presented the material. Although we talked mainly with individuals it is clear that the riot cannot be understood simply in individualistic terms. People were drawn into collective action, the collectivity became greater than individuals' own needs and interests.

Along the way we encountered resistance to our project—especially to our insistence that the rioters' voices needed to be heard. Given the extent of destruction and injury they had wreaked, it was argued by some that they did not deserve to have their views taken seriously, or perhaps that by doing so, we would be giving them a spurious legitimacy. Our view was that they had to be given the space in which to make sense of the riots for themselves and that in the process they might see the implications of their actions—and we might learn whether there were legitimate grievances here and how they could be addressed to avoid future episodes of destructive confrontation. At no point did we see ourselves as excusing violence for its own sake. We resisted the pressure to see the rioters only as villains, or indeed as either heroes or victims. In this book they speak for themselves, not as cardboard cut-outs, but as contradictory and very complex human beings. They made their own history, in circumstances not of their choosing, but they must also answer for the consequences.

Although we come from an academic background, we have written this book for the general public as an invitation to reflect on the events of a decade ago. We particularly wanted those parties who shared their stories with us to be able to access the accounts of the others so as to attempt some understanding of different perspectives and pressures on action. And we want to open up debate about how much or how little has changed since 2001. As the audience for the book is non-academic, we have avoided jargon and extensive referencing. However, later chapters draw extensively on the work of others, especially historians, which, for ethical reasons, must be credited. Of course we have learnt much from the work of other researchers and commentators and we include a list of books which may be of interest to those who wish to read further in this field.

# Contentious Terms

Some of us, academics or not, like clear definitions of key terms. First of all we need to clarify that 'Bradford' is both a city and a metropolitan district. It includes Keighley, which shares many of the same urban issues that Bradford faces. The District as a whole is more rural than urban and contains wealthy settlements like Ilkley, whose people do not always see themselves as fellow travellers with the residents of inner-city Bradford where the unrest was concentrated. The history of these distinctions is traced in chapter 5.

Two terms which figure hugely in this book are 'Far Right' and 'Asians'. In everyday life they are used casually and loosely and may cover a diversity of meanings—as will soon be illustrated in the stories people recount. No-one has a monopoly over their meaning, but we think it is important to clarify the range of usages, and to recognise that particular usages may denote a specific view of the riots.

In participants' accounts of the riot, the label 'Fascist' or 'Nazi' makes an appearance as often as 'the Far Right'. In Left and labour movement ideology these terms are embedded in historical analyses of Italy, Germany and Spain in the first half of the 20th century and in the holocaust and its aftermath. They became the terms of political debate to describe a particular kind of nationalistic, anti-trade union, anti-liberal and elite-led mass movement, often underwritten by racist ideology. Today they do not have a clear and consensual meaning, but are more commonly used to refer to racist parties with unrealistic ambitions to state power. In Bradford, both anti-fascist groups and the rioters used this terminology as a form of abuse, though only the former were historically informed and politically organised. Looking at the reports of the Bradford riots it is notable that these terms also surface in the media in a factual way, whilst even court judgements occasionally refer to 'youths with Far Right Wing affiliations' (*Yorkshire Post*, 10 June 2003). It was the National Front (NF) that called for a march on Bradford on 7 July 2001, but the NF was but one of a cohort of Far Right organisations (including the British National Party and Combat 18), much subject to splintering and factionalism, often without formal membership lists and with many informal hangers-on. Asian youth in particular referred to all such groups by the name 'National Front', or simply

'NF'. In several cities these activists were augmented by 'football hooligans eager for trouble' (as Paul Harris put it in the *Observer* of 1 July 2001). Bradford football fans had an organisation known as the Ointment who were present in the city centre in 2001. This is not to say that all Ointment are to be seen as Far Right supporters. Many were just crazy about football. Beyond this, men might be labelled as 'NF' simply by their appearance—for example skinheads, white, tough-looking male youth wearing certain types of clothing. The lack of clear definition allowed for many to argue that those involved in the violence were 'just football hooligans' and there was no 'fascist threat', whilst others used this language (of fascism) to argue that the riot was more than the outbursts of a mindless mob. Although some anti-fascist groups have seen the EDL as a successor to the National Front and other racist parties, their anger is directed towards a religious rather than an ethnic group whilst they promote a narrow version of English nationalism.

The label 'Asian' or 'Pakistani' is also less than precise, though these terms are used interchangeably by all commentators. Academic writers sometimes strive for a more specific geographic label like 'South Asian'; others are critical of the way these blanket names disguise significant social differences between Indians and Pakistanis, Muslims and Hindus, Sunnis and Shia, as well as between classes, sexes and generations within the category. The point for us is that people do use these terms to describe themselves and others. They can be taken as statements about identity, but identities are not fixed or singular. The majority of those arrested for riot were of 'Pakistani background'—this generally means that they, or their parents, were born in Pakistan and nearly always means that they are Muslim by religion. In 2003, when we conducted our interviews, there was beginning to be a shift away from the more inclusive label 'Asian' and towards claiming a narrower religious identity of 'Muslim' within it. This echoes an earlier shift from the 70s and 80s when Asian political activists had been happy to embrace an even wider 'black' identity (see chapter 6).

Not all the rioters were 'Asian' or Muslim. A small minority were African-Caribbean or white or of mixed backgrounds (with white mothers). Of those convicted and imprisoned around 10% were categorised as 'white' or 'African-Caribbean', even in one case as a 'dark European'. That not all the rioters were Asian or Pakistani raises questions about the common assumption that this was a race riot in which whites fought pitched battles with Asians. And even though the majority of rioters were Asian/Muslim/Pakistani this does not necessarily mean that the riot was about ethnic identity or religious adherence. That remains to be investigated, which is what this book tries to do.

The terms 'race' and 'ethnicity' are often confused with each other. Race describes physical/biological traits which are of no scientific significance but which have been given social significance. Racial differences have been used in the past to justify conquest, colonization and even slavery. Ethnicity refers to a sense of belonging based on presumed common ancestry, history and shared culture. A problem arises with the term 'white'. We often mark it with inverted commas to indicate it is problematic. 'Whiteness' is usually an invisible 'identity' because in Britain the majority are 'white'. Unlike black and minority ethnic groups, 'white' people tend not to think they have a 'culture' because it is built into the mainstream and it goes unnoticed. Most of our institutions are predominantly 'white'. By using these categories at all, group differences are highlighted. Why would we want to do that? One reason is that for minority 'groups', it draws attention to disadvantage. If 'white' is a category, it emphases a characteristic of advantage. None of these 'group' categorisations, however, reveal the marginalisations within them, such as the working class in the category 'white' or women across all the categories. The use of racial and ethnic categorisations are topics of much debate and should be treated with great caution.

# Acknowledgements

We began this study as a team of three—Janet Bujra, Marie Macey and Jenny Pearce—who all contributed to carrying out the interviews which are at the heart of this book. It is not unusual for researchers to disagree about their interpretations of the evidence, but as we proceeded we (Bujra and Pearce) found our positions increasingly divergent from that of Macey. Eventually we decided to go our separate ways, whilst continuing to share the data. Despite our differences, we want to express our admiration of the work which Marie Macey put into this investigation as an indefatigable and dedicated researcher, brilliant both at listening and meticulously recording. Without her commitment and passion for the 'truth' as she defined it, this book would have been the poorer.

We cannot end without thanking all those who agreed to share their recollections with us, especially those for whom the memory was still painful. We would like to think we gave them all, from prisoners in their cells, to police officers on the beat, the opportunity to make sense of these events for themselves. But without their willing participation we could not have drawn this complex and vivid picture of events and of those who were drawn into the action. Our promise of confidentiality prohibits our naming them, but this book is dedicated to them all. We also want to express our gratitude to the young men who became our research auxiliaries—Altaf Arif, Abbas Ali, Baasit Arif and Naweed Hussain. They helped us to understand the experience of being a young Muslim male in Bradford and became almost as enthused by the investigation as we were. The project was originally initiated by a small grant from West Yorkshire Police under the auspices of Neighbourhood Renewal Safer Communities Fund, in an endeavour to understand 'why the rioters rioted'. We appreciated that opportunity to begin an investigation which then became more far-reaching and lasted several years rather than the few months originally planned. For their unstinting assistance in accessing material, their good humour, and most important, their insistence on our freedom to draw our own conclusions, we will always be grateful. Along the way we were also indebted to the Prison and Probation Services, Bradford Vision, the Youth Service, Bradford Council of Mosques, the City Council and the Programme for a Peaceful City in the University of Bradford (especially Lisa Cumming) and many individuals without whom this study would have been impossible.

Finally, we pay homage to Alan Sillitoe, one of the 1960s 'angry young men', from whom our title is borrowed, and who died in 2010.

# Setting the Scene

In the months leading up to the Bradford riots there had been major disturbances in two other Northern ex-mill towns, Oldham and Burnley, and in Leeds. In Oldham and Burnley incidents of tension, fanned by Far Right activity, led to confrontations between white and Asian young men in or around areas with high Asian populations. A Far Right march took place in Oldham, even after it had been banned, and there was considerable support for these racist parties amongst local white people in both towns. Pubs were flashpoints of violence where Far Right groups and their supporters met. These pubs were often attacked in reactive explosions of violence following real or rumoured incidents of racist attacks on persons and property. Considerable damage and injuries on both sides were the outcome. The significance of Burnley and Oldham to the riot in Bradford was indirect, based on the fears engendered amongst Bradford Asians about possible Far Right incursions in their city. As we shall see, the riots in Bradford were by no means a repeat performance of these earlier disturbances, though there were some parallels. These earlier disturbances heightened tensions in Bradford in the weeks leading up to 7 July.

A week before the Bradford events, Paul Harris wrote a prescient report for the *Observer*, reflecting on the preceding riots in Burnley and Oldham and asking: 'Bradford Next?' Based on interviews with Pakistani youth in Bradford it confirms that they had heard the reports from Burnley and Oldham with dread and fury and were intending to respond violently if Far Right activists descended on Bradford as they had announced they were planning to do. 'If the NF comes here on Saturday they will be dead', said one. One youth claimed to have secreted a sword, others spoke of petrol bombs stored in derelict houses, knives and other weapons collected. They anticipated that drug gangs might be involved and shooting break out—neither of which predictions was borne out by events.

Harris also reported on the plans of the Far Right—he cites the National Front and Combat 18—to march in the town on 7 July, drawing off the police, whilst attacking Asians in their own areas to provoke retaliation. Seeing them as 'hardened racist criminals' he describes Bradford as a tinder-keg with a 'large pool of disenchanted white working class youths vulnerable to racist scaremongering' as well as a 'deprived' Asian population. Paul Meszaros relates how the British National Party (BNP) held a meeting in Bradford North (site of several white working class estates) the night before the riot, with over a hundred present (*Searchlight*: 30 August 2001). In the event, the assumption that violence would pit whites against Asians in a racial confrontation was unrealised in Bradford's riot.

City authorities, West Yorkshire police, and other concerned citizens were also planning to pre-empt the threat of mayhem. The police and city council successfully applied to the Home Secretary for a ban on the Far Right march. The council also cancelled the final day in the city centre of what had been a peaceful multicultural festival. Bradford has a long-standing tradition of opposing the Far Right and both Trades Council activists and the Anti-Nazi League prepared for a rally of opposition on the same day as the banned march, inviting MPs, Councillors and other worthies to express their views on fascism and racism. The stage was set.

# 1

# REPORTING THE RIOT

## From Rally to Riot

July 7th was a beautiful warm summer's day. In Centenary Square, in front of Bradford's imposing Victorian town hall, the anti-fascist rally began in the morning—the *Telegraph and Argus* (*T&A*) has it beginning at 10.30am. The police were assembling nearby and reports and rumours had already reached them of Far Right elements trying to beat the ban on their march. A rumour that 200 Belgian skinheads had arrived at Leeds/Bradford airport was discounted, but police reported turning some right-wing extremists back on the motorway. From before mid-day, National Front (NF) and Ointment youth (football hooligans linked with Bradford City Football Club) were reported to be gathering in pubs—at Rafters, at the Thornhill Arms in Stanningley, at the Queens pub in Bridge St, at Addisons in Ivegate and the Boy and Barrel in Westgate. They were also seen in the city centre streets, in one case reportedly distributing NF literature, and gathering in Bridge Street, where skirmishes took place.

The *T&A* noted 'numerous reports of National Front members and other right-wing extremists roaming the city on Saturday' (9 July 2001). The numbers were put at 'between 12 and 30', whilst Assistant Chief Constable Greg Wilkinson claimed 'between 12 and 20 . . . right-wing extremists', conceding that they acted as a 'catalyst' for later violence. Anti-Nazi League (ANL) organiser, Robina Siddique, was reported in the *T&A* as saying that 'a Nazi sympathiser' had been seen in the Square and had spat at Asian women and produced a knife. Meanwhile, she said, other 'NF people' were in a bar nearby but police did nothing. There is a long quote from Altaf Arif, 'a regional young volunteer of the year' with a record of anti-racist activism and whose father had been killed in a racist attack, saying that, 'The police have admitted they made errors . . . They failed to arrest a known Nazi who was roaming the streets. They searched him but didn't arrest him'. The last sightings were of a big group of around 50 Ointment in the Bedford Arms on Wakefield Road (5.58pm) and another group of right-wingers in Chapel Street (6.12pm). By this time though they were far from the action. The *T&A* reported that by then, 'The National Front were long gone—no-one was even talking about them any more'. During this period the police logged two arrests of men taken to be Ointment.

Some of the Asian youths were also gearing up early on. The police logs report CCTV footage of youths carrying metal bars onto the 618 bus at 12.38pm, another caught 10 minutes later in Centenary Square trying to hide a monkey wrench behind a wall. Minor confrontations between white and Asian youths were recorded in the Square and a more serious disturbance in Bridge St, where the logs speak of 'factions' of white and Asian youths verbally abusing one another. At 1.30pm a cordon was established at Bridge Street to keep the rivals apart. Police report more NF arriving in the city centre, including 'a known agitator'. These seem to have joined the crowd in Bridge Street.

Despite these provocations in the background, the anti-fascist rally passed off peacefully, lasting for over four hours. As the *T&A* reported, 'The Anti-Nazi League Rally in Centenary Square was earnest, multicultural and peaceful'. The crowd was diverse, white, black and Asian, with people of all ages, from babies to the elderly. Amongst others it was addressed by two of Bradford's MPs, Marsha Singh and Terry Rooney, Ian Greenwood, leader of the Labour group on the council and Mohamed Amran, member of the Commission for Racial Equality. A message of support from Tony Benn was read out. The speakers emphasised that despite Far Right provocation—they 'want to divide Bradford' (Singh) and 'The National Front wants us to fight the police' (Amran)—the crowd should stay calm and not resort to violence.

As the speeches came to an end, around 2pm, the crowd began to disperse, though a large group remained, especially young Asian men, who appeared bored and restless. Ateeq Siddique, an ANL member, is reported as blaming it on the cancellation of the Festival. At this point one of us was in the Square and noted Ateeq with a loud hailer, appealing to the crowd with an ANL slogan: 'Black and white, unite! Out the National Front!' They looked at him bemused and no-one responded. An elderly Asian man began shouting 'Allahu Akbar!' but was similarly ignored. A ribbon of participants from the Festival dressed in costumes for revelry snaked through the square. There was an air of anticipation, but nobody seemed to be sure what they were waiting for. There were rumours (purveyed by mobile phones) that the NF or British National Party (BNP) were in the city. It was a shock when, at around 2.30pm, as the *T&A* report, 'A ring of officers surrounded protesters' in Centenary Square. A cordon of at least a hundred officers, kitted out in what looked like riot gear, with dogs, horses and video vans, was suddenly on the scene, preventing anyone from leaving, in a tactic now referred to as 'kettling'. The police called the strategy 'contain and disperse', but the crowd became agitated and angry and a lot of pushing and shoving was going on. Youth workers were trying to calm hotheads. William Stuart, a reporter from the *Yorkshire Post* felt personally threatened by the dogs (*Sunday Business Post* on-line, 15 July 2001). Police told us later that they put out a tannoy message around 3.20pm, assuring the crowd that the National Front were no longer in the town, and the ANL urged people to go home.

Shortly afterwards, the cordon was forcibly broken as news reached those in the Square of a confrontation in nearby Ivegate and rumours that 'an Asian youth had been beaten up by a group of skinheads' led to those contained pushing their way out. Ivegate is a steep cobbled street leading down towards the Square. Half way up there was a bar, called, at that time, Addisons. It was fronted by large plate glass windows so that those inside could be seen by passers-by. As early as 12.30pm police logs had recorded Asian and white youths hurling abuse at each other in this area.

Not long after 3pm a group of Ointment are seen to enter Addisons bar, though Altaf Arif, already quoted, was reported as saying they were accompanied by a 'known Nazi'. At 4.20pm tension exploded into fighting when a youth named Kasel Altaf was reported by William Stuart to have been 'viciously assaulted by up to 30 white men' (*Sunday Business Post* on-line, 15 July 2001). *The Guardian* (9 July 2001) reported a witness seeing 'a large group of white men, throwing bottles really hard . . . They'd grabbed a young Asian lad and beaten him senseless'. They were chanting 'Come on! Come on!', but at the time he had thought they were just 'Bradford Saturday afternoon drunks'. Altaf Arif blames the 'known Nazi' who was seen 'stamping on an Asian guy's head . . .' A photograph of the attack accompanies *The Guardian* report. Much later (just after 6pm) the police log records an unsourced report of the same incident, in which it is claimed that the 'police had allowed [the name is deleted] to jump on an Asian man's head and shout "Come on you fucking bastards" to a group of youths being beaten back by police officers using batons'.

If this was the first incident which triggered the shift from rally into riot, the next followed almost immediately in Sunbridge Road. By now the crowd was dispersing from Centenary Square in all directions and shopkeepers locked doors as youth rampaged over the town, breaking windows and throwing bricks at the police. Damage and disturbance was recorded in the police logs from Godwin Street, Sunbridge Road, James Street, Market Street, Thornton Road and Sackville Street, with shop windows put through and pubs attacked as well as Asian and white youth chasing each other. A large group left the Square up Sunbridge Road, throwing missiles and with the police in hot pursuit. Asian and white youths were engaged in a scuffle on the sidelines. According to the *T&A* whites were chasing an Asian and attacked him, after which time other Asians set on the attacker. Two white youths were then stabbed—one trying to protect the other. For William Stuart they were 'suspected far right activists', one with 'England' tattooed on his back. Both the *T&A* and *The Guardian* of 9 July have a photograph of this incident, which occurred at around 4.50pm.

During the next hour and a half the police are stretched to the limits, receiving calls of mayhem from all over the city centre and beyond. Police helicopters are out surveying the scene. At Hall Ings, Godwin Street, Charles Street, Bank Street, Market Street, James Street, Westgate and Forster Square, pubs are being attacked, shops smashed, cars attacked, gangs of white and Asian youths reported running amok. And yet people are also observed still shopping and driving between warring factions. The first signs of preparation for a longer fight are also in evidence. The police log records that at 5.18pm a large group of Asian youths is observed piling up bricks at Westgate—they appear to have demolished a wall, and at Forster Square others are seen with baseball bats.

Further out, at Lumb Lane, the log records that between 5.25pm and 5.42pm, 'helicopter reports large group of well-armed youths have demolished wall', someone is assaulted and a car window smashed, whilst a resident reports 'large number of Asians carrying bottles "looking for trouble"'. The source of some of the bottles later becomes clear. 'Haighy's Bar reports group of youths have taken six crates of empty bottles from rear'. Youth are still causing damage in Westgate, Thornton Road and Godwin Street, but towards 6.30pm the action is moving towards White Abbey Road. Around 6.30pm the police regroup at the bottom of White Abbey Road and bring in reinforcements of a dozen police vans, maybe 200 riot police, dogs and helicopters. The diverse gangs of youth creating mayhem around the town are also 'grouping up' in the same area which thereafter becomes the main site of riot. The police report 'we will have problems'. Some youth appear to be sucked in from Lumb Lane 'with hammers and bats' (police logs) whilst others are heading away from the trouble and towards Manningham, but leaving a trail of damage, throwing bricks and breaking windows. Almost certainly they turn round to join the action at the bottom of the hill, where by 7pm the police logs report 'barricade across the road'.

It is now that the police begin to liaise with community elders (i.e. Asians thought by the police to have local influence). They also contacted other police forces for assistance—in the end, reports the *T&A* and *The Guardian*, over a thousand officers are involved, from eight other forces, some from Yorkshire, others from as far away as Merseyside. The uncontrollable explosion of violence could no longer be dealt with by the local force and a state of riot was declared (although there is no record of this in the contemporary reports).

# Riot

During the next several hours a pitched battle ensued, with police facing a 'rioting mob of five to seven hundred people' (*T&A*, 9 July, quote from Assistant Chief Constable Greg Wilkinson). No-one in their right mind would have chosen this battle site, as it put the police at a disadvantage from the start, stranded at the bottom of a hill with their opponents raining down missiles at them, and with reinforcements racing down from 'Asian areas' like Manningham and Girlington to join the riot. White Abbey Road is fairly flat, but it soon turns into Whetley Hill, wending upwards and then turning slightly left. The Lower Globe pub and Whetley Motor Company are on the right. Higher up there is an intersection with Carlisle Road and Whetley Lane, with the Labour Club on the left corner and a little higher up, the Upper Globe pub on the right. These were the main scenes of battle in the period up to and beyond midnight.

Many in the crowd of youth were now hiding their faces with sweaters, scarves or bandanas, although the photographs show that many were not, unaware perhaps that the police are already videoing the scene for later arrests. The mob was now composed mainly, but not wholly, of young Asian men whose adrenalin and anger was running high. They began to set bonfires, throw firebombs and overturn and torch cars. *The Guardian* reports 'Six rows of police officers, 30 to a row, confronted Asian youths who threw beer kegs, bricks, stones, petrol bombs and fireworks' (9 July). The *T&A* has the most vivid account:

> Cheers and whistles rose up from the mob as [a] missile hit its target. Seconds later, the wounded officer was carried from the battle line by two colleagues. The jeers were soon lost beneath the deafening thunder of concrete crashing onto riot shields. Another stricken officer limped away from the ranks, and then another . . .

It was a few hours before police were effectively reinforced by forces from other authorities. In that period they did little more than move the crowd onto the hill and then hold their ground. When they were able to push forwards they were soon driven back and the rioters reused the same missiles they had thrown earlier. Hiding behind burning barricades the rioters also used halogen lights to blind the police and torched cars to beat them back. At the Whetley Motor Company (an Asian-owned business) six cars on display were set alight and the derelict Lower Globe pub next door was severely damaged. The crowd was chanting 'We want the NF!' At White's View, a little way up Whetley Hill:

> . . . the brick-throwing rioters stood their ground, taking advantage of their elevated position on the hill . . . Suddenly . . . a car burst out from behind the mob. The blue Nissan raced straight at the ranks of officers who dived for cover or lunged at it. As it screeched to a halt, some officers clambered onto its roof and bonnet, trying to break its windows with batons and riot shields. The driver threw it into reverse and jolted away to be swallowed up by the swarm of rioters (*T&A*, 9 July).

The whole area was now in fiery contention, as 'broken bottles crunched underfoot and the road was thickly littered with rocks, sticks and other weapons dropped or hurled by the gangs'. At 7.50pm 'Asian males' were reported to police 'pouring petrol into bottles' at Jasmin Terrace. Police logs report '40 Asians and whites fighting with metal bars' in one of the streets off Whetley Hill.

There is also a big crowd of onlookers and people watching from gardens and houses on the route. The *T&A* report at one point that 'onlookers in nearby houses express concern at heavy-handed police tactics' but as the violence intensifies a white woman says 'Why don't they call in the army to stop this?', whilst an Asian man is horrified: 'Why are they pushing the violence up here to our homes? This has nothing to do with us'.

Whilst the major incident was stretching police to the limit, cases were still being reported of incidents throughout the city involving gangs of youth. At Undercliffe, Asians were milling around 'with bats and hammers'. At Church House in North Parade they were smashing windows. In Leeds Road '200 people were fighting'. In Eccleshill the police station was receiving threats to damage local pubs. Above the main site of action young men were massing at Duckworth Lane, 15 observed 'with metal bars', whilst below the riot Melbourne Hotel was 'taking petrol bombs' and in Westgate outside the Boy and Barrel 'white youths were taunting Asians'.

There were several attempts at peaceful intervention and mediation between 8.15pm and 10.30pm. The *T&A* reports Asians near Melbourne Hotel trying to intervene (unsuccessfully) when police roughly arrested a man who appeared to be making no trouble. Later the first attempts by 'Asian community leaders and business people' to quell the riot, led police to draw back temporarily, but the lull was short-lived. An Asian restaurant owner (Omar Khan) claimed they tried to intervene, but police were unhelpful and did not recognise them. Talks break down, violence resumes and intensifies with mounting police injuries. Police logs record a call for fresh units, with those on the line saying they are 'taking a battering'. A police horse is stabbed. An officer asks if they can consider withdrawal, but this is not followed up. Again at 9.30pm there are attempts by 'community intervenors' to stand between the rioters and the police, but 'mediators' claim that many of the rioters are outsiders 'from Halifax and Burnley', that the 'crowd [is] hostile to them', and that they 'cannot do anything'. Now the police report they are 'hopelessly outnumbered' and entries in the next few minutes report six more officers injured and ambulance crews unable to cope. Again the mediators try to intervene and as the fighting abates for a while the rioters demand that those so far arrested be released. The *T&A* describe Rabnawaz Qureshi joining Mohammed Riaz to try to calm the situation—they pleaded with police to free two arrestees, but met with refusal. 'We tried our best'. Police logs note that 'Riaz and Amran' are 'winding up the crowd' and they are spoken to. For a while it seems that the intermediaries are convincing the rioters to fall back, but soon afterwards a burning car is pushed towards the police lines, and the mediation collapses. A *T&A* reporter expressed his view that 'there could be no negotiating with the gangs because they had no demands, just one aim, annihilation'.

The Lower Globe is now ablaze, and a youth is reported to police to be threatening the front line with a crossbow. 'The front line cannot hold much longer' record police logs at 10.45pm. And between 11 and 11.30pm the police are being forced back, under heavy attack from petrol bombs and asking for authorisation for 'baton rounds' (rubber bullets) as 'lives [are] at risk'. Lawcroft House police station on Whetley Hill is under threat from 'Asian youths' and is closed to the public. Just before midnight it is recorded in the police log that 'Asian youths trying to gain entry' and bottles and bricks are being thrown. At the Lower Globe 'hundreds of Asians' are 'smashing up' the ruins and erecting barricades across the road. Meanwhile there is still trouble in other areas of Bradford—in Barkerend Asians are seen smashing car windows, whilst in Frizinghall a large group of white youths is reported.

But now another threat is apparent, as the log records: 'Manningham Ward Labour Club—multitude of Asians outside with masks on'. At the Labour Club drinkers were enjoying an evening out, apparently unaware of the mayhem erupting around them. Just after midnight the windows were smashed and it was set alight. BBC News On-Line (8 July) reported that:

> Landlord Roy Glister . . . described how 28 terrified drinkers inside were lucky to escape with their lives. 'All the windows were smashed and then they fire-bombed it', he said. 'We locked ourselves in the cellar and waited for the fire brigade. By this time they'd firebombed my car. We'd no way to get out at all'.

Police logs record 'distraught female—trapped in cellar' and begging for help, and an elderly man with heart problems hiding in a toilet. The *T&A* reported that 'rioters pushed burning cars up against the fire doors . . . firefighters and police eventually cut a safe route our of the building, which was burned to the ground' (9 July).

Whilst this incident is still underway, some of the rioters begin to split off into gangs which wreaked havoc as they went. The *T&A* says that 'rioters were forced back to Toller Road junction'. Carlisle Road is 'bombarded' (police logs) and Whetley Garage set on fire. The Upper Globe and the Junction Pub are torched as one large contingent ('hundreds of Asians') turns up Toller Lane. Police report many are armed with golf clubs. At Lawcroft House Police Station several vehicles are damaged in the yard. Arthur's Bar on Heaton Road is set alight, after the drinkers have been turned out, and on Lilycroft Road another barricade is set up, drivers are threatened and the windows of a bar smashed. By now the police are chasing youths up Toller Lane and they are scattering. But still 'Around 100 stood on the grassy roundabout [at the junction with Duckworth Lane] as cars screeched around it. Two youths swung golf clubs menacingly'.

By 1am Asian elders are again seen pleading with the youths to disperse and they begin to do so, calling out to police officers 'mockingly, "time to go home now"' (*T&A*, 9 July). However, not all went home—a large gang of about a hundred separated off and headed towards Oak Lane where they are reported at 1.15pm breaking into Listers large glass BMW showrooms, smashing its windows with bricks and setting fire to cars. Other vehicles were being stolen and driven away by youth, 'joy-riding, crashing and torching the performance cars, treating them like expensive fairground bumper cars, as the building itself burned to the ground' (*T&A*). A silver BMW was used to ram-raid a popular local hardware shop (McCann's).

Local people expressed shock and fear at what they described as anarchic mob violence and with neither police nor fire brigade in sight. 'Terrified residents of a residential home in nearby St Mary's Road were evacuated', after a call to police at almost 2am. A middle-aged Asian man is quoted: 'The National Front have got what they wanted. They have sparked off the trouble and then left the youths to destroy their own community'.

And still there were sporadic incidents of terror around the city. The police log an electrical shop in Duckworth Lane being looted, 60 people evacuated from Lilycroft Working Men's Club as they could not get home, a Girlington pub petrol bombed, a chemists looted and the Girlington Conservative Club set ablaze. On Keighley Rd youths are smashing up the Mitsubishi Garage at 2.40am, damaging and burning cars. Outside the Park Hotel in Emm Lane at 3.32am, police logs report, 'people are rioting—where are the police?' The Co-op in Legrams Lane is ram-raided and looted. Elite Motors on Keighley Road is also looted and on fire. In Whetley Lane at 6.35am a BMW car is on fire. The last entry in the police logs is at 10.53am on the Sunday morning, reporting from McCann's hardware shop that 'pick axes and accelerants have been stolen from the premises and may be used later today'. Meanwhile Bradford Royal Infirmary treated 82 people injured in the riots. Sixty-three of them were police officers and 19 were members of the public. Three had been kept in for further treatment.

The riot had now spent itself and there was no further trouble. The whole of Bradford had watched television footage of the unfolding riot (pictures which had flashed around the world) and on the Sunday shocked and curious folk wandered around the scenes of devastation, as one of us did, recording in a field diary at the time:

> Three or four fire engines are still at the smoking scene of the Labour Club at the corner of Whetley Hill and Whetley Lane, police vans and police guard the wreckage, whilst media folk with cameras and mikes at the ready wait for the next instalment. On the opposite side of the road there is the blackened and abandoned face of the Lower Globe pub . . . on Oak Lane, knots of young men—from early teenagers to men in their thirties (nearly all Asian Muslims), are standing at street corners and lining the road opposite the site of one of last night's conflagrations—the burnt out wreck of the BMW showroom, with 15 or so grey skeletons of cars piled up in its forecourt like so much rubbish.

But at the same time 'shops were open for business, mosques open for prayer, the normality of everyday life going on eerily side by side with a watchful and edgy suspense'.

# Aftershocks

Although the main riot had involved only minor confrontations between white and Asian youths, and some of these were begun by Far Right provocateurs, incidents followed which looked like revenge attacks. In the very first Riots Special issue of the *Telegraph and Argus* (9 July) it is reported that in Greengates an Asian restaurant and a garage had been smashed up by '30 white youths'. A few days later it was reported that Asian-owned shops and restaurants in Bingley, Girlington, Wibsey and Little Horton had been attacked. Arrests of both whites and Asians followed in this and the previous incidents (*T&A*, 9 and 13 July), suggesting that the owners or other Asians had tried to defend their property.

On the Monday following the major riot, Ravenscliffe, a largely white estate was the scene of a disturbance, described in the press as a 'smaller-scale white youth-led riot' (*T&A*, 13 July 2001). Between 50 and 100 youths ran amok in the middle of the estate, where they were immediately penned in by police. After a few hours of stone throwing and arson, 15 arrests took place. The contrast between the two disturbances is powerful in more ways than one and will be returned to in chapter 2. The most immediate difference was that the Ravenscliffe rioters were charged with 'violent disorder' which carries a five-year maximum jail term, whilst those involved in the earlier and much larger-scale riot were sentenced for 'riot' which carries a maximum 10 year sentence. The difference was endorsed at the Court of Appeal in London over a year later (*T&A*, 17 Oct 2002) when Andrew Chapman, arrested in Ravenscliffe, fought to have his three year sentence reduced as 'manifestly excessive'. Many of the main rioters however received sentences of four years for similar actions.

During the major riot 55 arrests were made, the overwhelming majority young men from Bradford. The police warned that 'we have an excellent record in follow-up arrests. The people who have been involved had better keep looking behind them' (*T&A*, 9 July). A massive exercise to achieve this, called Operation Wheel, was soon set in motion. The Chief Constable's Report for 2000–01 confirms reports in the press that 320 officers were injured in the riot. He commends the bravery and fortitude of his officers facing the mob for hours on end. He also clarifies the cost of the riot—£3.4 million had been spent on the police operation, but another £7.5 million was due for insurance claims for damages, for which the police were liable under the Riot Damages Act. (To put this into perspective, another operation that year, to investigate the death of a teenager, had cost £2.3 million.) What he does not discuss is what police acknowledged in the immediate aftermath of the riot—that they had lost control, that their strategy of 'contain and disperse' had failed. 'There were times when I didn't feel we were completely on top of the situation and . . . when we were completely stretched' (Wilkinson, quoted in *T&A/Guardian*, 9 July 2001).

Saturday Night and Sunday Morning

# Instant Reactions: Why was There a Riot?

Already, just two days after the riot, people are trying to make sense of what happened. The press is full of instant opinion and explanation, some of which has endured to form the stuff of academic debate. It is worth looking at some of the opinions immediately expressed. In the middle of almost overwhelming condemnation of the rioters there was a range of views, including some attempts to justify their actions or to put them into a wider context.

For some the riot was essentially a 'race riot'; *The Guardian* headlined its report of 9 July with these words. Not everyone agreed. For William Stuart this was 'to miss the point' in so far as the whites involved in fights with Asians were taken by the latter to be Far Right activists. He concludes that 'The rioting . . . seemed to be aimed more at the police than at white people in general' (*Sunday Business Post* on-line, 15 July 2001). The immediate response of Assistant Chief Constable Greg Wilkinson was that 'criminality was more of a motive than race'. Certainly the major action pitted the police against mainly Asian rioters, and criminal acts of looting, arson and damage to lives and property took place on a large scale. There was genuine fear of escalation, and the police considered using more force than they did. Wilkinson noted that rubber bullets might have been used if there had been loss of life (*T&A*, 9 July 2001). There were many calls for enhanced police equipment, especially from MPs and city worthies. They were given encouragement by the Home Secretary, David Blunkett, who also commended the police for their bravery. A correspondent to the *T&A* perceived political dangers in this development. Riot generates the demand for more violence to quell it—this road leads to 'water cannon, tear gas, rubber bullets, finally the Army . . . the military becomes political; democracy ends' (Jack Mawson, Letters to the Editor, 13 July 2001).

That Asian racism rather than white made this into a 'race riot' is forcefully voiced by Jim Greenhalf in a *T&A* opinion piece immediately after the riots. He claims that only white-owned businesses were attacked and that the riot could be seen as an attempt at 'ethnic cleansing'. He also sees race and religion as interlocked. Some of the rioters were 'convinced that they are taking part in an intifada (uprising) against the infidel (non-Muslims)' (*T&A*, 9 July). That the major battle took place between police and rioters rather than between black and white could have a racial significance. Manawar Jan-Khan, spokesman for the Manningham Residents' Association, writing an opinion piece in *The Guardian* on

26

12 July, expressed his anger: 'The police turned on our community, herding us like animals . . . the coppers were all white and we were all Asian'. This does not prevent him exposing differences within the 'Asian community' when he writes about 'community leaders that don't lead . . . the old men in suits and salwar kameez who are out of touch [and] need to be retired'. In no respect were Asian Muslims in Bradford of one voice about the riot. Ayoub Ansari, an elderly Asian who had witnessed the final scenes of violence in Oak Lane, described the rioters as 'wild and mindless . . . We live here and we want peace. This is not Muslim; this is not Islamic'. Mohamed Ajeeb, ex-Lord Mayor, complained that the police had not reacted quickly enough to criminal damage in predominantly Asian areas: 'they were more interested in the city centre and ignored damage in the Asian areas'. Fears were expressed in Manningham that 'property prices will go down, insurance will go up' in the aftermath of the riot. Conversely there were those Asians who blamed local MPs for not having 'done anything for Bradford' and one said 'the children throwing the firebombs have got nothing left to lose', and that 'the government has got to learn the lesson' (all quoted from *T&A*, 9 July).

A middle-aged Asian man blamed the Far Right, but not in terms that give credit to the rioters: 'The National Front have got what they wanted. They have sparked off the trouble and then left the youths to destroy their own community' (*T&A*, 9 July). The youth did have some backing however. An Asian Muslim correspondent to the *T&A* writes that the rioters were right to resist attempts by the BNP and NF to 'force us out of this country' and that 'the police didn't do enough to protect us against white racists . . . our voices were not heard and the only thing we could do was to use violence against them' (though he condemns it: N. Khan, 13 July 2001). Understandably no-one is interviewed at this point who admits to taking part in the violence, though the Bishop of Bradford emphasises the need to listen to those 'who feel violence is the right way ahead' (*T&A*, 9 July).

A final strand in instant explanations is to point to 'underlying causes', summed up by Jim Greenhalf as 'social deprivation, heavy-handed-policing, institutional racism', but derided as 'the same old excuses'. Marsha Singh, the MP who had spoken against the Far Right at the rally, now says the riot 'was nothing to do with deprivation, this was sheer criminality' (*T&A*, 9 July 2001). Some linked it to the failure of state and local policy makers in relation to ethnic difference. Ray Honeyford, the headmaster who had been at the centre of a major row in Bradford in the 1980s, when he argued that accommodating cultural differences within schools detracted from the major aim of assimilating Asian pupils into British culture, now insists that the riot of 2001 has proved him right (*T&A*, 9 July). For others though it was the often enduring inequalities which link race with class and which gave the Far Right their opportunity to incite trouble. *The Guardian* points to the (limited) electoral success the NF and BNP had picked up in the recent election. Whilst agreeing that 'young men . . . let rip', they insist that: 'This reaction has less to do with race and far more to do with anger and alienation' (9 July).

Charles Husband, author of a study of Pakistani youth in Bradford, notes the 'disadvantage and exclusion' which they suffer, leading to a heightened awareness of difference, sowing the seeds of conflict (thisisbradford.co.uk: 15 July). William Stuart points to the long history of confrontations with the Far Right in Bradford, most potently the 'Paki-bashing of the 1970s and 80s' (*Sunday Business Post* on-line, 15 July). Darcus Howe recalled a different time in the 1980s when both blacks and Asians (those who 'had broken with mosque politics') were together members of Bradford Black Alliance, activists whose politics were underwritten by a common experience of work which created cross-community linkages. The collapse of the textile and related industries had now left 'isolated and alienated communities' and led to violent outbursts 'without organisation or cadres of any quality' (*New Statesman* on-line, 16 July 2001).

This then is the story and the range of understandings of momentous events at the time. What did the participants who were caught up in the turmoil think they were doing?

# 2

# MAKING SENSE: THE RIOTERS SPEAK

*There was going to be a National Front march . . . they were obviously coming down to cause trouble . . . When I got there the police had pushed them back and they made a barrier between the National Front and our lot . . . (it was a Bradford thing) . . . that's what made me angry—they come down, causing trouble [he means the National Front] . . . there's no way yer can say yer having a peaceful march, can yer? . . . telling us to get outa the country . . . they're saying stuff like that. So how can you expect to have a peaceful march and a peaceful demonstration—they can't, can they? . . . the police shoulda done summat about it, stopped them coming . . . the way I saw it, the police wanted em to come . . . they can't just come into our town . . . it's your home town . . . Next time they're going to think twice about it . . . If they hadn't come down, that day, there'd have been no reason for us to get together like we did . . .*
**(Rioter interviewed in prison, 2003)**

In September 1936, thousands of people came out on the streets of East London to protest against a march by Sir Oswald Mosely's British Union of Fascists. 'Mosely planned to send a column of thousands of goose-stepping men throughout the impoverished East End dressed in uniforms that mimicked those of Hitler's Nazis. His target was the large Jewish community' (*The Guardian*, on 50th anniversary, Sept 30th, 2006). Police formed a protective barrier to allow the march to proceed. The locals rioted and set on both police and fascists, bringing the march to a chaotic and violent end. *The Guardian* claimed that what became known as 'the battle of Cable Street . . . encapsulated the British fight against a fascism that was stomping across Europe'.

Around the same period, people in Bradford also engaged in violent demonstration against Mosley's Blackshirts, as we shall see in chapter 6, which also discusses how often the Far Right have come to Bradford in force. If there had been an actual invasion of 'Asian areas' in Bradford by the Far Right in 2001 the actions of a few hundred rioters might have been regarded as heroic—if not now, then in 50 years' time! The threat of the National Front to march in Bradford was diverted however, so we are left puzzled and bemused, wanting to know: 'so why did they riot?' And why do some of them talk as if they were re-enacting a battle most of them will never have heard of?

We have seen that many people suggested motives at the time, particularly ones of sheer criminality. The rioters themselves were effectively silenced—whilst they faced the full rigours of the law and very harsh punishments designed to deter them and others from any repeat performances, they did not have their day in court—almost all pleaded guilty and did not speak. As they were not politically organised before the event, they had no political platform of demands or rationales for action (as compared with those who organised the preceding rally, with leaflets and leafleting, recruiting of speakers and so on). Nor, in the melee of the riot itself, did any 'leaders' emerge to speak for the rioting crowd. Another factor also came into play, as we shall see. Whereas the rioters generally assumed that 'the community' of other Asian Muslims was on their side, after the violence they were generally spurned.

Without asking the rioters themselves, it is impossible to guess or to judge their motives. This is what we set out to do. By the time we began our investigations in 2003, most of the riot cases had been through the courts, though they were to continue into later years. Out of 144 charged with riot, 107 adults had so far been given custodial sentences averaging over four years. From a listing of these, we drew up a 'random sample' of 25%—26 prisoners. These turned out to be scattered in 11 different prisons, though four had already been released. One of the prisons was too far away for us to reach—we decided to limit ourselves to locations in Yorkshire and Lancashire, reducing our sample to 25. When we approached the men for their permission, all but three agreed (one of these was going to appeal) and we failed to trace one of the releasees. This left us with a sample of 21 (20%). The point of a random sample is that the diversity within the whole population (here meaning all the adult prisoners incarcerated for riot) has an equal chance of being represented. The sample can speak for the whole.

Getting to some of these prisons could mean a round trip of nearly a hundred miles, and occasionally arriving to find the man we had permission to interview had been removed to another prison the day before. At the best of times it meant being frisked and depositing our belongings at a reception centre and then being taken by guards down long corridors to the clank of keys and arriving in a bare room to await our man.

Each interview lasted approximately one and a quarter hours. In prisons we were allocated a private cubicle in which to do the interviewing. Releasees were interviewed either at the University or in a friend's house (they did not want to be interviewed in their own homes). Interviews were tape-recorded, though three of those in the sample refused to be taped, whilst in another case the prison authorities refused permission. Where tape-recording was impossible, extensive notes were taken. Despite the prison setting of nearly all the meetings, we found most eager to talk. Each interview was carried out by one member of our research team of three. We were all women, white and no longer young. The prisoners were young men with an average age of 24 (age range 19–35), and all but one were Asian Muslims (one was African-Caribbean and two had white mothers). In order to reassure the men and to enable us to understand their responses better, we employed three young Asian men from Bradford, none of whom had been involved directly in the rioting, but were similar to the rioters in many other ways. One of them accompanied us on each visit and they usually contributed some questions of their own. We had a set of guidelines for the interviews so that they covered similar ground, and they were deliberately conducted in an informal, almost conversational way. All the men were assured of confidentiality.

We do not rely wholly on the transcripts of these interviews for our understanding of the rioters' views. We also commissioned a small survey carried out by a young Asian interviewing six of his peers about how they made sense of the disturbances. Their views revealed raw and sometimes intemperate reactions in the immediate aftermath of the riot. We also talked to many other lads on a more informal basis. About a year later (2004) we followed up our interviews with visits to the rioters' homes to ask if they would take part in a workshop where we could feed back our overall findings from the research. Although several were still in prison and one or two had moved, we gleaned an impression of families with residential stability living in a wide range of properties all over the inner city, with the majority occupying small terrace houses.

In the course of our work we decided to see if we could get any comparable understanding from Ravenscliffe, the 'white estate' in which the much smaller disturbance had taken place on the Monday after the main riot. Would the 'rioters' there have the same or different rationales for their violent actions? Only nine youths from Ravenscliffe had been convicted—but of 'violent disorder', not 'riot'—and they had received much shorter sentences—averaging 21 months. This difference in treatment would continue to rankle for many months, as we shall see later. Our foray into Ravenscliffe exposed some surprising contradictions. On the one hand Ravenscliffe people described themselves as close and with long-standing family connections within the core population. However, our attempts to trace those who had been convicted (all but one had been released by mid-2003) disclosed the shifting and short term nature of many tenancies on the estate. Not only did the releasees no longer live at their previous addresses but the present tenants had never heard of them. We traced only a couple of those implicated, but as well as interviewing them we talked to other residents about their views of the riot and life on the estate. We were struck by the contrasts between streets of blighted and boarded-up houses in the midst of neat properties with beautiful and well-tended gardens. We do not claim that our investigation of the Ravenscliffe disturbances was extensive, but it did give us some insight into a very different way of thinking about the city and its problems.

Asking violent young men to explain their actions is often seen as a waste of time. It is assumed that they will provide cover-ups and that they will lie. At best one will only hear self-serving accounts. Several of the young men that we interviewed admitted that they had indeed lied, to police and to parents—and they felt little or no shame in trying to get themselves out of trouble in this way. Police videos show them hurling missiles or trying to set vehicles alight and they denied that it was them—one even insisted the youth in the video was a 'lookalike'. Another says, 'I knew it was me, yeah, but obviously to save my own skin I was saying, no, it wasn't me'. One tells the police that 'I didn't throw no bricks' whilst to us he admits throwing many. Several said they had owned up only to what was on video, whereas they had perpetrated many other violent acts. One says: 'in the police station I was denying it, I was telling my father nothing happened. I was hoping to get away with it'. Many owned up only when their pictures appeared in the press. In an extreme case, one lad had devised a whole catalogue of lies to evade punishment. He denied to police that he had thrown a petrol bomb, but freely admitted to us that he had done so, and he lied to parents and family that he had been in the riots. This young man had a job and no previous convictions. Once he was charged he saw he might lose his job, so he invented an expedition to Africa in connection with some volunteer youth work he was doing—this stratagem was successful as he only got a short sentence and returned to work.

In general, the rioters' stories were designed to put themselves in the best possible light—as indeed most people would like to do. If the audience for such accounts were parental, community or public authorities then various defensive rationalisations might be offered. Some claimed to have been drunk, or to have been drawn in to help others, or to have responded to police brutality. We shall return to some of these accounts, not all of which were false. Conversely if they were recalling events to their peers, they were full of bravado and bragging, exaggerating their fearless heroics. In this case they were less self-consciously aware of editing the record, but definitely doing so all the same.

So why bother to ask them for their side of the story, when we could not completely trust them? We had other sources against which to check—police files and videos—and from these we also found that many had not lied, either to the police or to us about the details of their involvement in the riot. For us it was important to acknowledge all these accounts as representing truths in some sense. We needed to understand how the young men's perceptions of the situation led them to act. Were their judgements clouded or distorted by rumour or by prior and threatening experiences? Was there indeed any justice or reason in the way that they understood the unfolding events? How do they see themselves in relation to others, or judge the consequences of their actions? We gave them the opportunity to make sense of the riot and were struck by how much thought many had given to this reflection.

## Rioters: Social Profile

In 2006 a Channel 4 'docu-drama' on The Bradford Riots had as its main character a young man who was a university student. We later interviewed one ex-rioter who had been on a degree course at the time, but his case gave a misleading impression of the rioters, who were by and large lads without much education or prospects. All but two of those we interviewed were from Bradford, with more than half of these from the BD7–BD9 areas which have high Asian populations. Half were born in Bradford, another quarter elsewhere in the UK. A quarter were Pakistani born, but most of these arrived as young children. Except for one lad of Jamaican descent and two with white mothers, their parents were born in Pakistan or India. When they spoke about others in the riot they usually identified them as 'Asian'. Asked to identify themselves, they usually offered a dual tag, for example 'Asian Muslim' or 'British Pakistani'. Only three left out their formal status as 'British', but added to it a more personal status—'Pakistani' or 'Muslim' were the most popular.

Although sons were sometimes vague it seems that the majority of their fathers were initially manual workers, many in the textile industry. They would probably have experienced a period of unemployment on its collapse in the 1970s. Some families have suffered periods of real hardship and still live on the poverty line. Other fathers had worked hard to build up savings or pool wider family resources, which some now invested in a taxi perhaps, a restaurant, or buying and selling property. By 2003, most of those still working would seem to be on modest incomes whilst others are retired with other family members working. Few of the mothers seem to have worked in the formal sector, and this was taken for granted by their sons. One, asked if his mother worked replies, 'No, she comes from Pakistan'—and the three exceptional cases were all non-Pakistani women. This is not just because of women's lack of skills or fluency in English. Being able to afford to keep a wife at home is an assertion of male status. The point is that most of these young men have been used to mothers at home, and to fathers with cash power but often out working. This pattern is very different to that of the white population at a similar socio-economic level.

Family expectations were high for their sons' education and work prospects, but these had not been realised. Although almost wholly educated in Britain and mostly in Bradford, educational outcomes were poor. Over half did not even achieve GCSEs and had dropped out of school by age 16 or before. Of those who did complete their GCSEs (or returned to education later) none had completed any further study courses—they had dropped out again. Hence their horizons were narrow, even though some clearly had ability. Conversely most had received some formal Islamic teaching, though their practice of religion was often lax, as we shall see.

Seeking work with very limited qualifications, it is hardly surprising that almost two thirds of these young men had only been able to acquire manual jobs or routine white collar work. However, on their imprisonment only a quarter were unemployed. Police records for all those charged suggests almost double this percentage and undoubtedly some of the work was hidden, being off the books or additional to benefit claims. Of those in work, one man was a textile worker, several worked in the building trades, in shop work, catering, factory work or packing. A couple had skilled jobs as chefs, with others working in telesales, customer services and accounts. One had a semi-professional position, whilst one or two others had been helped by family to buy rentable property or takeaways. At least one seemed to be earning from illicit activities (drug dealing). Family connections (family businesses) have been important for almost a quarter of these men, though they have gone in at the bottom, not the top of such enterprises.

Although nearly two-thirds of these young men were single and without dependents, over a third were already settled, all but one with children. A lot of marriages seem to have been arranged familially, through Pakistan. Even young men without wives felt they had family responsibilities towards parents and siblings. These men cannot be understood as unattached hotheads—the family is important for their lives.

At the time it was said that many of those arrested for riot had no previous convictions. Police records suggest 40%—which still means that the majority had a record. Our sample was of men incarcerated for rioting and only five of these were first offenders. Three-quarters (16) of them had a string of previous convictions, though mostly of the kind that many young men in Bradford accumulate—drug, drink, car offences and shoplifting loom large. However, six had convictions for violent behaviour. On the whole they regarded the police with suspicion, some even to the point of hatred. Drink and drugs were often what led them into petty criminal behaviour. Despite their Muslim backgrounds 63% of our rioters are (or recently were) drinkers of alcohol, with four claiming this as the reason for their involvement in the riot. As we shall see, this puts in question the assumption that arson attacks on pubs had an anti-alcohol, religious motivation. Nearly 80% admitted the use of drugs— primarily cannabis. Conversely, nearly 40% insisted that they were non-drinkers. Given the Islamic prohibition on both alcohol and drugs, the 'confession rate' is quite high here.

There is a good deal of diversity in this group of rioters, but considering the whole social profile we might have expected some restraint on violent action. Most became involved despite having jobs, even 'good' jobs, family responsibilities, some maturity in age, and a religious upbringing. Nor were they cut off as Asian Muslims from the whites who lived around them. Listening to the lads talking about their lives we found that two thirds of them freely mentioned significant social relations with white people. They had white workmates, friends and neighbours. One had a white wife, children and in-laws, two had white mothers and many lads had, or used to have, white girlfriends. Again we are left asking, what then led them to riot?

# Routes into Riot

The riot of 2001 did not begin in Manningham or any other area of Bradford with a high Asian Muslim population. It began in a shared public space, Centenary Square in the city centre, and involved Asian youth coming together with people of other and diverse origins in a peaceful protest against 'fascism'. It started as a legitimate public political event. This is despite the fact that many of the Muslim youth may never have attended such an event before and may not have come with the same understandings as those who organised it.

And some youth who were later involved in the riot were drawn in after the peaceful rally had ended. Indeed young men joined the action at all stages of its later development and for reasons possibly unconnected to its origins.

Some of the lads claimed that they knew there would be trouble in town.

> When the riot started I actually knew it was going to happen . . . There was word out that there was going to be, not a riot exactly, but . . . a National Front march. And that had been displayed on stickers and stuff on phone boxes. It was the National Front themselves that put stickers on in our area [West Bowling].

Several said they'd seen 'posters', though probably these were to advertise the Anti-Nazi League rally, like those handed out at the Mela the weekend before. These leaflets said 'racist parties shouldn't be allowed to come into a multicultural city'. 'There were, what do you call them, leaflets handed out saying there's a big protest, because of BNP doing a march . . . So that's why everyone went down there'. 'But', added another, 'we had no idea of a riot'. None thought the riot was organised in advance. '[Police] officers tried making it out as if, oh, the riot was planned and they had some big planners and—that's all bullshit . . . it was just one of them things, yeah, where people just got together'. For most of these lads, coming to Centenary Square was a spontaneous last minute decision, often made with friends. It was a Saturday morning and some were at home, others cruising idly around town in cars, others shopping. 'I just got told by a friend (they were drinking together at the friend's house)—there's going to be a demonstration, the NF's coming down'. Another said he went 'just to see what was happening' because 'everyone knew . . . there was a protest, the Anti-Nazi League was going to come down and they were going to make a march and there was a lot of people there making a protest . . . Just to stop the Nazis'. 'I knew they were coming' said another:

> . . . a week before, I seen it on the internet, how they were going to have a march in protest coming through Bradford. An' I think three days after that there were going to be one in my home town in Keighley, yeah.

The sense that 'everyone knew' the Far Right were coming was powerful. 'So at this time, yeah, everybody were ringing and saying oh, NFs are coming, big coaches, and they're coming on trains and this and that—and they made it into a big thing, d'ye know what I mean?'

Around half of the lads we interviewed had been there at the beginning and most of them had then been around to see the mood in the Square turn ugly after the rally had ended, had seen or immediately heard of the incidents in Ivegate and Southgate which had turned disorder into mayhem and violence. One or two were still part of the action until it faded away many hours later at the BMW garage in Oak Lane. Most of them were involved in the stand-off on White Abbey Road. Some had multiple entries. It was not uncommon for lads to be in the thick of it and then go home and have some tea, visit friends or 'drop in on grandma' and then rejoin the riot later.

Other rioters were drawn in after the rally, not having planned to be there. Two young men were driving about with friends in Huddersfield when they got a call from another friend in Bradford, saying that 'police and everybody, they're fighting in the city centre'. They turned their car around, zoomed back to see what was going on, found a scene of chaos and joined in at the top of town. Another lad was with a friend in the early evening when they heard two police helicopters hovering overhead and thought 'there must be summat going on here'. He and his friend went to White Abbey Road where they could hear the mighty roar of a crowd approaching in the distance 'like a football crowd in the stadium'. They were unaware of earlier events in the Square. He got drawn into the action when he saw a friend of his being man-handled by police: 'I wasn't there to get involved . . . but, heat of the moment'. Another man had been brought into Bradford by friends from his home in Halifax to do some shopping. When he tried to get back to the car at the end of the day the unrest was taking hold and police blocked his way, calling him, he claimed 'a fucking Paki . . . me head went' and he evaded them and joined the rioting crowd. At least two told us they were drunk—one said he had been drinking in a pub off White Abbey Road and had come out to see what all the noise was about and found himself in the middle of the riot. He was so drunk that he fell down, but picked himself up and joined in. It was not until the following day that a friend told him that it was all about 'the NF, who had come from Oldham in 19 coaches'. Another man said he'd been at home when he got a late evening call from his (white) neighbours who were in the Labour Club, begging him to come and help them to get out.

## Rising Tensions

From those lads who had gone to see the demonstration in Centenary Square we get accounts of how a peaceful protest spiralled into violence. Once in the Square few of the lads paid much attention to the rally itself. However, one said:

*Saturday Night and Sunday Morning*

. . . there were people who were saying we don't want those NFs here and they had anti-Nazi stickers and posters and stuff . . . what I think they believe, yeah, is ethnics and whites should have equal rights and you know we shouldn't get thrown out of the country if we're Asian.

Only two others mentioned the speeches and the stewards with armbands. What they remembered were:

crowds of people, standing together . . . Asians, white people, black people . . . all different kinds of races . . . I was not really taking much notice what they was doing, because I was standing around waiting to see if I did see the NFs . . . Yeah, everybody was just waiting, to see what was happening.

Another said that 'people were just stood there in protest'. They wanted 'a peaceful demonstration'.

But then the mood changed:

something just kicked off, and they started running about for a minute, and then the next minute there's fights going on in there, people throwing bottles and police pushing people about and that.

Most of them found police already in the square, and estimated them at between one and two hundred. The police were also wearing what looked like riot gear. As one rioter said, 'they had no reason to stand there in riot gear', given this was a peaceful event. Another man described how the police 'formed a line, like they were trying to split us up from the NF, but like I say I never seen no NFs, know worra mean?' He agrees that at the time he thought there must be NF on the other side. 'The police were charging forward like, to disperse the crowd . . . Everyone were running all over the place . . .' Another talks of being 'surrounded' by police, whilst a third saw men that looked like 'NF':

I don't know if they were skinheads or whatever they were, they popped up out of nowhere . . . near where the Hilton is . . . And there was a few confrontations and er, everyone just started throwing bottles around an' stuff . . . .the police started chasing everyone on horseback, past the police station . . .

Clearly the presence or otherwise of the National Front or other Far Right elements was central to the lads' perception of what was going on in the town centre. They had come down expecting to confront an enemy—and some of them did see white youths that were taken to be the enemy. Many more heard rumours on their mobiles, 'loads of NF'—of coaches arriving and said to be parked up near to St George's Hall. The lads who had driven back from Huddersfield reached the bottom of Manchester Road and stopped to talk to some other friends, when one of them started shouting:

'National Front, National Front'—right, so I looked in the mirror and there must have been, I'm not going to exaggerate but, you know, about 20 to 30 lads, you know, walking down with big beer bottles, crates . . . White lads, yes. They were coming out of these back streets now [Clifford Street], I've seen them coming out.

Two claimed to have seen ten to 15 of them 'by the police station . . . chanting slogans . . .' Later on others saw presumed Far Right youths near to pubs. In the early evening one man drove with a friend:

> . . . through the town centre and they were all there, you know, all the NFs and everything, drinking, you know, just having a laugh . . . . [outside the Boy and Barrel pub]. And when we drove down—we had our windows open, cos it was warm. We had our windows open and they seen us, yeah. They started shouting abuse, yeah. And then they come running at us with, like, yer know, like glass pints and stuff. Throwing it at the car. So we sped down . . .

Although the lad who saw 'NF' by the police station claimed they 'had them stickers on supporting National Front and stuff like that, BNP party and all that', most of the youths presumed to be Far Right were not labelled in this way. Indeed when we asked the rioters how they recognised 'NF', their answers induce doubt. They were 'skinheads with white t-shirts and jeans, yer know, yer don't think twice . . . they're wearing these kind of braces with blue jeans and black boots—it's like a uniform'. Others were even more specific— they were 'white lads who wore "Burberry caps" and sweaters with certain brand labels'. They were 'the sorta people yer see at football matches'. 'They all dress the same: shaved heads, green jackets or bomber jackets, jeans, red Doc Martens . . . yer know what the National Front look like'. Some associated them with the Ointment (Bradford football fans). Others identified them as 'skinheads' with 'tattoos on their heads'. Many were absolutely sure that 'yer can tell who's who', they were not just any white lads, 'yer can tell the difference'. A few identified them by their actions rather than their appearance—they were into 'swearing' and 'racist abuse', 'they can look like anything, but they're racist'.

Having said that, they generally knew them by repute rather than as a result of personal experience. One spoke of a fight in a night club where he was 'punched out of nowhere'. Another spoke of being beaten up two or three times by youths he took to be NF, and how he 'hates them'. 'Paki bashing' was mentioned in West Bowling, but others spoke more generally: 'A lotta people I hang around with, yeah, they know the difference with NFs an that, they get into fights an that. I don't want to go too much into that'. Others said it was all in the past: 'You hear stories from the older generation, my Dad says back in his days you couldn't walk down anywhere without getting bashed up, spat on, called Paki or whatever. But things have

Saturday Night and Sunday Morning

changed a lot since then'. One lad had never heard of the holocaust or of Nick Griffin (the BNP leader) though he talks of 'Nazis'. For others the threat of the Far Right is all pervasive: 'a lot of Asian people feel threatened all the time'. Although their hatred was palpable, it was almost theoretical, until two key incidents confirmed all their prejudices.

# Trigger Incidents:
# Ivegate and Sunbridge Road

Around 3.30pm, 'they say, the police . . . went on t'mike and said the National Front haven't turned up, so will yer go home, disperse now—know worra mean—peacefully.' He did not hear this himself, nor did any of his friends. The police now attempted to break up the crowd: 'the police were charging forward like to disperse the crowd . . . Everyone were running all over the place . . . ' And when the lads:

> tried to scatter all over, the coppers an that get more violent . . . We got through eventually, by pushing an' that. No point just standing there, yer'd just get trampled all over the road . . . [the police were] pushing people onto t'pavements, swearing and everything and getting violence.

Any orderly dispersal was stopped by lads bursting out of the cordon in response to rumours about a fight in Ivegate nearby. One rioter spoke of a 'stabbing' and of 'loadsa people' blocking the entry into the alleyway at the bottom. 'There were coppers up at t'top. And t'coppers charged down and everyone started running down'. Outside Addisons Wine Bar, a noisy crowd of Asian youths were being held back by the police. In the pub were the 'NFs'—white men and youths, who came out shouting 'Paki bastards'. 'Bottles and glasses were being thrown from inside the pub at the Asian youth'. The Asian lads were throwing them back and the police were trying to keep them apart. This youth thought that the police were protecting the NFs: 'they knew the NFs were there and they knew they [the rioters] were going to attack 'em'.

In this chaotic scene, none of our rioters saw Kasel Altaf being attacked (he was not stabbed), as they were pushed back or forwards, away from the scene. But the rumours spread far and wide. One man was drinking with a friend in a car near to Skipton in the early evening when they heard news of the riot in Bradford on the car radio and returned to Bradford. There he heard that his friend Kasel Altaf had been attacked in Ivegate and joined in to avenge him on White Abbey Road, although 'I was totally drunk'.

The second trigger incident a few minutes later near to Sunwin

House affected only one of our rioters whose friend was later charged with the stabbing of a white youth:

> we felt we had been provoked by that white youth punching one of my friends . . . It still doesn't justify whether they are NFs or from the BNP, it still doesn't justify to go around stabbing people that had punched him . . . but at the time we were angry.

A 'white youth got injured and hurt . . . and that's what started it all'. Soon, many came to hear of this incident too—'I heard . . . a Nazi got stabbed by somebody'. As the rumours spread, passions were inflamed.

> The Asians down town were going crazy, chasing everyone. This is how we see it, they come in to cause trouble and take us out, if I know he's going to take me out, I'll take him out before he takes me out . . . take out means fight and defend yourself all you can.

Although people had scattered in different directions they were drawn back in and towards Westgate. As one said, there were 'police everywhere. They surrounded in such a way that we ended up in White Abbey Road . . . [police] chasing us, batons everywhere, flying . . .' At the Marlborough pub one recalls seeing a lot of white men 'with pints in their hand' who came out of the pub to see what was going on. Another lad went into the pub to buy cigarettes and then stood outside with the white landlord, 'The police is there and lads chucking stones and everything at the police'. 'Police was pushing them out of the city centre.' Some said that 'It was only when the police arrived [on White Abbey Road] that everyone started to gather up'. Some claim that the police drove people into a 'full Asian area'. 'They wanted to push them into their own area . . . with them charging at us, swinging their bloody batons'. By now, the talk of 'NF' is over—'cos by the time [the riot] took to White Abbey Road that racist thing about the BNP . . . that was all down the drain, that was gone'. 'They came in, a few of them, provoked it, and then got outta there and left it at that'. The hatred of the Far Right was gone because now, as they saw it, 'the police is targeting against us' and 'It turned into a riot against the police'.

As far as these men were concerned, the Far Right had definitely been on the scene, and moreover the police were complicit in this—'they were protecting them and they should have been protecting us'. 'Because the police know that NFs don't get on with Asians, right so, they let 'em in, yeah, to cause all the trouble, so there is racism there'.

Saturday Night and Sunday Morning

# A 'War Zone'

By now it was evening and White Abbey Road had turned into a battleground, the police piniored at the bottom of the hill. Any and all materials that were at hand were used as weapons by the rioters. There was equipment left by road building works, beer barrels, a mesh barrier used as a shield, bricks and stones—'they was on the road' or the lads were 'breaking the walls' as they passed. 'It were like extreme situation . . . so extreme measures are going to 'appen'. Soon there were petrol bombs to hand as well: 'there were lads there with crates . . . petrol bombs and stuff'. This rioter insisted that the materials for these were easily to hand—bottles from anybody's doorsteps, petrol from cans kept for an emergency in cars, wicks made out of torn shirts. The Lower Globe pub which was derelict and later set on fire was said to have a store with empty bottles and gas canisters in it. Our rioters denied pushing cars at the police, though this happened, or setting fire to pubs. For some these pubs were 'their locals' and 'I'd say 70% of them lads . . . they drink themselves'. 'I don't agree, yer know, wi' pubs getting attacked' said another, 'I don't because I used to go into 'em meself . . .'

By now the number of rioters had swelled as mobile phone calls drew in more excited youths eager to see what was going on and to join others like themselves: 'it's a brotherhood thing'. 'When I stood at the top of White Abbey Road I could see nothing but people . . . there were just hundreds of faces'. Some had raced in from Manchester or even Birmingham or other places, responding to media coverage or calls from friends. During the next few hours most were heavily involved in the violence and anarchy. 'There was this great massive fireball, yer know, the whole road was on fire'. There were lots of cars 'smashing an getting burnt' and 'pubs getting attacked'. One rioter admitted 'I threw a petrol bomb and I hit a few policemen with it . . . and one of them's rolled on the ground . . . they had protective clothing on and nobody was hurt [but] I could have killed somebody'. This man was arrested at the scene. Cars were rolled down towards police lines. 'I'm sure one of t'police got squashed', said one rioter '. . . it was dark then an that', and there had been people 'injured when the stones were being thrown, people getting hit'. Another remembered with horror:

> I seen, like-rolling cars down the street—they weren't saying to people to move, people were just getting mowed down by cars as they were pushing 'em down, I could see people just lying over the windshields an' stuff like that, an' I thought this is getting too hot and I might as well go.

The rioters were actually injuring each other as the volleys of stones came over, and the ambulances couldn't get in as the crowd attacked them. People around had to help those injured—one man had seen people being carried off. As one rioter concluded, 'This is war'.

At the same time there was a sense that this was an unequal combat. The police were accused of 'barbaric brutality'. They were 'kicking people like animals'. A youth was standing:

> . . . and the police come with a police dog, and they let their dog go, and the dog was chasing the guy, and I actually saw it . . . blood all over. There were 30–40 guys watching and they couldn't do anything—they started throwing petrol bombs at him [a police officer], but t'copper, guy that was injured and the dog were all on fire, so . . . definitely that dog incident wound em up.

Another lad described seeing 'one man down, he got a right gash in his head, cos he got hit by a baton'. The police:

> . . . were ready outright for war, weaponry . . . they didn't have guns, but they had shields and batons and truncheons and helmets. None of the youngsters had helmets and truncheons . . . I can't see the police as victims. I actually seen them . . . attacking people.

They also excused their own violence as self-defence: 'police charging with a truncheon . . . summat inside me just snapped. I picked up a stone'.

Because the police were wearing riot gear, the lads ceased to see them as human beings, because they 'had all them bloody . . . helmets and the lot, they were like Roman soldiers'. They couldn't tell the difference between men and women police. 'If they mix the coppers, male and female, yer can't do much about it'. One says that by this time he and the other rioters were beyond taking account of whether there were women there or not. 'I waren't bothered', whereas another says that if he had realised it would have brought him up short. But on the whole they felt 'police is police', no matter what gender or colour.

The rioters were also critical of police tactics: 'Every time the young lads were calming down, the police would charge at them and wind them up again'. 'The further up they were pushing 'em, the more violent it became'. The police became trapped at the bottom of the hill, when 'what they shoulda done, they shoulda come from the top of Abbey Road and trapped 'em, shouldn't they?' So why didn't they do this? 'They wanted to push them into their area [Manningham]'. And the police over-reacted, 'If the police even calmed down even a few minutes an that, yeah, they coulda settled that crowd down. But they didn't think. They shoulda been there, doing their job'.

# Arson and Looting

As the riot built up, properties began to be attacked. One of the first to suffer was probably the Whetley Car Company, up Whetley Lane, which had many cars for sale on its forecourt. The semi-derelict Lower Globe Pub next door was also burnt down. Later, and in the most serious incident of arson, the Labour Club at the top of Whetley Hill was set on fire with many customers still inside. They were rescued but only with difficulty. And so it went on, with looting and firing of properties ending with the BMW garage at the bottom of Oak Lane.

One question raised was whether white businesses were targeted in this orgy of burning. The lads we interviewed understandably denied this claim: 'if it was a race riot, a lotta white houses, people's houses, woulda been burnt'—which they were not. And the Whetley Garage was Asian-owned. 'The bloke who owns the car thing, he's Pakistani, isn't he? They pushed [the cars] down the hill and set them on fire'. One rioter admitted that he saw people setting fire to the cars: 'I did, but I'm not saying owt on that'. He claimed that he 'just watched, let them do it', and he agrees 'it was exciting an that, but I didn't get involved with it'. It was said that the pub next door was owned by the same man, but 'it were derelict', with the implication that it did not matter that it got burnt down. A betting shop, part of a national chain, with two white managers, was set alight at the top of Whetley Hill, by 'two white people . . . and a couple of Asian people. And they were smashing up the shop, yeah, and trying to torch it and burning it'. One youth claimed he had pulled out a burning carpet in a bid to stop the fire, The Asian barber next door was known to one youth who saw this incident: 'I live near him back home, he came out shouting, oh, you know, my shop's gonna get on fire, don't burn it, this and that, but they wouldn't have it, you know what I mean. Once somebody's head's gone . . .' Fortunately the fire did not spread.

One of our sample was initially accused of being involved in the burning down of the Labour Club, though he said he had not been at that site and the charge was dropped in court. Like many of the others he distanced himself from this potentially catastrophic event: 'there were people still in there, that should never have got burned down'. Another admitted he had seen lads involved in the arson and had thought:

> . . . oh that's a bit over the top, yeah. I seen people with big golf sticks and you know and I thought whoa that's just bang out of order that— do you know what I mean. That's just taking it a bit too extreme. That's taking it too far that.

Another wonders why the perpetrator did not get a life sentence. 'He's not for the community, you know what I mean. There were children in there. That's totally . . . that man was wrong. He was wrong . . .'

The Labour Club was not the end of it. Some of the rioters headed up Toller Lane and Heaton Road and were involved in the destruction of the Junction pub and Arthur's Bar. By now the rioters had completely lost any sense of mission. As one said of this phase, he was with others, 'taking drinks, smashing up cigarette machines and bandits—just for the sake of looting it. To destroy it'. In one pub they'd found two Asian men drinking—they left, whilst the bar workers had already fled. The same man was still in the thick of it as they marched down Oak Lane towards the BMW garage. At first he claimed just to be watching as others smashed their way into the BMW garage, pushed cars out of the showroom . . . and 'then they set it on fire'. But then he confesses, 'I think I did go in there . . . it was really dangerous. There was cars in the back behind the car park, I think I was in there'. But he claims he didn't push any cars out. Some lads found the car keys in the garage office and took them and drove off cars, 'driving them up and down Oak Lane', some just smashed them up. At that time, he claimed, there were no police on that road at all, none there when he arrived and after the building exploded, 'I just decided to go home because everyone was just walking'.

# Going Home

Most of our lads had left the riot long before this. Two were arrested on White Abbey Road. One of the drunks claimed he'd sobered up and gone home to sleep, whereas another man just 'got bored with it, there was just smoke everywhere . . .' He was 'tired and hungry, I just wanted to leave'. Five of them had become afraid for their own safety in the midst of this huge crowd, seeing others injured and thinking 'that could be me'. Matters were going 'too far' or getting 'outa hand'—they were fearful of being trampled by police horses or beaten by police or they were shocked by their fellow rioters' extreme actions: 'people were setting cars on fire'. Some felt they could not trust themselves: 'what if I might do something stupid?' Or they suddenly found themselves lonely in a crowd: 'at one point I was stood there alone, watching'. One described how at about midnight he had reached the top of Lilycroft Road where the roundabout and the 'cop shop' is, and he and a dozen other youths were so exhausted that they collapsed onto the grass in the middle of the road. They had drinks—though this turned

Saturday Night and Sunday Morning

out to be 'cans o'pop' rather than alcohol—'one lad were dishing em out'. He started walking home, sat on a wall to rest and saw 'massive mushroom clouds, there were explosions' coming from the BMW garage—'I were drained of energy'.

Some admitted that family pressures had eventually forced them away from the mayhem. 'Cos I seen me father an me brother and they said, come on, you'd better go inside now'. They had been out looking for him—they were not involved themselves. He was near to the Labour Club when they found him and had seen it alight. Another remembered 'Yeah, I got picked up by me brother on his way home from work'. His mother had said 'you'd better go and find him':

> An he picked me up and I were on t'top o' Toller Lane. And he told me, he sez, BMW's getting burnt down, you're at the wrong place. So he took me down there and that's when I saw the cars flying out yer know an back ends burning. I thought, what's this!

He had gone home earlier in the evening and 'they were going to give me up'. Despite this—his awareness of their anxiety, he went out again, disregarding their pleas. 'They couldn't really do much. They did try, yes. Me mum, me sisters—me brothers warn't there— they were at work . . . Ladies can't do that much—they know I'm on the drink an' all'. He didn't have a row with them:

> I just kept it low, kept it quiet, just tried to get outa there, cos I didn't want to take it to them. It's easy done when yer' angry, already boiled up from the riots an then coming home and then someone says something and yer off with them then—and yer've got yer own little riot at home.

He laughs at the memory.

Like many of the other rioters, this lad received mobile calls from his family in the thick of the battle: 'Me mum, me brothers an sisters, they all rang me up—but I didn't answer' (though he noted the phone number, so he knew it was them). 'They were telling me to come home . . . They know what kinda person I'm like—they know I'll go down into something like that. They were saying we're here, we're here, we know yer having a riot'. Another lad had been rung by his sister who lives in Birmingham. She realised from all the noise in the background that he was in the midst of the disturbance, so she said 'just get home . . . She just kept ringing me, so . . . I had no choice'. The reason for leaving was not because he thought he would get caught: 'it didn't occur to me that I would get caught'.

There was clearly a tension here between commitment to family and the assertion of independence. One man told us how his mother kept ringing him 'Get 'ome, get 'ome!'. He ignored her pleas, insisting, 'But I'm a grown man'. Several however mentioned that they had prevented their younger brothers from joining in. One said his brother 'watched it on t'news and wanted to come down but I told him he couldn't, so he stayed at home . . . I just feel protective of him . . . He listens to me'.

# Mediation Attempts

If the lads were not under family constraint during the riot, they also assumed that they had the backing of the local community, even of that audience of bystanders, mainly white (of whom there were hundreds, women and men), on White Abbey Road:

> . . . you got houses on the right yeah, and they're mostly white houses and they were just coming out and watching and stuff and they were sort of cheering it on . . . people don't like the police, know what I mean?

Some of the lads had themselves tried to restrain others, telling off youths who were throwing stones in town, or who were swearing at the white owner of the Marlborough pub. One described how an Asian elder called Zulfikar, with a beard and traditional dress, was going round 'telling all the lads—what are you doing? Put your stones down. I thought he was the sanest person there'. Later he tried to support an elder who had been allowed through police lines with a loud hailer and was shouting to the lads, 'Disperse! Nothing will be done'. He approached him and said, 'look tell the police just to calm off a bit'. They did not, and soon rioters snatched the man's loudhailer. Another man admitted that he had backed off a bit, when they were approached by elders asking the rioters what they thought they were doing: 'they were the same age as ma dad'.

This level of respect was rarely accorded. The lads largely ignored any attempts at mediation or peace-making which took place during the riot. One man had seen 'one or two Asian councillors. They were trying to say . . . don't do it, don't do it, but nobody was listening to 'em . . . what do they ever do for us?' Another had seen older men, 'voicing their concerns, saying: Shame! Go home, messing up yer own area!', but had ignored them. Some of those who intervened sparked particularly abusive responses:

> . . . some MPs did come on [but] who the fuck does he think he is? What the fuck has he done for us? He's only picking himself up in front of the police, so he gets his name even bigger. Why is that? . . . Community leaders as well, because I will not listen to someone I've got no respect for.

This man accused politicians and self-styled 'leaders' of being corrupt and self-serving. Like others, he 'didn't listen' to their demands that the violence stop.

Religious leaders, Imams, were not present at these attempts at mediation. Maybe the youth would have listened to them. However, one rioter was dismissive of a younger religious man from West Bowling mosque who had tried to intervene. This lad had no time for religious people: 'I just don't trust em'. All but one of the rioters we interviewed were nominally Muslims—the exception was an African-Caribbean with strong bonds with Asian Muslim friends and who told us he was 'not deep into' Christianity—indeed he had occasionally attended Friday prayers in prison. About half of those we interviewed counted themselves as religious, some of these because they came from strict families, others who had found religion themselves and prayed regularly, fasted every year. 'I know my Islam' said one; another that his religion was 'for life'. It should not be assumed that they thereby avoided drink and drugs—at least half admitted to drinking and/or smoking cannabis. One of the lads who claimed to have been drunk in the riot was in this category, as were many who admitted violence in the riot.

The rest of the young men were more lax in their practice of Islam—though nearly all of them claimed to at least attend prayers on Fridays. As one said, 'I'd never lie to yer. I don't attend mosque regularly, except Friday prayers'. Only one man said he did not pray at all, and indeed ate secretly during Ramadan. Another told us he did not need to pray, though he did so occasionally. Three of these who were not particularly religious were also non-drinkers, thus fracturing the usual assumptions. In general though, it is clear that religion played little part in restricting those who took part in the riot, and religious leaders made little attempt to intervene.

Some young men had their own explanations for the lack of respect for elders and betters. One man spoke at some length about the 'lack of respect for the older generation today—the youth think they can do as they please, no-one can tell them anything'. In his view this was because Asian parents are not allowed to physically chastise their children any more. One lad said that elders did not understand—they thought that matters could be sorted out by 'talking, but sometimes talking is no good'. In the riot, anyone viewed as a 'community leader' was ignored. The riot assumed a compelling power of its own over the participants.

Almost everyone speaks as if there is a single 'community' amongst Asians in Bradford, but in truth divisions are large, even amongst Asian Muslims. The young men also speak in this misleading way as if 'the community' were indivisible. They spoke of assuming initially that they had 'community' backing—after all, were they not defending the community? One said that at first 'I was applauded for my actions'. But within days it was clear that the rioters had little support. Some lads were angry that afterwards they were 'grassed up' ('my community gave me up'), and they were shocked that so few expressed a negative view of the long sentences they received. One described the process at length—how, soon after the riot, local politicians, who just wanted 'a name for themselves', called meetings of elders, saying, 'we're backing the police . . . And now the whole community is saying what happened is wrong'. The police then, according to him, took advantage of this to claim community support for publishing the pictures of rioters in the press. The elders were then shocked to see their own sons and grandsons amongst the rioters. This man felt that his own father had given him up to the authorities when he told him in front of his probation officer: 'you should respect officers, officers is like an elder because they put their uniform on, he's like a father figure . . . He has to look after the community—I'm thinking, oh what are you saying, dad!' The humiliation of being treated in this way is mixed with disgust at his father's grovelling acceptance of police authority. But the father is also making a point about the respect due to elders and fathers, and which has been breached in this case. At best they could say that given a common experience of racism, 'Not many people agreed with why [the riot] happened, but they understood why it happened'.

## **Making Sense of the Riot**

By the time we interviewed these lads, they had already had considerable time in which to find explanations for the riot. A few were remorseful, others felt sorry for themselves for being caught and imprisoned. The strongest reaction was to cast blame on others for the riot—and in particular Far Right elements who were thought to have incited and provoked the local population, and the police for what was seen to be a heavy-handed and unnecessary response, punishing local youth rather than the 'fascists'. Bradford was the stage on which the battle was set and the lads' feelings about Bradford were part of the story they told.

Before the 'NF' were in Bradford they had been in other Northern towns—Oldham and Burnley are cited—where they provoked violence and were said to have broken into houses 'where there were just women'. What they did was 'intimidating to people, just put the fear in them'. The lads believed that the intention was to attack the Asian Muslim community in Bradford and that they were

Saturday Night and Sunday Morning

called on to defend it: 'if you bring NF, this is what we'll do to protect ourselves', and 'we've got to defend our territory, we live there'. Although the territory in question is not seen to be just Asian areas, but the whole of Bradford, Muslims are particularly threatened: 'the Muslims in Bradford, we've had trouble with the NFs all the time . . . we didn't want 'em here. They just want to take over . . .' They saw the National Front as 'Nazis' and racists: 'trying to call me Paki, go back to my own country'. The rioters 'thought the Nazis were probably going to take over the town'; their goal was 'only to get us out of here'. The riot was 'a big conspiracy', said one, 'the BNP have it all planned'. Another noted that the Far Right 'set the flame . . . and watched us being sentenced'. The BNP 'fooled people' (by threatening and then not turning up in any numbers) who 'eventually vented their anger out on the police'.

The police became the target of the rioters' anger for two reasons. Firstly because they were perceived to have allowed the National Front to enter the city, and once there to have protected them against the fury of local people. Secondly they were accused of provoking and taking part in brutality against the rioters and of being racist. Several of the men had not understood or accepted that the National Front's planned march had been banned and they blamed the police: 'they let 'em in'. Some went so far as to assert that 'the police wanted 'em to come' and 'the police, man, they set it up'. In their view it was 'the police's job' to keep these thugs out. And once they were in the city the police should have focussed on them, not on those who protested against them. They should also have let the crowd know that the NF were no longer there. When Kasel Altaf was beaten up in Ivegate 'the police . . . did nothing'. 'The police were concentrating on the Asian youth whilst the whites were getting away with everything—they should have dealt with it equally'. And later it was strongly believed that the police had driven the crowd back into an Asian area. And so it turned into 'a riot against the police'.

In the resulting confrontation, the police were seen as provocative. Initially at the peaceful rally 'they had no reason to stand there in riot gear . . . they were stood there like they wanted a fight'. And many of the lads insisted that the violence was started by the police: 'they should know better than how to incite a riot'. One said, 'it turned violent like when the police were pushing people onto t'pavements, swearing and everything . . . shoving them outa the town centre'. Others spoke of intimidating tactics—the use of barricades, dogs and horses, police baton charges. Several said they had joined in after seeing or hearing friends being beaten with truncheons. The sense that police action was unnecessary and not 'normal policing' also led these men to feel that they were being targeted: 'the police is racist' and 'we're humans, not aliens'. More than one spoke of the police using racist language ('fucking Paki'). Discriminatory police action made one man feel 'like I didn't belong'. The apparent failure of police officers to drive off the 'NFs' made it easy for these lads to jump to the conclusion that the police sided with the Far Right.

We have seen that most of these men have had previous experience with the police and more than one admitted that the riot gave them an opportunity 'to get their own back'. As one rioter said, some had 'anger in their faces—they just wanted to hurt the police'. The police are seen by many as continually harassing people like them: 'we're living under oppression' said one who had been stopped and searched many times. Some had a more politicised view, the police were 'part of the government . . . a police government'. The response to the riot was evidence of a conspiracy, said another, ('freemasons innit') in which government was in cahoots with judges and the police to ensure that people like them were punished disproportionately.

If the view of the police in the riot is almost uniformly negative, these lads did compare it with what they saw as 'normal' policing. 'I think police are there to protect people and to keep the peace . . . but they haven't done what they're supposed to do'. 'They don't hate us, they are human, they have to protect the community'. That the police are seen not to have done so on this occasion meant that they did not deal with the riot 'in a political way', whereby 'they have to do everything by order and by law', not swearing or using physical force—'their job is to calm things down, not provoke us even more'. Several mentioned better relations with community constables, the 'everyday police', some of whom were described as 'decent' and 'fair'. One was volunteering in a youth club run by the police and another had even considered becoming a police 'special'. They noted that the police were mostly white and that more Asian and black officers were needed.

By blaming the riot on the Far Right and secondly on the police, these young men were also often expressing a commitment to what they saw as under threat, 'home'. The value they placed on family and community and their commitment to the town in which they had been brought up is obvious. 'I'm proud of Bradford' said one, 'the biggest part of my life'. 'I just love it, Bradford', it was 'our town'. 'Bradford's where you're from', said others. The riot was about preserving Bradford as a 'multicultural place' and so they had 'no choice but to stand up'. As they saw it they were also protecting their families and community from the specific racism of the Far Right. They knew their parents had experienced racist intimidation

*Saturday Night and Sunday Morning*

and been unable to retaliate through fear and lack of numbers and felt they were righting these historic wrongs:

> . . . in those days people used to call 'em monkeys or raisins . . . me dad used to tell me how it used to be, even me mum. This country is a very racist country . . . now the Asian people, Jamaicans, won't stand for it, know worra mean?

'The new generation is angry' declared another. Whilst being prepared to do battle themselves, they had generally tried to prevent younger brothers from involvement ('I just feel protective of him'). As we have seen there is contradiction in this claimed support of family and community, for they ignored family pleas to stop the violence and come home and they despised self-proclaimed community leaders. They acknowledged that there was a generation gap with lack of respect for elders by youth. But it was in the aftermath of the riot, as we shall see in chapter 7, that the youths had recognised the contradictions, when 'my community gave me up' and families were shamed. Most had prevented their mothers or sisters from attending court hearings and were unhappy about their families visiting them in prison. One said of his mother 'she's a queen in my eyes' and she did not deserve to undergo prison searches and humiliation to see him.

The experience had left them with a profound distrust of community politics, and for some, a confirmation of conspiracy theories, but not one which had yet led to them questioning their own politics. For example: 'Nobody votes . . . an Asian lad or an Asian. I can guarantee you at least 65–70% of them will say no . . . Our parents . . . understand the value of the vote, whereas us lot it doesn't affect us'. They were caustic about community 'leaders' but simply expected them to deliver, not for this to be a collective effort: 'we want good people to sit on those seats, not corrupt'. The riot itself was not the outcome of prior political organising or consciousness raising, and even within the action no clear leaders emerged to formulate its demands. Whilst it is clear that, 'no-one was organised, wa they? . . . they just went . . . yer just go for it', nevertheless they had turned up positioning themselves against the National Front and for some the riot had a meaning, for 'people to listen'. 'Organising' then took the spontaneous form of networking:

> One person, once he rings a friend, and then the friend rings a friend and then the friend rings a friend of the friend and then they all get together—but the officers thought, yer know, Asians had sort of organised it—but that's not true.

Some of the lads had indeed found themselves alone in the riot and this became the basis on which they questioned the charge of riot as action with a 'common purpose': 'I don't know the crowd. I don't know him . . . or him, he's not my neighbour, he's not my friend'— he was not 'part of a crowd'.

Though these youth were not politically organised they did have some political views. They had general grievances about their lives ranging from the lack of facilities for young people, to segregated education systems and the need for more black people at higher levels of society. After all, one said, everybody's 'tax goes into the same pot'. At the time we interviewed them (after 9/11 and the Afghanistan and Iraq invasions) there was much angry talk of 'Blair n' Bush'.

Finally, there is a powerful strand in the accounts that the rioters give which offers an additional explanation for their actions. Most of them spoke of the excitement of participating in the riot in a way that suggests that young men were here defining their masculinity, as 'hard men'. The length and extent of the violence is neutralised and excused as, 'just guys throwing petrol bombs at the police . . . we were just having fun really . . . it was blown out of proportion—it were just t'lads and t'coppers having a laugh'. Another described the 'battle' as a 'game' in which the army could eventually have been involved. It was a 'fight to the finish. It does mek yer feel strong, cos yer done it with a load of guys and lads'. There was a bravado in seeing 't'police get squashed'. They conceded that 'the adrenalin kicked in', and that it was 'like a mission . . . James Bond'. There was a pleasure in fighting. Some saw themselves as 'soldiers': 'they . . . wanted to show off, it was like *Braveheart*'. Doing it together added savour: 'everybody got involved . . . there's an excitement and then there's a joy to it'. Being in control was not part of the picture: 'I'm in the middle of a war zone . . . me head went'. For some this bravado was boosted by alcohol—as one explained, 'it were the drink . . . it does get yer more violence'. During the riot he had 'a bottle with me, charged up'. For others it may have been the assumed expectations of their peers: 'I know people'd be ashamed to say this, but I were afraid'. Some were even fearful of their own strength and of how they might 'kill someone'. Images of war and hardness abound, linked compellingly to honour and revenge.

# Ravenscliffe

A common theme in the rioters' stories is their sense of injustice at the sentences given to them compared with the much more lenient ones enjoyed by those involved in the violent, but much smaller disturbance in Ravenscliffe estate a day later. Shocked by the high tariff of up to 10 years for the offence with which they were charged—'riot'—they had come to learn that the rationalisation was the collective action ('common purpose') of more than 12 participants. Most of them denied that they had come together with the intention of initiating a riot, although it could be said that a sense of identity with others developed in the course of the battle. As already noted, the Ravenscliffe offenders were charged, not with riot but with 'violent disorder' and therefore received much lower sentences. As one of the rioters noted, there were 'more than 12 of them [in Ravenscliffe] . . . so why didn't we get charged with violent disorder?' Many of them had an answer to this question—it was 'just because of the colour of their skin'. Like the police, they tended to dismiss the Ravenscliffe disturbance as 'copycat' action and at least one saw it as more racially motivated than the main riot: they thought 'the Asians are coming'. Few of the lads in the main riot had any first-hand knowledge of Ravenscliffe. One described it as a 'no-go' area for Asian youth, not somewhere he would feel safe. When asked why he thought they had rioted, he said: 'they were just being bad'. The main rioters were not being 'bad': 'because actually, yeah, we were trying to stop National Front members from coming down'. The point being made here is that the main riot was not 'racist' but rather positioned itself as political action.

We cannot claim to have a clear view of the motivation of those convicted for the violence in Ravenscliffe as we were only able to trace a few of them. One had been sentenced to nearly two years in prison, and had served half of that. What we discovered by talking to these and other Ravenscliffe residents was firstly that their explanations contained more racially-charged language. Secondly they had an overwhelming sense of grievance about their lives, in which the 'Asians' had come to be seen as the major cause. However, there was a more complex relationship with 'Asians' than this might suggest. They made distinctions between local Asians who had lived on the estate for years, and the general population of Bradford Asians. There were also many mixed race people born and brought up there. In the event, local lads were prevented from venting their rage on any actual Asians, and they had taken the police as proxy in the same way as the main rioters had become locked in battle with the police in the absence of Far Right combatants to attack.

The triggers to the disturbance in this case are not very clear. We were told that the police had swamped the estate from early on the Monday morning, and that they had had earlier warning of possible trouble. But the 'trouble' itself was externalised as 'a loada Asians' were coming down 'for a riot'. People thought that they were 'all in their cars on Harrogate Road' (the main road leading past the estate) and that the police had set up road blocks there. 'The Asians were coming. They were all here at t'top of t'road'. 'The Pakis come causing trouble'. Another rumour was that a white lad from Ravenscliffe had been stabbed in the main riot, though this turned out not to be true. One lad said he had been having a drink with a friend on leave from the army, and they believed these stories, and came out to see what was happening. They had never seen such numbers of police in Ravenscliffe before, wearing riot gear and using protective shields. He knew all the other lads involved. They had been at school together and he joined them in hurling stones, 'people brought them in wheelie bins'. He admitted that:

> . . . it were totally wrong . . . but because I'd been drinking, I didn't think about it . . . Because of the excitement and because of the adrenalin of what were goin' on, it teks over . . . you haven't got to take part, but yer feel like outa place if yer don't—and everybody was doing it.

Another lad was just 'hanging about' on the streets when he got caught up in the disturbance, hearing that 'the Pakis were coming down' and the police were trying to stop them. Mid-evening, he was in the crowd that stormed up his own street and put a brick through the window of an Asian resident who was suspected of being a drug dealer and a 'pervert'. His family had watched this man bringing home 'bags of H' (heroin) and young white girls of 13–14 years old who were not prostitutes. The crowd threatened to burn the house down, but veered away when they realised the danger this might pose to other houses nearby. Everyone agreed that the mass invasion by Asians never materialised, but they had been prepared to defend their area—the Ravenscliffe lads 'were really ready for it'.

Many local residents found themselves in the thick of it. 'They were all outside our house. Loadsa lads—the police come and they started fighting. There were hundreds of them'. 'There were a loada people shouting and logging bricks'. There was a sense of excitement, with some saying 'we wanted a chance to kick off' and that it was 'a bit of fun' and 'a laugh'. The police were now taking the brunt of the violence and being accused of complicity: 'it were t'police, winding everyone up. People were geared up, they feared something would happen'. Another says, 'T'police let Pakis onto t'estate . . . T'police didn't get hurt—they were just putting it on'. The strong conviction was that the police were shielding the Asians from attack by Ravenscliffe lads. 'People don't like the police, they protect Asians'. At the same time it was said that Ravenscliffe people generally regarded the police with suspicion. In all of this there are similarities with the main riot.

Exploring why these young men and other Ravenscliffe residents were so ready to see 'Asians' as a threat, we uncovered some surprising responses which went further than the occasion itself. One of the rioters himself had a half-Pakistani mother and sister, though he had not been brought up in an Asian setting and it was his mother rather than he who disclosed this fact. He himself felt extreme resentment against Asians. Most of this was directed towards young men and related to competition over girls: 'that brings most of trouble'. Asian lads were said to 'steal white girls' from their boyfriends in the course of clubbing and drinking in the town centre. He had much personal experience of verbal abuse and fights with Asians in such settings. 'Asian youth, I never really got on wi' em. They have got no respect'. They also behaved badly in their cars, cutting across others in challenging ways. Another said, 'Asians take the piss'. Nor were things expected to improve, 'it'll never work, they live separate lives'.

Given this hostility it is surprising to find that the small cluster of shops in the estate were mostly run by Asians. They were seen as different: 'those Asians are all right with us'. They had gone to school with their children. The daughter of one of them was described as 'one of us'. And people of mixed parentage, like the rioter's mother and sister—'half-castes' was the term used—were also accepted: 'I'm not prejudiced—me sister's half-caste'.

Of more general concern was the sense that in Bradford, Asians got an unfair share of the resources, 'I think they like to get a lot more than people expect . . . a lotta white people feel a threat of how the Asians is getting bigger n'bigger and taking over everything'. It was resentfully conceded that Asians were smart: 'them Pakis . . . they save their money up. They send their money home. They're rippin' off our system. I know Pakis mesel' . . . Pakis want to own Bradford. They own everything anyway'. And their response was adamant: 'They're not tekking our area. It's all outa order'.

A few were more reasoned: 'Everybody believes the Asians took all our jobs. I don't think that'. But the sense of being cheated by life is powerful: 'there is a lot of discontent on Ravenscliffe. No jobs, no peace' and there was 'nowt to do here so you cause trouble'. Unlike the Asians, lads here did not have a love for their city—they felt trapped and would have preferred to live elsewhere. Things had gone downhill: 'This used to be the best estate'. They had little confidence in the capacity of external authorities to improve their situation: 'They're just trying to buy us off. We're the ones on the ground'. In many of our conversations with people in Ravenscliffe we noted a profound defeatism and lack of self confidence. Here too they may compare themselves with Asians: 'Asians don't like a shit-hole like we do. Even our club—look at it! And houses all boarded up . . .'

We were aware that the BNP had been active on Ravenscliffe and enquired about its impact. 'On this estate they're not racist at all. They've got black sisters and brothers—loads of 'em', insisted one man, 'they wouldn't vote for the BNP'. But the mother of one of the lads showed us a small poster the party had produced in support of a campaign to get the rioters' sentences reduced. She also admitted voting for them in the following local election. But her son was wary, he thought it would be 'quite scary if they did actually get in'. And he had never heard of their leader, Nick Griffin.

What we learn from comparing these two violent events is that despite many parallels, the Ravenscliffe disturbance was not an exact mirror image of the main riot. The deep-seated grievances that were exposed in each case were not dissimilar, and in both cases the police became proxy for the enemy, never seen as standing neutrally between warring parties but as a target for bitterness and resentment. Both events became a stage on which young men (often lacking in self-esteem, insecure and marginalised by their communities) expressed their masculinity through bluster and bravado, a delight in the adrenalin high of battle and descent into anarchic criminality. And both disturbances exposed the tensions of a post-industrial city with a history of immigration. One explanation for the Ravenscliffe events is to see it as an intervention in a legitimate political debate—about the distribution of public resources in the city, in which they claim to have been unfairly treated. Their response is not to blame those who distribute the resources, but those whom they see as more successful than themselves in getting a share. In Ravenscliffe the 'Asians' had become the scapegoat for thwarted ambitions and deep insecurity. Conversely, the participants in the main riot made political claims about the threat of 'fascism' as a rationale for their violence, lifting this upheaval beyond a 'race riot'. These were unanswerable claims in so far as they were not supported by political organisation. Unsurprisingly the police saw their actions as 'a riot without a cause'. Acknowledging that both these sets of rioters had legitimate grievances does not in any way lead to us condoning the violent means by which they expressed them—there are other ways of making political demands and getting one's voice heard, which in other times they might have pursued (see chapter 6).

# 3

# UNDER FIRE: POLICE PERSPECTIVES ON THE RIOT

*The riot was 'yet another kick in the teeth for Bradford . . .
I felt like shouting . . . can't you understand what you're
doing to Bradford? The bottom line is, I was born here,
I've lived here all my life . . . how the hell are you ever
going to get people to invest in Bradford when all you're
gonna do is burn things down . . . I was angry.*
**(Operational Officer)**

The forces of law and order received high public commendation for
their handling of the 2001 riot. This is understandable in that so
many of them were injured in the violence. However, they had failed
to prevent disturbance turning into riot. In the very first reports of
the violence the police were subject to criticism. The *Telegraph and
Argus* (9 July 2001) expresses astonishment that:

> . . . despite a tip-off [that] there would be serious violence, police
> chiefs so badly misjudged the situation, were unable to snuff out the
> first hint of trouble and ended by being totally outnumbered by
> rioters (9 July 2001:2).

They had, in fact, lost control of the situation.

Despite the commendations, and behind the scenes, there were
police who were more critical of their actions on that day. They
conceded that many mistakes had been made, whilst still laying the
major blame on the rioters. Our awareness of this more analytical
stance derives from 10 interviews which we carried out with a range
of police nearly two years later. Memories were still very raw and
vivid, especially for those who had been on the front line, four out
of five of whom had been injured, two seriously. We chose our
interviewees from a list of volunteers, aiming to cover a range of
positions, from those who bore the brunt of the violence to those
who coordinated the response. All except one were Bradford

officers; the exception had been drafted in from a neighbouring force. Two were women, one an Asian. When asked about their social identity, they mostly said 'white European/English, whatever', not really appreciating ethnic labels, but some added their class origins with pride: 'I was just a working class kid', 'we're just the plebs aren't we' and 'we're not posh but we had a nice clean home'. Class outcomes as well as origins were important—one officer insisted that social class was far more significant than ethnicity:

> I live on a [private] estate . . . lots of Asian people round there—but I don't look on them as being Asian, I look at them as being my sort of social class . . . I've got a certain standard of living and I like to live amongst people of that social standing.

Religious identity was not so important to most, with one or two describing themselves as non-believers. They had lengthy service in the police force, from seven to 29 years. Most of these were long interviews, some lasting over two hours, mostly carried out in the police stations where they worked or, with a few, at the university where we worked. The police permitted their personnel to speak openly in these interviews and we were struck by their frankness. As with the rioters, we have not identified individuals and have not disclosed their precise job titles.

In what follows we take first the accounts of front-line officers and then their commanders. Despite the differences in experiences, we uncovered some common themes. There is a real sense in these accounts, missing from the public record, of the challenges and difficulties faced by police officers in these chaotic circumstances, as well as their feelings about the unfolding violent events. Police, like rioters, do not generally have a public space in which to voice their reflections on such an experience, and they took full advantage of the opportunity these interviews provided.

# Front Line

## Prelude to Riot

Those called out on the day had little idea what was in store for them. Certainly most could not have imagined that they would be on duty for over 18 hours without relief, and how fast a peaceful rally would be transformed into violence on an extensive scale. One officer was expecting to work from 8am to 6pm but did not go home until the early hours of the next day. She was assigned to a Police Support Unit (a PSU) and given a 'briefing' beforehand, but there was no warning of what was to come. It was just 'the usual stuff . . . whether it be football or a march'.

Saturday Night and Sunday Morning

They began the day patrolling Centenary Square.

> To start with there were just the Anti-Nazi League in Centenary Square, setting up a little stall and giving out badges and balloons and stuff like that. And then more and more people were gathering . . . the Anti-Nazi League were—they had a megaphone . . . shouting stuff and obviously making some sort of a speech but it was really poor quality and I couldn't tell what they were saying.

At that point there was 'no trouble' but she noted the unusual composition of the crowd:

> . . . the official Anti-Nazi League protestors who'd actually set up on the morning, they were predominantly white I would say, mixed sex and probably I would say they were all aged in their late twenties, maybe in their thirties and some older. And everybody else virtually were Asian males, aged, I don't know, 16–25 possibly.

However, she also saw white youths: 'they weren't the BNP who supposedly were gonna arrive but they were white males of a similar age, a little bit older perhaps. I wouldn't say skinheads but I suppose they fit that description'. She saw other officers stopping some of them and assumed there had been intelligence that they intended trouble.

And then the mood changed and suddenly 'the atmosphere was awful, really, really heavy . . . quite aggressive'. They were sent to change into their 'full protective gear'. Within minutes they were dispatched to the top of Ivegate with orders to stop youths coming down. 'That's when we got the first bricks there. We didn't have our shields then . . . our shields were still in the van, cos we'd been running up Ivegate so we couldn't run with our shields at the same time'. However, they did not understand what had happened in Ivegate: 'there'd been an incident in Ivegate in [Addisons] bar with some white group [but] I didn't know that at the time'. Almost immediately she was hit on the leg by a brick but then they retrieved their shields from a police van and were back into the melee. They saw a woman's car attacked, the back windscreen put through, and commercial property being smashed all around—windows at an estate agents, a shoe shop, a bank building. They struggled to cope with this mounting and widespread eruption of violence.

Another officer had been similarly deployed. She experienced the initial mood in Centenary Square as a 'festival atmosphere . . . fun', and 'you could feel the excitement', though she also noted a 'yobbish element'. She too saw no identifiable 'BNP', but a lot of white lads 'itching' for trouble.

> There were some white lads hanging about you know, and I remember some sort of confrontation where like an Asian faction and

> a white faction had words across the road . . . the Asian side were
> stood . . . on the Centenary side of the road you know, and I don't
> know what was said because I just heard, you know, the tone and you
> look round and you could see these, you know like this white lad
> shouting something . . . and then some officer took hold of him and
> he was arrested and taken off . . . and then it just, from there, it just
> seemed to escalate.

Asian and white youths were shouting aggressively at each other, pushing and shoving, and the police were in between. They were sent to get 'kitted up' in their helmets and protective gear. It was a beautiful July day, hot and sunny, and they were soon sweating inside the heavy clothing. A nearby bakers offered them all free pasties, but this interlude ended with the eruption of the Ivegate incident.

She was also deployed to stand in line at the top of the narrow alleyway and saw nothing of the actual confrontation with Kasel Altaf. She spoke vividly of the difficulties of communication:

> . . . you have an earpiece to your radio, but the noise, you can't hear
> anything—you hear very little of orders coming through on radio, I
> mean, I could hear a garbled blur through it occasionally, that were it.
> So you're relying on your sergeant to, you know, relay whatever's
> happening. So you don't know what the big picture is.

But by now there was abusive chanting and bricks were coming at them, buses were passing whose windows had been smashed and still there were ordinary Saturday shoppers milling around, bewildered and terrified: 'people were coming to us for protection and we were having to say to them don't stand next to us, we're the target'. The police were in the thick of it, but barely comprehending what was going on. Then they heard:

> . . . some guy got stabbed [in Southgate] . . . there'd been these
> running battles through the town which of course we hadn't seen all
> that because we weren't involved . . . but you could hear the noise
> and you could hear glass breaking, you could hear chanting, you could
> hear running, you know.

They were sent back to Centenary Square: 'The general idea . . . was to herd everybody into Centenary Square'. They tried to identify ringleaders and she did see some men 'running round telling these lads, you do this, you do that, you go there, you go there, right we're heading this way now. So there was organisation'. There were running battles all over the Square by now 'it were just like mayhem . . . it's like one sheepdog trying to herd 1,000 sheep in one place, because they wanted us to contain everybody in Centenary Square' and then disperse them back home. This proved to be impossible and she had doubts about the strategy, but, 'We're just foot soldiers and you do what you're told to go and do'.

An officer whose task was 'evidence gathering' had sensed the mood in the Square was 'confrontational' from the beginning. He now thought that the initial responses of the police had been 'too soft', and that the reason for this had been their fear of bad publicity. He denied that the rioters had at any time been encircled in the Square, though he conceded that police were blocking the streets leading out of it. 'They're not gonna let a large group of Asian youths who are all angry, they're not gonna say, yeah go up this street'. He too was sent to Ivegate, but he was stationed at the bottom of the street and did not observe the fight outside the wine bar. The public—and the rioters—may assume that the police act according to a plan and that they are directed according to rational decisions in terms of clear information. In reality, most of the police on the ground, like the rioters, gleaned their understanding of what was happening from rumour, 'stories going about'. Nevertheless, by the time we interviewed this officer, he was sure that Kasel Altaf was implicated in his own beating up—he was not 'an innocent bystander'. He also heard about the Southgate stabbing incident, but was convinced that the 'stories' were just 'excuses to cause trouble'.

Front-line officers we spoke to insisted that they had no prior intelligence about the likelihood of serious confrontations in the city centre, but they noted that the press, local and national, seemed to have had warning. The media were there in force and in the way of police work, as well as setting up photo opportunities with young men in the Square. One officer also said that an Asian-owned car dealership in the city centre had closed very early in the day: 'he knew something was gonna happen, somebody told him, cos he'd shifted his cars'.

Of the other front-line officers we interviewed, one had been redeployed from a neighbouring force in the early evening and whilst waiting for instructions in Centenary Square heard about the massing on White Abbey Road, but also that there was some anxiety about a possible invasion of the Central Police Station (which was then situated in the Square). He commented that:

> Bradford Central's actually got windows on every corner of the building . . . And you could see people running around causing disorder . . . because we had quite a good vantage point. We . . . were extremely frustrated hearing officers calling [by radio] for assistance on White Abbey Road and we were stuck in the building waiting for a senior officer to give us instruction.

Arriving in White Abbey Road he was astonished to find that the police had 'lost control', having 'chaperoned' the rioters to a site which he described as the 'worst case scenario because it was one that we could never hope to control'. He denied, as did most of the others, that the rioters had been 'driven' to White Abbey Road, though of course he had arrived after this had become the site of battle. He claimed that the police's main concern was to get the rioters out of the city centre with its 'high value' property and it was simple chance that they ended up in White Abbey Road.

Other officers had different explanations. One claimed that the rioters 'had their own agenda, they had their own plan and they got us to herd them where they wanted to go, you know, they didn't have to be herded, you know . . . they ran up White Abbey'. Her view was that they had chosen this area because it was high ground and because it was familiar to them: their 'comfort zone, they know all the ginnels, rat runs through streets . . .' She here attributes to the rioters a degree of solidarity and organised consensus that does not square with the anarchy of the situation. Others thought the rioters were simply going 'home' (though around half of them did not live in that area). However, it seems clear that the police did not want to be accused of deliberately driving the rioters to a predominantly Asian area.

Another officer was deployed on normal duties elsewhere in the city and not called on until 7pm, when he was ordered to head a team in 'full riot gear' on Whetley Hill. This was the only officer to use the term 'riot gear'—we shall see the significance of this later. He described the chaos, the lack of transport to get to the scene, and the lack of information—he had not known in advance what was going on, there was only 'gossip'.

Although this man had not observed the earlier upheavals in Centenary Square he was a veteran with experience of action in earlier riots—at Orgreave in the miners' strike of the eighties, in Nottingham and in Leeds. His views of the way the riot began—and why—are worth hearing. He saw the Anti-Nazi League (the 'left-wing . . . white Anti-Nazi League' as he described them) as culpable in a minor way—they were, from his perspective, 'whipping up hysteria'. Conversely the Far Right did not make a significant appearance—those who were thought to be followers were in reality just thugs and bullies, particularly youths associated with the Ointment football fans.

> I didn't see anybody who were described as National Front. They certainly didn't come in with the banners, they didn't come in with the arm bands and stickers like they usually do . . . I don't really think the National Front or the British National Party played a huge role . . .

The Bradford Ointment, who are just known thugs really, who support Bradford City, they do a lot of their drinking in one or two of the pubs in Ivegate . . . I don't think they've got the brains for right-wing tendencies [but] I think they'd been winding themselves up for this, I think there were easy targets there. I think that whatever Asians were going to be in the area, they were going to get picked on by this lot . . .

Whilst contemptuous of the rioters' claims to legitimate grievance, he also questions police tactics and strategy. In the initial stage they should not have cordoned off the crowd in the Square—'encircling a crowd does nothing apart from create confrontation' he insisted. 'There's no safety valve for people to go, and when there's no safety valve you get a build-up of pressure don't you?' And once the violence had evolved into a head-on confrontation between rioters and police, he is even more critical of the police response. And he was not the only one.

## Into Battle

Officers arriving in White Abbey Road found a scene of utter chaos—it was now after 7pm, but still light. Police vans were parked up, horses charging into the crowd and the police seemingly overwhelmed and already exhausted. One of our interviewees explains how they were met by officers who were angered by the delay in reinforcements, they'd been 'getting bricked and we'd no idea of that'. Soon all were in the midst of what one called 'a war zone' and facing what would be 'probably 10–12 hours of constant rioting' without any relief. Moreover the police saw that they were at an immediate disadvantage compared to the rioters—'they'd taken high ground, so we're at the bottom of the hill'. Although the rioters were massed and already hurling missiles at the police, there was an audience of people in nearby houses: 'terraces, council houses . . . drinking beers on their doorsteps watching it'. People 'stood there with a pot of tea and what have you in the garden watching, people hanging out of their windows'. The riot had become a spectacle for some, but a horrifying ordeal for others.

One officer's vivid memory of the next few hours is striking:

. . . we ran forward and got bricked and then we were told to retreat so we ran back, and the rioters ran forward, picked up all the bricks and . . . threw them back at us . . . there were bricks coming and bricks coming and bricks coming and petrol bombs and it was just bang, bang, bang, bang, bang, bang, bang, bang, bang . . . the sound was getting louder and louder and louder as the night went on . . . at that point I thought we were dead.

Another officer describes how the rioters came 'marching at the lines, flames going, all bricks flying and they're all walking down going "We want NF, we want NF!"'

Horizontal lines of police were formed across the road, several deep, each unit dependent on their sergeant for instructions, and the sergeant dependent on commands from higher up. But the lines of communication were hampered by the excessive noise and by radios which did not work effectively and a command team which seemed distant and ill-informed of the realities on the ground: 'the organisation was poor, the communication was exceptionally poor, which resulted in officers being stood not knowing what to do'. Another officer noted that:

> . . . there were hundreds of police lines all the way back, when you went back there were people stood there at the back, no idea what's going on at the front. They'd left the front line there for hours, just taking all these bricks, they didn't swap them over.

One heard his PSU sergeant calling up, 'he was saying it over the radio, I want my officers relieving'—but for hours his pleas went unheard. Other PSU sergeants found themselves stretched to breaking point: 'there were other units with no supervision at all and you're trying to keep them in straight lines as well . . . once the line starts to lose it, there's a danger . . . the rioters will come through the middle'.

The onslaught was unbelievable and officers were ill-prepared. Their heavy shields were too short to protect their lower legs and once damaged by missiles, difficult to see through. The visors on their helmets 'continually misted because of body heat'. Some did not have the full complement of kit. Probationers were not authorised to carry batons. One officer described their equipment as 'sub-standard'. Given these inadequacies they were very vulnerable to attack.

> The bricks, you just couldn't see where they were coming from, but the combination of the bricks and the petrol was that when you were trying to avoid the petrol, then you were being hit by the bricks . . . from skidding along the ground to being launched so that they were literally dropping on you . . . cars were being rolled down . . . colleagues were falling left and right, people were being injured which caused the lines to weaken.

The bricks were continuous, brought in shopping trolleys seemingly on supply lines—as one officer said, 'I wouldn't have believed there were that many stones in Bradford, never mind in Whetley Hill'. And at one point 'a kid appeared to the left with a crossbow and at that stage—fear. Fear that somebody was gonna get killed'. When a police officer became stranded they were terrified that he would be lynched—like 'PC Blakelock in London, that's probably what happened to him', reflected one, recalling the Broadwater Farm incident of the 1980s. Worse, some of them felt that calculations were being made, that rather than use rubber bullets, 'the loss of an officer's life would have been an acceptable risk'.

Fortunately no deaths occurred, though there were many injuries: 'we'd started up on about the fifth row back . . . all those people in front of us had either been injured or whatever, and we'd ended up on the front'. Police officers were shocked at the rioters' glee as officers collapsed and were dragged away: 'what disgusted me was each time a police officer fell due to injury there were huge cheers'. This added to their sense that they were set up as 'the enemy' and brought it home to them 'what it's like to stand there and get so much hatred'. The police became the 'targets, they're Aunt Sallies'. In the grip of the violence, the rioters were correctly understood as not perceiving the police as human beings: 'you were just a mass of blue and if a brick hit one of you then that were fine, it didn't matter who it hit'. The majority of those we interviewed returned to the battle despite serious injuries: 'I went back in and carried on'.

Nearly all the officers commented negatively on the tactics they were told to employ. On the ground the police could not believe that they were prevented from acting more effectively. 'Instead of all those officers being there, the horses, the vans, you could have gone round and pushed in from the back or from the sides of those people . . . drive a wedge in . . . you'd have split them'. 'I think our strategy was wrong' concluded this officer. Another said that an outer cordon would have been effective, whilst conceding that their resources would not have stretched to it. As for the way they became immobilised on White Abbey Road and later Whetley Hill, unable to move forward, another officer commented in tactical rule-book terms: 'a static object reduces morale and it gives them [rioters] time to congregate and build up'.

It would not be excessive to say that many officers lost confidence in their commanders whilst they continued to hold the line. One said he felt 'frustration at my own senior officers for the apparent lack of control they had and apparently lack of leadership'. 'I think with a bit more thought from the people who were running this thing in the special operations room', said another, '. . . we could have been split up . . . to chase, to disperse . . .' Another emphasises in retrospect 'how in danger we were and how we'd got ourselves into such an incredible position . . . we really should never have suffered the losses that we did in terms of injuries'. More than one describes themselves as 'cannon fodder . . . you just do as you're told'.

More surprisingly they credited their opponents with being smarter than they were. 'I think we walked straight into a trap and they had better tactics and better plans than us. They took the high ground, they left us to run up a hill and down it, and up it and down it and up it'—the very repetition of phrases underlines the monotonous horror of the situation—the rioters 'had the ammunition all ready . . . they had the troops, everybody was fed and watered'. Their numbers were continually replenished, as their home area was seen to be under attack—'we're going into . . . a big Asian community' said one officer, who nevertheless saw the rising tide of violence as a 'spontaneous' reaction, not a carefully managed plan. Nearby house walls were knocked down to supply the missiles, and petrol bombs could easily be made by rioters who went away and returned. They had mobile phones which were 'a very effective means of communication', compared to the police's own faltering equipment. They also used imaginative ploys to hinder the police advance—barricades built of torched cars and debris. Or they turned the tables on police technology:

> The torches that we used to try and single out offenders or to illuminate when it had got dark . . . was then mirrored by them shining torches at us. And so it was almost a battle of wills and it was a battle of techniques and they were simply using our own techniques against us. But I have to say, with greater effect.

Whilst their protagonists seemed to have the upper hand, many police officers felt abandoned. Not only were the front lines not relieved, they had barely any access to food or water: 'dehydration was a big problem'. A plastic water bottle was handed on: 'we had a swig and passed it on'. 'We weren't looked after' said the evidence collecting officer, 'we didn't actually get fed all night, we didn't get any drink or food . . . you're on the front line'. He was free to go to 'the officers' vans . . . they've always got tea, coffee . . . [but there was no plan] it was an afterthought'.

Despite these impossible conditions, the officers did have a sense of their own expertise and professionalism. One who did not suffer injury commented that he felt 'utter confidence because of the training' he had received in dealing with petrol bombs. And his gear also made him feel invincible:

> Once that first brick hits your helmet or your pads or whatever . . . and you think, oh that didn't hurt, suddenly you become Robocop . . . I remember being hyped up with adrenalin, thinking this is great you know, this is what I've trained for . . .

—and he adds, significantly 'they [the rioters] must be feeling the same thing, this is great'. They denied any acts of police racism: 'I would have been horrified' said one. A woman who was badly injured insists:

Saturday Night and Sunday Morning

> I never lost my professional calm . . . there was no retaliation. I saw
> officers acting so professionally in such a highly . . . emotional and
> really pressure-filled time . . . there was one rioter I saw snatched
> [arrested], brought back through lines, and they put him on the floor
> to cuff him and the bricks were coming over the lines and bouncing
> around him, so this officer put himself in the line of fire to protect the
> rioter from being hit by the bricks . . . I mean that's the ultimate
> professional.

Trying to stay 'professional' was an effort in such a situation. One officer says 'the one thing you really wanted to do was pick a brick up and throw it back'. It was partly the hyped-up fury at what they had to endure that kept them going into the small hours.

It is difficult to get a sense of how the log-jam on Whetley Hill was eventually resolved. But there is a suggestion from one or two that it did not involve orders from above, but officers seizing the moment on their own initiative. An officer leading a unit was heard to say:

> . . . 'we must go forward now, if we pull back now . . . we'll totally
> lose it', and . . . at the same time he just says—'right line forward!' So
> he obviously took it upon himself to go forward and that's when they
> pushed them right up to the top of the hill.

Another officer gives a slightly different account:

> I don't know if there was an order or not, but it just seemed like
> everybody thought, sod this—one took a step forward, everyone else
> took a step forward and we just ran at 'em, because we'd like, we'd
> nowt left to lose . . . we were gonna die so we just ran at them, you
> know and it broke the tide.

By this time reinforcements had begun to arrive from several other forces and there was some relief. The British Transport Police were said to be particularly supportive and skilful in tackling the problem and the riot began to break up. But the police officers questioned why reinforcements had not been called for earlier in the evening, given the severity of the violence. They believed that the army had offered to intervene but were told to stand by. They could only think that their commanders were reluctant to admit that they had lost control. It might be construed as 'a sign of failure'. 'Nobody wants to, you know, be thought that they couldn't cope . . . It's a macho thing isn't it?'

Arriving at the top of Whetley Hill was not the end of the battle. Behind them lay burning cars and buildings and a road littered with the debris of violence. A garage with '40 or 50 cars' on its forecourt had been caught up in the mayhem and many of the cars damaged. Ahead of them was the Labour Club, still with customers drinking inside. One officer described the scene at the top of the hill: 'they'd

lit a barricade . . . you literally couldn't see anything com
you'. And then one describes what he heard over the rad'

> . . . they asked for units to try and make their way to the I
> because it had been set on fire with people trapped insiuc.
> that time I felt physically sick, because while we'd been taking bricks
> and what have you . . . other lives [were] put at risk . . . I would have
> thought . . . police would have taken some form of initiative to try
> and advise people not to open the pubs . . . my understanding is that
> [the rioters] barricaded the fire escape doors . . . which may indicate
> that they knew people were inside and I hope to God really that they
> didn't because I find it incredible.

Because of the case coming up at the time (Mohamed Ilyas was later
sentenced to 12 years in prison for arson) he declined to say more.
Another officer's prejudices were shaken when he went with others
to the Labour Club to investigate.

> An Asian guy came up to us. We were stood, there weren't many
> bricks or anything . . . but there was a car on fire outside the Labour
> Club and there was still a few [rioters] running around. And this
> guy . . . said, 'there's people in there, you need to get them out . . .'

The officer called for help but meanwhile 'what struck me was it was
an Asian that said there's people in there'.

We know that there were no police around when the 'BMW
garage was burned to a crisp' but these officers went on working for
hours after this, chasing up the different strands of rioters as they
began to disperse, some newly armed with golf clubs. Many police
officers were not laid off until early on the Sunday morning, and
some resumed normal duties later in the same day.

## Riot Without a Cause?

Front-line officers struggled at first to make sense of what was
happening and why so many Asian youth had turned so violent.
'Nobody expected the degree of ferocity'. They were united, as we
have seen, in their rejection of the rioters' own rationale—that they
were defending Bradford and their communities from Far Right
thugs, basing this firmly on the insistence that 'they [the Far Right]
didn't come'. When police report seeing white youth who seemed to
be just as 'ready for trouble', they did not perceive them as likely
members of the BNP or National Front. They live in a different world
of perceptions of threat and danger and to them 'there didn't
appear to be a cause . . . to warrant a riot of that scale'. Abhorring
the violence, one officer insisted sagely that 'there are so many
other ways in a democratic society of expressing your opinion'. Given
the lack of a legitimate 'cause' they were more inclined towards
other explanations—that the rioters were 'attracted by violence',

that for some it was 'pure entertainment', peer pressure or grievances against the police. At its heart for several was 'a large group of hardcore criminals and hooligans'.

It was not a simple case of criminality however. Except in prison, criminals are not known to riot. They conceded that this event had a political edge. Some blamed the Anti-Nazi League for fomenting trouble, seeing them as 'left-wing . . . professional agitators' who should have been stopped in advance. But one of them insisted that the ANL, 'don't preach violence at all . . . one of their chants is *black and white unite*. So to say the ANL caused it . . . is wrong . . . but your violent extremists will tag along'. His examples of violent extremists however, were the Socialist Workers Party and CND.

They were not totally unsympathetic towards the rioters. The police have been trained in forms of political correctness and the value of multicultural communities. One had leant Urdu in order to do his job better 'I'm trying to reflect the community I serve'. He had served with an Asian officer for some years which helped him not to see things 'through a white man's binoculars'. He acknowledges the intensity of feeling against the Far Right and says that the police failed to understand this—though it is he who voices scepticism about the rioters' rationale for violence. Many police failed to see beyond the façade of good manners: Asians 'they're lovely people, I've been in where they've got the best china out, biscuits, we've all sat on the settee . . .' Other officers viewed the rioters first and foremost as young men, often spoiled by their families, groomed as sons to feel omnipotent. They thought they lacked good role models, no longer being so attached to religion or the mosque. They explained their behaviour in the Square initially as that of male adolescents, in love with fashion:

> so even if you're going out to . . . cause a riot you don't want to look a mess cos what if you bump into a girl you fancy, or a mate? . . . I don't suppose any of them were really at that stage thinking about the consequences of being filmed.

One derided the explanation that the rioters were protecting 'community values'—she could see that this might explain the torching of pubs, but cannot understand how 'a BMW garage offends against Islam'.

They viewed the rioters as having racist tendencies in so far as they targeted white businesses, but they are not surprised by this response: 'if there's a mixture, as there should be, a good mixture, you'd never ever get all this'. This officer also linked racism to poverty and unemployment and lack of communication between people. Other officers confirmed that ethnic relations in Bradford were not close. 'It's them and us because we don't mix'. Conversely they were cautious in using the word 'racist' about the rioters' behaviour, in case it might boomerang on them: 'I'm terrified that I'll be construed as racist'. One did assert that: 'The rioters are racist, they're racist against the police because . . . they're predominantly white the police. They're racist against the businesses they attacked'. On the whole though, they did not see this as a 'race riot' as it was perceived in the media. Riots had been a part of Bradford's history, said one. He produced a print of a riot in 1871 and said he had seen footage of riots against the National Front in Bradford in the 1970s which were 'mainly whites rioting. Lots of Union Jacks and flared trousers and long hair'. Even in this riot of 2001 there had been whites as well as Asian lads throwing missiles and shouting abuse.

Given their own grim experience of the riot, the police viewed the sentencing as basically fair, though some concern was expressed that those with previous convictions got the same tariff as those with none. They thought the sentences would act as a deterrent at least in the short run, though for some 'it's like a badge of merit' and they might well be 'hero-worshipped'. One expressed her pride in the 'community' for handing the young men in, saying it took 'guts' to do this and they might have acted differently if they'd known the length of the sentences. 'The older generation of Asian, Pakistanis and Indians, they work hard, you know, they keep their noses clean'. Basically they are 'nice . . . law-abiding people'.

There is some understanding here that there were generational divisions within the 'Asian community'. This is also apparent in their comments on attempts at mediation.

> The ones who were trying to stop them from doing it were the older ones, they had traditional dress on, but they were obviously parents . . . older people . . . they were bloody brave, because they got in front of them. Tried to stop them.

It was not just generational differences which they saw exposed here. One officer talks about 'peacemakers' and remembers his astonishment when one 'stood out and told [the rioters] "fuck off back where you come from you black bastards, this is Bradford, this is our area"—and it's this Asian guy!' He was surprised that none of those who intervened got injured. 'The Bishop of Bradford just walked up to the front line and said, "who's in charge, I'd like to speak to them"'. He was a 'sitting target there but they were all prepared to come out . . . all denominations were there—Muslims, everybody were trying to calm it down'. We shall see in the next chapter that little support was given to the peacemakers and they had little chance of success. One of the policewomen commented that her own preferred way of dealing with conflicts was by negotiation, but that the situation of riot offered a hopeless context. 'I'm a talker you know. I can talk people down usually. But—bit hard to communicate with 1,000 people!'

After their ordeal, these front-line officers expected some review of what happened and what lessons could be learnt about policing riots. One said she had understood that there would be some 'policy document', but 'how long it will take is another thing'. None of them had been interviewed about their experiences and views of how the violence could have been better managed, even those who had a wealth of knowledge distilled from previous engagements. Not surprisingly some felt let down. 'I think I was really disillusioned, we are just part of the machinery'. 'Nobody's ever said, "you did a bloody good job", or asked "how do you think we could have improved?"'

# In Command

Understandably those in charge of operations were more defensive than officers on the front line, though in the last analysis they applauded their performance: 'I think the police showed tremendous discipline . . . they operate under instruction and what they were doing was holding the line'. They were also adamant that policing itself had not been a cause of the riot: 'I don't think policing was a catalyst at all'. Unlike the officers on the ground, their commanders had some prior intelligence that trouble was brewing. Following earlier riots in other Northern ex-mill towns, they had visited Oldham to discuss possible scenarios, and had deduced from this that the NF would not come in force, maybe less than 50. 'Those are the sort of numbers that we were anticipating, both from Oldham's experience and from our intelligence sources'. They had advised the council to cancel the last day of the Mela festival which would have taken place in Centenary Square. The NF march was banned, but there were no powers to ban rallies or demonstrations, though they did try to persuade the ANL not to go ahead. They had intelligence officers picking up on rumours around the town which indicated rising tensions and they had cleared debris which might be used as weaponry from around the streets. The Youth Service had been alerted, the mounted section, dogs and helicopters put in readiness. However, 'nothing could have prepared us for that [riot]'.

Operational officers were divided as to whether the riot was pre-planned, even a conspiracy. Some strongly believed that the lads (having also learned from Oldham) were 'ready for trouble'. 'We knew milk had been stolen [for the bottles], there were all sorts of rumours about petrol bombs and we knew that . . . machetes were bought'. Another officer was just as adamant that there was no pre-planning to speak of and that the story about the milk bottles was a misunderstanding—the stolen milk float was recovered intact. According to one officer, National Front members had been seen driving around Bradford the previous week. Tabs were being kept on known BNP members in Eccleshill and Queensbury. One officer was convinced there was 'an element of pre-planning' because the lads came with 'disguises' of hoods, scarves and gloves: 'If I were going to a peaceful demonstration in Bradford on a nice sunny July day, I would be wearing a polo shirt and a pair of jeans or even a pair of shorts'. The reader should refer back to the more tuned-in woman officer's observations of young men and fashion—hoods are fashion irrespective of the weather, and Muslim youth do not wear shorts. However, early use of petrol bombs led him to suspect 'they had some supplies nearby'—perhaps in White Abbey Rd, and that they had stock-piled milk bottles in advance. And of course, he continued, it was the intention of the ANL to confront the Nazis and stop them marching in Bradford—in that sense, 'disorder was planned'. An outright conspiracy was suspected by others: 'there were people behind the scenes [unspecified] pushing the buttons . . . I don't think we'll get them . . . a lot of them did go back to Pakistan'. These were 'the ones that were on the phones . . . and already had the petrol bombs'.

They were as equally convinced as the front-line officers that the Far Right did not show up and hence did not provide a reason for riot. That they were coming in force was just 'a wild rumour', albeit a potent one. One officer noted:

> the tension across the North of England, you know, the threat of right-wing extremism coming to Bradford and a little bit of a siege mentality in the sense that people were so incensed that they felt the need to take action.

However: 'In the event, BNP didn't turn up . . . maybe a dozen'. The white men who were assumed to be NF were really football fanatics. Of the incident in Ivegate, for example, one says Kasel Altaf is 'not lily white . . . to my mind he started all that, everything that happened in Ivegate . . . the first drinkers that were attacked . . . were just football supporters, not racists'. Others agree that the Ointment is racist, but not that it is a vehicle for the Far Right. Conversely they did see Far Right manipulation behind this event and as its beneficiary: they had set up a situation in which Asians riot and are blamed: 'People are scared to say anything in case they're branded racists . . . but . . . these riots [are the reason why the] NF or . . . the BNP are making political gains'.

They were also sure that the rioters were to blame, but their identification of motives was varied. One spoke of 'testosterone-filled males of whatever colour being wound up' by ANL provocation and by rumours. For some it was 'almost like a party'. One officer expressed the opinion that young adult males 'call the shots' in Muslim homes and certainly outside, and that they could no longer be controlled as they were in the past: 'we've got a male culture that is loose from its cultural roots, it's formed its own identity, it's got hip hop and California and drug culture and all of those things wrapped in there'. Many youth drank alcohol and police found this hard to square with their assumption that pubs were torched for cultural reasons—'because we don't drink'. They had been trained to work with 'communities' and towards cohesion, and they were disconcerted to find their sense of positive change confounded. They thought they had learnt from disturbances in the city in 1995 which also involved Asians: 'We're more transparent, we're more open, we've more connection, we've more involvement'. These views need to be set against their perceptions of ethnic relations generally in Bradford: 'there's such a gap between the two societies . . . It's that cultural difference' . . . 'segregated communities'. When police did not deride the rioters' claim to be defending their communities, there was evident resentment of some at their claim to be Bradfordians. Many police were themselves Bradford born and they had a sense of their birth-right being violated. Viewing the chaos, one said bitterly, 'I sat there and thought about mum and dad—they must be turning over in their graves really'.

For many operational police the riot was simply 'thuggery', perpetrated by a criminal element who 'hated the police anyway'. The police were struck by the unpalatable outcomes of their own just behaviour. Although their 'role is to protect those people and enable them to have protests . . . yet we become that face of authority that ends up getting attacked on the night'. The crowd 'took their anger out' on the police. But at the same time there was a racist element: 'it started off as anti-BNP and then it was anti-police but I do believe it became anti-white'. Evidence of this was to be seen in the targeting of white property. Listing all those which were attacked, one officer concluded that the young men saw 'successful white businessmen, making money out of Asian people in an Asian area' as a legitimate target. And there was simple envy such as the stealing of expensive cars from the BMW garage which they couldn't afford 'unless they were drug dealing'.

Like the front-line officers, police in command also conceded that they faced an enemy that threatened to outwit them at every turn:

> Their ability to mobilise outstripped ours. A certain person . . . who is well known in Bradford 7, had one phone call and half of West

Bolling's young people were over there—young men, tooled up, ready to go.

The police at operational level thus had a rationale for why they did not quickly quell the riot and why the police themselves were not a 'catalyst'. They admitted however that lessons might have to be learnt. One says that they were not prepared, their officers lacked training in riot techniques and most police officers have 'never been on a front line'. Their equipment was inadequate and 'the shields were wrong'. But most of all they were appalled by the speed with which their communication system broke down. On the one hand there was the 'overwhelming' rate of calls coming into them from the public, reporting sightings of violent activities and destruction all over the town, about which they could do little. On the other was their poor communication with the front line, where information was either not getting through, or was not being adequately absorbed and acted upon by the operational command teams. There are hints of differences of viewpoint and culture amongst groups at the top which further hindered effective response and left some officers feeling 'immense frustration' at their limited capacity to influence events on the ground.

They were disconcerted when the police became paralysed on Whetley Hill, with repeated retreats. The job of one officer entailed trying to coordinate police activity with other services such as the fire service and experiencing that:

> it's virtually impossible to get through on the phone. The phones are red hot. So I'm either sending a runner [or asking someone else to contact them] . . . for three, four hours I am just totally snowed under.

And yet in another way they had an overview that was unavailable to officers on the ground. More than one mentions the large windows of the Central Police Station giving them a vantage point from which they could view the rising tension in the Square. This view seems to have increased rather than decreased their sense of control as they watched attempts at dispersal failing before their eyes. Nevertheless, reports came to them of all the localised confrontations so they understood the direction of events better than those on the ground. And then they were able to access footage from the police helicopters which were continually circling the disturbances. Towards the end of the evening, two of the most senior commanders watched film of the torching of Manningham Labour Club, and were shocked by the sight:

> Sickening really. Sickening . . . a really bad moment . . . the whole place was in flames and I remember feeling absolutely gutted because—and we both talked about it, you know, about how you

> know everything we work for all the time, you know, it's just undermined by this, you know, [the] division going up in flames . . .

The public might assume that the police would have clear strategic plans for dealing with public disorder, but this one, with its scale and anarchic emergence, caught them unprepared. Some denied that they had tried to cordon off the crowd in Centenary Square. They confirmed that there was a tannoy announcement that the National Front were not in the city and that the crowd should disperse. One officer concedes that dispersal—his own favoured tactic—failed, noting that the rioters regrouped and 'that's when . . . we . . . sort of lost a grip'. Certainly there was no decision to drive rioters to White Abbey Road. They were focussed on protecting 'the commercial heart of the city' and this was just the way things turned out. Indeed they would have preferred the crowd to disperse up Thornton Road. A senior officer insists that there was a secondary disturbance near Infirmary Fields (on White Abbey Road) involving the stoning of passing buses and cars, to which the police responded. Hence the rioters 'actually chose the point of conflict', as the police were then deployed to deal with that disturbance. The rioters were then drawn to that site, and hence the stand-off on White Abbey Road and Whetley Hill. It was said that alternative strategies of circling and trapping the rioters from the top were impossible as they had too few resources. And so it came to a point where they had to admit that 'we cannot cope' and calls were made for police reserves despite the embarrassment—it was like an 'admission of defeat'.

Some decisions were made which turned out to be controversial. One was the impact of when to don 'riot gear'. Senior police officers insisted on referring rather to 'personal protection equipment' and emphasising that:

> Police have to do a risk assessment of what they do and then take control measures. If, as employers, they fail to provide such equipment and comply with risk assessment they are liable as individual employers.

The plan had been to 'police Centenary Square in normal kit, but . . . be ready to respond proportionally to whatever happens'—in other words to change into more protective gear at an appropriate moment. They denied that the change of uniform was provocative: 'people always say, well the police in riot gear are—they're just a green light, oh they've got the riot gear on now kids, come on let's brick 'em', and yet at another point this same officer concedes that 'riot gear' does dehumanise and facilitate violence: 'it's that blank wall they [rioters] see as the riot police'.

Then there was the decision to call in civilian mediators. A list of potential 'community leaders' who might act as peacemakers was available to police and early on, one officer reports liaising with the Community Police: 'what about intervenors . . . who can you contact to try and get them to talk to these people?' At operational level there was an assumption that these men (they were all men) could influence the lads to stop rioting: 'the community leaders . . . are quite powerful people . . . and they were trying to break into [the crowd]'. Also, 'religious leaders . . . were trying to break it up'. There is 'respect for law and order within the elders'. Realistically, however, they soon realised that, in this case, the problem 'was beyond defusing—nobody could have stopped that and prevented them you know'. Another strand to mediation efforts was to utilise the Youth Service who had been alerted and were early out in the Square. We shall see in the next chapter what a difficult position this put them in, and the police acknowledged this: 'they don't like to be too closely associated with us out there because it affects their credibility with young people'. At the same time this officer hints that the Youth Service wanted the police to pull back but were not listened to, hence 'the relationship broke down'.

Other serious possibilities were discussed.

> There was a request for baton rounds [rubber bullets]. These were taken to the scene and the Chief Constable made a decision not to use them. I don't think he wanted to be the first one in the UK to use them.

This raises a significant debate about the extent to which, in situations of civil unrest, each side may respect certain constraints. Interestingly this officer suggests that neither the police nor the rioters crossed a certain boundary: 'the crowd themselves didn't go beyond that boundary but could have done'. After all guns are readily available in Bradford. It is noted that in other places—like Northern Ireland or the London riots in which Keith Blakelock was so brutally murdered, other boundary lines have applied. And over time, the situation has also changed in Bradford. One long-serving officer remembered many years ago responding to disorder on the streets without body armour and 'using a dustbin lid' when lads set fire to two police cars. 'At the time we thought that was unbelievable, we thought that was way beyond the line . . . Well, we've gone way beyond that boundary now'. And yet the only deadly weapon seen in the 2001 riots was a crossbow, which seems not to have been used.

The decision not to use rubber bullets was surely wise as it would have been inflammatory and led to escalation with incalculable consequences. However, this illustrates the general problem faced by those who commanded operations in the riot—everything they tried seemed to fail and they were not in effective control again until they brought in reserves and the rioters themselves began to flag. The question is, could they have done any better?

## Ravenscliffe

One thing that front-line and operational officers agreed upon was the irrelevance and insignificance of the disturbance in Ravenscliffe on the Monday following the main riot. And yet their comments suggest that there is more to it than this, as well as illuminating some aspects of rioting in general. None of these officers had actually been involved in the policing at Ravenscliffe, but they had views. One spoke of 'lovely Ravenscliffe'—she had done a lot of policing there. But 'that wasn't a riot . . . [it was a] scuffle generated by an almost educationally subnormal criminal element to have a go at the police'. Another said that the disturbance there was indeed an 'echo' of the main riot, but also 'light relief'—and 'on such a small scale' that the events were incomparable. However he added that police were again the target of frustration. 'It was the same background, bar the ethnicity—it was white, sorry males, in their late teens causing disorder, there were more females there, slightly'. It was a lot easier to police given the geography of a confined estate. He pointed out that 'it wasn't sustained' but there was 'still the same ferocity . . . there was still the same goading'. Another officer described the incident as 'just a lot of thugs at Ravenscliffe who fancied having a go at the police then used the riot as a cloak to do so'. Some of the youths were just 'having fun'. The level of violence was not so high—according to him, on a Saturday night cars often get bricked.

A female officer agreed that there was no comparison between the two events. However, she noted thoughtfully that the white lads used the Asian lads' riot as an excuse—and the same excuse—'we're protecting our community'. She heard there was a claim that Asian lads were coming to pillage the estate community. 'And I find that quite interesting, that these two groups of people who think they're chalk and cheese, it's amazing how similar they think, isn't it? But yet they're so dissimilar they can't possibly live together'.

They were aware that it was the differential sentencing that had set up questions about the two events. But: 'You cannot compare the sentences because you cannot compare the incidents'. And some were suspicious that the comparison was made simply to fuel 'accusations of racism', which they did not think were justified.

The basis on which one senior officer dismissed the Ravenscliffe disturbance adds more to our understanding of how the bigger event came to be classified as a 'riot': 'normal life as we know it had totally broken down, buses and transport couldn't pass the scene, rail transport into the city had been cancelled'. If a riot was more than 12 people with a common purpose, Ravenscliffe involved more than 12 but normal life did not break down, it was spontaneous, the police were there and it was quickly nipped in the bud.

Despite this, the same officer draws connections of another kind when he refers to one of the key trigger incidents in the main riot:

> . . . the events in Sunbridge Road, the stabbing behind Sunwin House, could have actually been the catalyst for widespread white disorder, cos that went out on *Sky News*. People saw the stabbing on *Sky News*. White man on the floor, Asian people stabbing him. They highlighted the knife going in.

He thinks this may have had an impact on Ravenscliffe. Other officers emphasise the reactive nature of the events there: Ravenscliffe 'was a reaction by white society against what happened, because they will also see [Bradford] as their city'. And that bitterness of white youths which we described in the previous chapter is understood to have potential political consequences. Ravenscliffe is 'a white council housing estate where the BNP have got quite a lot of support'.

# Unheard Voices: Police Perspective

There is one story here about the riot which has not been heard until now, and that is how it was experienced by police on the front line. The endurance and fortitude shown by those who were under continuous onslaught for so many hours deserves to be disclosed. More surprising perhaps is the extent to which these troops felt themselves to be poorly served by their officers and their equipment. Given the extent of the injuries that were suffered, there was scope for them to sue their employer for sending 'ill-equipped and under-trained employees' to face 'violent mobs', but it seems that loyally none did so (*T&A*, 10 July 2003). Certainly there were lessons to be learnt here, but there is no evidence that any effort was made at this stage to learn them. Equipment has been improved, but the collective knowledge of how the incident was policed was not shared and dissected for better practice.

The account of the riot which is given by the police is very different to the story of the rioters. That is partly because the experience looked, felt and was understood very differently from opposite sides of the barricades. Both sides regarded the others as on the offensive, themselves as brave defenders of the city. It must be emphasised that the officers we interviewed were volunteers and we were convinced that they were being frank and open about their

*Saturday Night and Sunday Morning*

actions. If there were officers who—in the heat of the moment—lashed out indiscriminately and used abusive racist language, then we suspect they would not have volunteered to be interviewed. That some did behave like this seems likely, not just because so many rioters spoke of it, but also because we hear from the officers we interviewed of the enormous stress they were under to remain professional and not surrender to their consuming anger at what was happening. Not all will have resisted. An expose of racism in the police service in 2003 (*The Secret Policeman*, BBC) did not implicate any officers from West Yorkshire, but the Chief Constable found himself having to respond with an admission that 'Unfortunately, our recruitment processes cannot screen out all of the cross-section of ignorance and bigotry which feeds racism in society' (*T&A*, 13 Nov 2003). Not only this, but the way the riot was policed was seen by many observers as 'heavy handed'—we will hear more about this view in the following chapter.

There is very little sympathy or even understanding for the profound sense of threat that rioters felt when faced with the possibility that Far Right thugs were in Bradford. Neither police nor rioters seemed able to distinguish between racist white lads and card carrying NF or BNP members—and maybe in the end, when it comes to confrontation on the streets, there is little difference. And for the Asian rioters, living in a racist society, such youths are indeed a threat to their security and to their futures. For the police they are just ordinary trouble makers, no better and no worse than Asian youth

Nor did the police appreciate the full import of themselves becoming proxies for the Far Right in the eyes of the rioters. Any pre-existing hatred that young men harboured for the police (given their minor petty criminal activities and the level of stop and searches which go on) was magnified in this situation. All the virulent anger that is felt against the 'NF' and the BNP is foisted onto the police, especially once they find themselves fighting in their own area.

The police were obliged to respond to the events of that day, but with more understanding and less heavy-handed behaviour during the initial build up, it seems to us that the violent escalation which followed might have been avoided. Thereafter it became practically a no-win situation in which, for many hours and on all sides, 'normal life as we know it', totally broke down.

# 4

# LIMITS TO PEACEMAKING

*I think you should protest, every time that the Fascists think that they're gonna intimidate people. Even if it is in small numbers. I think it should be learnt straight away, you've no place here. We should learn some history. The Nazis in Germany started off very small . . . they turned into a mass movement and stamped on every form of democracy. People didn't unite in the way that they should. And the Nazis were able to gain power. They should be exposed for what they are.*
**(Anti-Nazi League organiser)**

[The rioters] *are not going to see you, because you're fifty or sixty years old . . . they're not going to stop, throwing bottles or throwing stones or a brick at the windows. You're probably going to get hit with a brick, yer know?*
**(Youth worker, explaining the problems facing elders who tried to intervene in the riot)**

In 2001 everybody claimed to want a peaceful city, even the rioters. Everybody blamed others for disturbing the peace. As we have seen, the organisers of the preceding anti-fascist rally are blamed by some in the police for inciting the crowd and 'whipping up hysteria'. The rally organisers in their turn vehemently denied any complicity in the riot and reasserted their right to peaceful protest. Everyone blames the rioters. Once the situation had become violent—and polarised between police and rioters, the police themselves tried to involve third parties who might intercede between them. But third parties were unable to make any real difference in this highly charged situation. In the end there was a collective failure by all parties to achieve their objectives. We want to explore the reasons why other participants in the events of that day and night had so little authority over rioting youth and so little capacity to restore the peace.

# Right to Protest Against Fascism

Both the ANL and the Anti-Fascist Group of Bradford's Trades Council (TC) planned to demonstrate their opposition to 'fascist parties' like the National Front and BNP making any inroads into Bradford. They had watched with horror as the Far Right had descended on other Northern ex-textile towns like Burnley and Oldham earlier in the year and 'provoked a number of riots'. They were aware that in Bradford 'the Asian community did feel under threat'. Both groups were angry at the way the council, at the behest of the police, had cancelled the final day of the 'multicultural' Bradford Festival on the grounds that public safety could not be guaranteed. For them this looked like 'capitulation' and 'a victory for the National Front'. Worse, it left a 'void', which their planned rallies tried to fill. Their hope was, as an ANL organiser put it, that 'the Fascists will be put off by the large numbers turning out'.

These two associations did not organise together to mount a rally. They saw themselves acting separately—the rally 'was called by the ANL . . . I think the Trades Council . . . their Anti-Fascist Group, they were [also] doing stuff'; whereas the Trades Council group insisted that 'we have different positions entirely'. Their differences are buried in left-wing histories and ideological disputes (see chapter 6). There was a sense amongst Trades Council activists that they represented working class interests, 'it's working class communities that rightfully understand that they have most to lose from Fascism', whereas the ANL was perceived as largely composed of 'middle class liberals' influenced by the Socialist Workers Party. Their membership did not overlap. They had cooperated in various campaigns in the past—particularly in leafleting on estates in the run-up to elections where BNP candidates were standing, but there was no formal collaboration between them.

To an outsider these two political groups seemed to share more than divided them. They espoused the same objectives and used the same language in which to express them—a vocabulary of 'Nazis', 'Hitlerites' and 'Fascism'. This is the same language incidentally that was deployed by many of the rioters, though for anti-fascists embedded in historical consciousness and political organisation. Nor was it just their common stance against the Far Right, which in the case of the Trades Council included campaigning against anti-semitism and organising an annual Holocaust Memorial gathering. It was that both organisations were predominantly white. Each had some Asian members, and indeed one of the key leaders of the ANL in Bradford was an Asian, but they seemed to have few organic links with Asian youth from working and lower middle class backgrounds. At times they appear to adopt a paternalistic tone in relation to such young men.

Another feature which these two groups shared was their rejection of the authority of police and the local state. Whilst working within the law they had little trust in its representatives. For the ANL, the police are accused of 'provocation' and of antagonism towards 'people organising themselves'. Citing the Macpherson report, they insist that 'the police are racist'. The Anti-Fascist Group tended to put their negative view of the police into class terms: 'this cuts across any kind of ethnic divide, innit—young working class men don't like coppers'. But they also accused the police of racism—in this version misinterpreting Macpherson to mean they should 'go softly, softly in non-white areas' which led to 'massive resentment' amongst the police against ethnic minorities. For both these groups, their hostile perceptions of the role of the police in society framed their analysis of the events that unfolded on 7 July.

Both groups leafleted their intention to hold a rally but on the day, they were unwilling to share responsibility, with both claiming the public space of Centenary Square. It was the ANL who organised speakers—very much at the last minute and in quite a haphazard fashion: an MP, Marsha Singh, local councillors, 'someone holding a baby in their arms', a message of support from Tony Benn—'I think it was just anyone who was against the Fascists and had come to town'. Their PA system was acknowledged to be inadequate. Meanwhile the TC Anti-Fascist Group also had a table, a banner and leaflets in the Square, but they devoted most of their energy to 'a big spotting operation', tracking any known Far Right sympathisers arriving at the local rail stations or roaming around town, with the remit of reporting their presence to the police. Very soon they spotted David Appleyard who was later involved in the fracas with Kasel Altaf at the pub in Ivegate. They rang the police on more than one occasion, expecting he would be picked up as he had a long history of racist trouble-making, but he was not. Thereafter they acted more as 'witnesses' to the events, as they made sorties through the town to see what was happening.

For the ANL organiser, the first disquiet came almost as soon as the rally began—'the police were outside the police station, getting into their riot gear, at that early stage, which I thought was particularly provocative'. There was satisfaction however that the crowd which turned up was 'a happy gathering' of ethnically diverse

Saturday Night and Sunday Morning

men and women, young and old, and 'kids in pushchairs', all wanting to protest against Fascism. When the speeches were over:

> . . . people were just milling around. It was a summer's day and people were chatting in groups . . . However it didn't take long before the whole of Centenary Square became encircled by police . . . Anti-Nazi protestors were hemmed into Centenary Square, surrounded by police.

The TC Anti-Fascist Group put it even more strongly:

> . . . the police saw a threat which was not coming from the Nazis, but actually coming from the people who were gathered there to oppose the Nazi presence! . . . an absolutely criminal response from the police . . . yer could just see by their whole body language . . . when all the police horses were there they were all faced into Centenary Square. This wasn't a police presence whose purpose was to protect the people against fascism, they'd all be looking outwards.

As the ANL activist was prevented from leaving the square she saw what she took to be confirmation that the Far Right was indeed in the city.

> They came to Bradford—the National Front and the BNP . . . At various points you could see out of Centenary Square. I saw a gang of these Fascist thugs seig heiling down the street. And at that point young lads tried to break away and charge towards them.

She saw the police arrest a 'white skinhead' and bundle him into their van, though she claimed that the same youth was seen later in the day, having been released. And she became aware that there were 'NF people' in nearby pubs. The conclusion seemed obvious:

> . . . the police turned out that day to protect the Fascists, to do what they wanted, which was to go on a drinking binge and roam around Bradford, whilst anti-fascist protestors were being hemmed into the town centre.

The rally was 'treated as a threat to public order'. One TC activist was abused by a white youth, who yelled 'Fucking Paki' at him whilst being arrested in the Square. The activist was incensed and went for him, but was restrained by friends, amongst whom was the same Kasel Altaf who was to be at the centre of the Ivegate incident. A little later the TC group was joined by some 'comrades' from Leeds who happened to be white and had shaved heads. They were taken to be 'NFs' by some of the Asian youth in the Square, who moved menacingly towards them, but dropped back after the TC activist hastily explained. Both he and the ANL organiser saw people becoming restive at their captivity and trying to push their way out of the Square—'the police presence was overwhelming'. In the middle of a surging crowd they were pushed backward and forwards. They judged the police to be completely out of control, using their batons freely against the protestors. Both of them independently reported seeing a youth set upon.

> I saw a lad dragged across the ground and some of his mates were shouting 'leave him alone, he's got learning difficulties', and he was deaf, he had a big hearing aid, and he was being dragged along . . . and he wasn't actually doing anything except surging backwards and forward . . . quite horrific.

The TC organiser concluded, somewhat intemperately, that: 'the police rioted in town. An just—quite random attacks on Asian kids, wi'batons, horse charges—they went mad . . . it were quite clear that they wanted to drive 'em outa town'. Indeed he went further: 'the reason there was a riot is because the police rioted first'.

They saw the youth break out and race up towards Ivegate as rumour spread about the confrontation there, but none of them saw it. The ANL organiser heard that 'an Asian guy shopping [sic] had been hit' by Fascists drinking in a pub, whereas the TC activist believed it to be 'police lashing out at the Asian youths who were being abused by Appleyard and his friends'. All agreed that the point had been reached where there was little more they could do. The crowd of their other supporters had dispersed, Asian lads were being chased by police, and they prepared to leave themselves. At around 6pm an ANL activist retrieved her car and drove through town, was surprised that she saw little damage to buildings, but then shocked to find, at the bottom of White Abbey Road, police massed with their vehicles and horses:

> I just couldn't believe it. I thought what the hell are the police doing, moving up to that residential area which is a largely Asian area? It looked like things had died down and I would have thought the sensible thing for the police would have been to go back to their station, disarm themselves.

Later in the evening some of the TC activists collected money amongst themselves and delivered food to the police stations where those arrested during the riot were being held—it was accepted at Toller Lane but refused at the Central Police Station.

Their view of the riot itself was that youth had immediate grievances against the police for their behaviour in town, as well as understandable and legitimate anger against the Far Right: 'things seem to be just so unjust to them'. High unemployment, poverty and deprivation amongst Asian families and having little to hope for were also relevant. They were shocked by the extent of the violence and destruction, but did not accept that they could have done more to prevent it. One conceded that 'some criminal gangs' also took advantage of the trouble. At the same time one who had himself been involved in riots in other places spoke of, 'the right adrenalin high. It's like being in a war, really . . . anger . . . [but also] there's just the sheer joy . . . we live in strait-jacketed lives . . . riot is an unleashing of all manner of emotions'. And young working class men found their class hatreds and their sense that 'their very existence is under threat from Fascism' expressed through this 'unleashing'. The Trades Council activists also struggled with some of what were contradictions to them: 'I were disappointed', said one, 'by some of the targets'. He meant the pubs and the Labour Club, although the latter no longer has any association with the Labour movement. He assumes that it was torched because it was 'white' and because it sold alcohol. He assumes that 'the Imams' have influence over Muslim youth given high unemployment rates (the lack of a counter influence from organised labour). He also recounted a report from one of his members that 'fascist' graffiti proclaiming 'kill the Jews' had been seen in Manningham and struggled with the realisation that: 'It's not Fascists wot's written that—it's young Pakistani kids what'd written that'.

After the riot the Anti-Fascist Group Trades Council hosted a semi-public meeting to try to make sense of the riot and to begin thinking about a defence campaign for those who were being arrested. The meeting 'was so heated' said an ANL activist. 'Some people were blaming rioters, some people were blaming the police . . . Some people were saying you shouldn't have ever protested'. One of the ANL leaders was accused of having fanned the flames by calling on protestors in the Square to 'go back and defend your communities'. This was denied—and indeed not all agreed that such words could be interpreted as an incitement to violence. A TC activist felt that the ANL had:

> . . . taken some quite unfair criticism. I think the temptation to blame that organisation or individuals involved with that organisation is quite grotesque actually . . . it ignores completely the fact of the police rioting in town.

A campaign mounted by Asian women who had been affected in the aftermath of the riot, when their menfolk received punitive sentences, seems to have disregarded offers of help from the ANL or the Anti-Fascist Group. 'The Fair Justice for All didn't seem to want organisations associated with it . . . they wanted it to be a family-oriented thing, I understood that partly [but] any campaign's better if it's bigger and it's broader', said the ANL organiser, whilst also applauding the positive outcome of 'women collectively organising'. A TC activist was blunter—he thought the women were mistrustful of 'white people in the Trades Council'. It would seem that Fair

Justice did not see either group as natural allies and perhaps suspected their motives (see chapter 7).

The supposition that anti-fascist organisations would have had the kind of moral authority over Asian lads which could have generated a riot or even that they could have marshalled dissension is absurd. Whilst they shared a political vocabulary with the rioters and a common view of the 'cause', the social relations between anti-fascist organisations and local youth were tenuous, in sharp contrast to the 1970s.

# Pitfalls of Peacemaking

The different sites where the riot developed and exploded—Centenary Square, White Abbey Road, Whetley Hill, the Labour Club, Oak Lane—seem at times to be acts in an unfolding drama where distinct sets of participants perform quite different plays. At the same time that the rally was breaking up, youth workers were actively trying to calm and disperse the lads in the Square. They had been organised and called out by the police for support. Later, on Whetley Hill, elders and 'community leaders' tried to mediate. Both of these groups—the Youth Service and the mediators—were Asians who were not rioters. Religious figures also made their mark—whether through active interventions like the Bishop, or through witness of the events. This latter group was largely white, for Imams were conspicuous by their absence.

The council-run Youth Service found its position in the Square highly exposed and difficult. Many are Asian, though not all Muslim. On this occasion they also recruited volunteers and 'community people' like themselves. They tended to see themselves as 'professionals', or, as one put it, 'high profile elements' within the Asian 'community', who have, in the words of another, a reputation for being 'influential mediators'. Whilst they were shocked by the riot, which one described as 'total criminal thuggery', and critical of the rioters, whom they saw as totally out of control, they nevertheless had sympathy for their hatred of the Far Right whom they also saw as a potent threat.

On the day they spent a lot of time liaising with the police and were called into the Central Police Station early on for a crisis meeting. However, their relations with the police became more fraught as they began to see the situation deteriorate. They had expected that the police would provide them with information about the intrusions of the Far Right so that they could speak with authority to the youth. They expected them to arrest Far Right activists in the Square when they were pointed out to them: 'we knew there were elements of BNP . . . inciting by presence'. One spoke of 'skinheads . . . shouting . . . swearing, they were using abusive language'. When arrests did not transpire they felt that both they and the public had been misled. This generated 'real, real anger at the police'. As one of their managers said, 'the initial reaction was, we've been set up, we've been lied to'.

They did not expect 'police officers to be kitted out in full gear', making provocative charges towards people in the Square. Most alarming to one worker was seeing a police officer near the Queen's pub (on the road leading out of the Square towards the Station) with a 'massive batch' of plastic ties (in lieu of handcuffs). He thought, 'it looks like they are ready . . . waiting for a disorder to happen'. He saw confrontations around this pub in the morning which he described as the police having lost control and become violent themselves: 'they didn't really know themselves what they were doing . . . t–otal chaos'. A volunteer witnessed a youth being violently thrown to the ground by police and confessed that 'if that had been me, I might have got involved in the violence'. In this situation they found themselves trying to calm and communicate with a huge crowd of young people, begging them not to get involved in the mayhem and to do what the police asked. A manager said: 'we were saying to the young people, "don't bite" and we were saying to the police "what are you doing? Move back, right, you know you're provoking it"'.

Both police and youth were deaf to Youth Service pleas. But it was the police they blamed, for their heavy-handedness and their over-reaction to events, even seeing them as part of the 'ignition tape' which led to the riot. As one concluded, 'I'm not saying just . . . let's blame the police' but 'I was really angry and my anger was with the police'. Moreover they complain that the police resist any criticism of their role and had not allowed any other parties into an enquiry on policing the riot: 'I don't think there has really been honest dialogue about how it was policed'. We cannot put this response down to pre-existing prejudice against the police amongst the youth workers we interviewed. One was ultra-respectable, believed strongly in law and order and had high expectations of the integrity of the police. He had never been in trouble with them. Another who had suffered many bad experiences with being stopped and searched, nevertheless valued his local community police and had begun training at one point to be a police officer. But on the day of the riot their perceptions were jarred. Whilst the youth 'were just pumping up testosterone and adrenalin . . . police officers also had adrenalin going, right'. And the Youth Service found themselves positioned 'in-between' with little room for manoeuvre. Indeed they felt compromised by their formal relation with the police, knowing that Asian youth would dismiss them as 'with the police'.

They were also unimpressed by the rally organisers: 'they didn't think about marshalling or any form of crowd control', and hearing one of their leaders calling for the lads to ignore the Youth Service and 'go back to your communities and protect your neighbourhoods' incensed them. But they felt they were largely irrelevant to what happened later. The police were seen as clumsy in their attempt to cordon off and then disperse the crowd. And once rumour of the Ivegate incident had spread, this was the 'spark that lit the torch'—'that's when the havoc really broke out'. In Centenary Square the atmosphere became 'very tense . . . explosive', because people assumed that there must be a huge crowd of Far Right thugs about to appear—they didn't believe police claims that 'there are no BNP in the city centre'.

After the crowd had broken out of the Square the Youth Service were no longer regarded by police as having a role to play. And yet many of them continued to be informally involved, often observing the riot from behind police lines. Like the police they were amazed at the behaviour of bystanders—'it was unbelievable!' said one. Perhaps one to two thousand people were watching:

> . . . it was like film shooting was going on in the background, *Eastenders* or *Coronation Street* . . . people chit-chatting about their own affairs, just having a nice gossip because it was a nice sunny day! . . . I found that really strange.

They continued to be critical of police actions. On White Abbey Road police:

> . . . were just standing there holding their shields, which I thought was ludicrous . . . I expected them . . . to send another hundred from behind us . . . to contain the damned problem . . . We assume [the police] are very good at containment of civil disorder . . . this was a great opportunity for containment.

By containment, they meant blocking off side streets, reinforcing from behind, but this did not happen. This worker was disconcerted to see what he viewed as police ineptitude—a 'game' of retreat and advance with little real movement.

A Youth Service volunteer was himself caught up in the violence at the Labour Club, when he and a group of friends saw a gang of lads smashing a window, climbing through and going for the cash tills. He was immediately anxious that he might be regarded as part of the mob. But then he saw a fire started up in the lower floor when there were evidently people upstairs. There were police in

Hollings Road nearby and he raced to tell them that people needed help, there was a fire. The police said that they already knew and a fire engine had been called, but they could not get through the riot. With a friend he begged rioters to help rescue the people trapped inside. In the end his friend got the doors open and with another Asian man, they ushered a group, including a woman and children to safety. Meanwhile the crowd was yelling anti-white abuse and he and his friends were shouting 'you don't touch these people'. Maybe this was the young man that the police encountered (see previous chapter). He makes light of his efforts—he doesn't want 'to take the glory—that was others'.

This man followed the riot up until its grim final stage at the BMW garage. We shall return to his story later. Meanwhile the manager was working the very next day with his staff and volunteers to prevent further flare-ups—they went around to talk to young men and warn them: 'you ain't doing that again'.

The work of the Youth Service was never sufficiently recognised in commentary after the riot. In discussions which we had with a wider group of Youth Service workers at a couple of workshops (it included white and black workers as well as Asians), we uncovered a broader range of views, with some seeing the rioters as 'extremists' whilst others had themselves gone to the rally: 'I was there to say I don't want these people [Far Right] in my community. I'm not justifying what happened . . .' An Asian woman said, 'I was there on that day . . . police were cordoning the Square, looking in, facing in, looking at us . . . [and behind them were] seig heil booted youths'. But we also found a disturbing sense of dissatisfaction and confusion amongst the Youth Service workers about their positioning in relation to ethnic relations in the city and what could be said about it without fear of losing jobs. Confirming that they had indeed been 'stuck in the middle' in the riot, in an impossible situation, they felt used and devalued by both sides. The assumption that they would be able to exert influence over the young men did not square with their remit to work with youths between the ages of 13 to 19, though they did know quite a few of the youth from past acquaintance. One had been able to persuade a lad he knew to give up a knife. They valued service to the community and the 'unpaid' work many of them do: 'that's the sorta people we are'.

Community leaders felt equally unsupported. Those we interviewed were an interesting mix. There was the elderly Asian businessman whose car showroom was attacked and many cars burnt; there was the educated, confident and younger Asian businessman from a neighbouring town called in by the police. There were white Christian leaders whom we describe here as 'witnesses' and who saw 'being there' as part of their 'true ministry'.

Limits to Peacemaking

All of these tried to intervene as the riot reached its height in Whetley Lane. When the younger businessman arrived he was introduced to police at the scene (who did not seem to have anticipated his arrival) as someone:

> . . . you could maybe use to try and get some kind of dialogue going with . . . the rioters . . . I was one of the first people there and I recognised a number of city councillors . . . and other people who like myself had been involved at national level . . . parliamentary candidates . . . business leaders, community leaders . . . about 10 people I recognised . . . It was raining rocks . . . violent . . . like a war zone.

He also noted the vast number of bystanders—he put them at a thousand—'people like to play for an audience'. The older businessman was rung by one of his employees as he was on his way somewhere else: 'there's a thousand people here, they're turning cars upside down, they put them on fire . . . and at first I thought, you know, he's kidding'. He hurried to the scene:

> I couldn't believe with my own eyes what was happening . . . when I reach two of my premises [a derelict pub and a car garage/ showroom] . . . I saw these lot of cars burning in the road and I saw one of my properties [the pub] was burning.

The fires were dangerously near to petrol tanks at the garage. Stones were flying and 'police people, they were absolutely to the last leg, and they were just laying or sitting on the floor'. He called several friends and colleagues, begging them to come and help: 'these are our kids who've gone on rampage'. Meanwhile most of the staff of the Anglican ministry in Manningham were on the scene from its White Abbey inception:

> . . . the Bishop was out . . . talking with people, meeting with the police, ministering to those who had had missiles thrown at them, talking with the lads, talking with people who were trying to intercede with the lads, trying to stop them . . . We were not seen as authority figures really so we could do our bit . . . we weren't perceived as the police although we were white and people were a bit aggressive.

None of them were able to make a difference and they were in considerable danger themselves. The younger businessman recalls that: 'It was frightening walking up to a mob and it was frightening standing there in the police lines because you had to be very alert for the rocks . . . I saw a lot of people injured'. With others he tried to talk to the rioters, but it was 'very hard to talk to those young— they were kids really' who were not in a state to listen. He saw people from the 'community' telling them 'Hang on, what you're doing's wrong you know, you really need to put these rocks down and go home. You know you haven't really got any reason'. The older businessman said he had approached the police and told them: 'we are on the same side for peace . . . give us a chance to talk to these boys . . . we want the safer city . . . don't make it bigger . . . give us a chance to mediate between you'. To his chagrin the police didn't recognise him:

> . . . they didn't want to know anything. I said [to the lads] why you doing this? . . . there's no gain there . . . And every one of them say, why don't you ask the same question to the police, why they doing it to us again?

A few tried to bargain: 'if you stop [police] charging at us, we will stop throwing stones on them . . . we will listen'. The younger businessman said that they negotiated with the police to release two arrested lads in the morning if the rioters went home. There was a lull of about 15 minutes, but then violence resumed. The Christian witnesses acknowledged that they were 'powerless' against 'a frenzied mob that would not be stopped' and who were consumed by 'a lust for violence'. One describes:

> . . . talking to somebody in the front line while some of us were negotiating . . . and there was a lull whilst we were trying to listen to what was being said—about five of us—talking to one of the lads and he said, 'Boy! We haven't had one like this for years, this is fantastic!' He was jumping up and down . . . and he was just totally high on violence.

All of them condemned the rioters, one saying that 'we can call them thugs' who bring shame to their families. Moreover, 'they like to have a drink, they want to be able to go with a girl, they want to have freedom'. They were 'not in our calibre of people [where] you're gonna have a civilised discussion'. They had trampled on 'Islamic values' of respect and avoidance of harm to others. 'The community as a whole was against the riots', says one of the Asian businessmen, whilst a Christian witness noted that 'there was not . . . community support behind these guys . . . there's been a real sense that the lads have let them down'.

This does not mean that they did not concede a real initial cause for the riot. One Christian witness says he was shocked 'that the whiff of a rumour of the National Front sent this chaotic response'—though he saw this as having been stirred up by the ANL with influence from the Socialist Workers Party. One of the Asian businessmen says: 'I loathe the BNP, the National Front, but . . . certain elements of the Anti-Nazi League are just as bad'. The other Asian businessman's views are more in line with those of the rioters. The police 'shouldn't have let [the BNP] come—what are the police for? . . . The BNP . . . should never have come'. The rioters 'believed [the police] betrayed them'. Unsurprisingly they therefore had doubts about the sentencing. One said 'I want fair justice . . . I don't want these rioters to be a scapegoat', even though 'nobody is above the law'. Another suspects that there was a 'political agenda' from central government—stiffer sentences were designed to deter any future unrest. But the sentences were not in line with normal practice, they were discriminatory and their harshness 'set community relations back'.

The peacemakers were apt to take a broad view and to locate the violence in Bradford's decline. Bradford was a city which was 'very poor . . . in its facilities . . . in its outlook . . . in its future'. Its people were 'living in ghettos', in overcrowded poor quality housing, with low educational levels, the only role models criminals and drug dealers. These were 'communities living in time warps'. The youth, eyeing Leeds—'probably the most vibrant city in the north'—feel 'we're being left out of this'. Another was distressed by the impact on Bradford: 'I was gutted, not for myself, for the city itself . . . This is our city, this is our place to live . . . we're all Bradfordians'. He asked himself why the youth had destroyed so much and concluded that the riot 'showed definitely anger and frustration amongst those youngsters' because there were few facilities for youth. 'Investment in the city has been absolutely nil'. Those who 'made the money out of Bradford' then deserted it. The people were poorly represented in parliament and City Hall 'haven't done a competent job at all'. One Christian witness pointed to the high levels of unemployment, saying 'jobs are crucial'—and yet one of the Asian businessmen employed largely 'traditional white people' in his companies, claiming that Asian youth lacked skills and didn't want to work.

The 'peacemakers' were critical of the police response to the violence. One of the Christians pointed to 'the policing, the way the police were facing off the crowd and all that kind of stuff you know—it was miserable'. He assumes that the police must now be doing 'some real radical thinking'. The businessmen were aghast to see the impasse in the police's efforts to control the crowd. They had chosen 'the worst place in the world' to make a stand. 'The police wasn't competent to handle it', said one, claiming that they didn't liaise with youth, and that 'there are not sufficient people of ethnic community . . . particularly in policing'. However one of the businessmen, shocked to see 'an anti-police riot' says that he is on the whole favourable towards the police:

> It was policed to the best of their ability. There wasn't any other way that they could do it. They weren't heavy-handed at all . . . they were empowered to do a job and that was to protect property and people.

Saturday Night and Sunday Morning

They did liaise with 'key people in the community', but they had limited links with the youth.

# The End

As the rump of the rioters stormed down Oak Lane towards the BMW garage, the violence took on a different character. Now the young men were not confronting enemies. The Far Right had long since disappeared as a target or perceived threat and the police had fallen back in exhaustion. The final orgy of destruction can only be put down to the frenzy of battle and a triumphalism that the lads had wrested control of the streets for themselves. There was very little reporting of this phase of the violence—the media had gone home, police video vans were no longer in evidence. Few of the rioters we interviewed had been in the thick of it until the end—or were not prepared to own up to their presence. But if we listen to the voices of other witnesses at the scene we can see how even in this most inhospitable of circumstances, some brave souls were still struggling to intervene and to deal with the impact of events.

Local residents thought the riot was over—they had been following its progress on television. They were unprepared for the influx of a violent crowd into their streets late in the evening. A Muslim elder describes what happened. They heard a great noise and 'so many crowds of the youth were coming straight, you know, down, and they start smashing . . . the BMW garage . . . and they smashed some cars also. And well, then, they start igniting the fire'. They estimated that there were about 100 of them, 'sticks in their hand and some they have cover up, you know, face. Also petrol bottles, yes . . . It is very very threatening and very frightening . . . experience'. He and his neighbour went outside to Oak Lane and his neighbour suggested, 'we should go and stop them. Tell him no, no, there is no way we can do that, they are so aggressive you know. Very danger. And we are waiting for police might be come'. They waited in vain. The police were rung repeatedly for help by many residents, but responded that they were 'very busy and the fire brigade say they could not come without police protection'. This was despite despairing residents telling them that there was an old people's home next door to the BMW garage. And so they looked on, helplessly: 'We are very regret we could not stop them. It's too dangerous and very ugly picture what we saw . . . Just taking a risk you know. No police protection.'

They later heard that the police were resting outside Toller Lane Police Station whilst they were left to face the mob alone. A youth worker who lived locally was also part of the small crowd of residents who came out of their houses to witness this terrifying scene. As well as torching the BMW building, he saw 'the young men started to have nice races up and down with these twenty to forty-five thousand pounds vehicles!' No-one appeared to know why the rioters targeted this site, though there was a suggestion that there was some animosity towards the white owner. The police did not arrive until 3.30am, by which time 'nearly all building is gone. And so much is lost. And all our houses is, erm, shaken. Explosions, yes! They go on the sky'.

Another of the youth workers was still tailing the rioters when they attacked the garage. There he saw one youth fighting another to try to prevent him taking part, but to no avail. He also witnessed the successful bid by local residents to stop youth attacking the long-established hardware store, McCann's, telling them 'this is not for you to burgle'. As a resident in the area himself he saw this store as 'one of our shops'. It was his view that the rioters were 'targeting white businesses'. The Muslim elder noted that 'there is a lot of Asian property on Oak Lane, they were save, they didn't touch them'. The other youth worker and the elder also spoke fondly of McCann's and described an ethnically-mixed business community in Oak Lane who 'have no problem between themselves'. One of the Christian witnesses described how:

> I stood outside McCann's when I saw it being ram-raided and somebody said it's full of gas canisters and I thought, all we want is for that to go up and we've had it. So I stood there for about three hours and prevented further looting of the place and any further destruction . . . Some other people came [local residents] when they saw I'd made the move and stood beside me, so actually we formed a sort of human barrier . . .

The Muslim elder reported that whilst the front door was broken down, the building itself was saved.

Meanwhile, the old people's home was evacuated by another member of the clergy with the help of two other people:

> because there were incendiary devices going off all around them, the police couldn't get in, the brigade wouldn't come for safety, the ambulance couldn't get in . . . so the local clergy had to evacuate this old folks' home and put them somewhere else.

One place to which they went for refuge was the house of the Muslim elder, where they rested and were given food.

These people saw the worst of the rioters, and yet they were as quick to understand as they were to condemn. We hear confirmation that the rioters had little support in the local community. 'They're mindless people I can say. I strongly condemn you know . . . extremist . . . We feel very shame, we feel very disappointed because they're destroying you know . . . totally unacceptable'. And yet this Muslim elder was also convinced that the Far Right 'definitely came that day' and he viewed their message of hate with concern:

> if somebody say you should go back [to Pakistan] I think this is very threatening for us. We are not going to accept that . . . Maybe I accept it, our youth not accept that . . . because they born here, they brought up here . . .

Still, for him, the violence was 'totally unjustifiable'. He also threw a much wider net of blame. 'I accuse also mosque people you know'. Imams were uneducated and had no training in teaching; few could speak English. They did not know how to relate to the young people or to the problems of the neighbourhood: 'They never hold any seminar or any gathering in which we share our problem—our youth problem and drug . . . They could not see the problem of the community you know'. He himself had been active in the running of his local mosque, but resigned after pressure was being put on him and others to vote for a certain candidate for councillor just because he was a Muslim. He is also dismissive of local political leadership: 'they are not representing community. Listen! They are representing their own caste and biraderi [clan]'. He is conscious that young people 'are thirsty, for knowledge, yeah, for leadership, yeah, and most [older] people are not providing them'. He is not surprised, however, to find that youth 'don't see anyone as leader you know, not Imam or [MP]'. He is also very concerned that many of the young rioters had no jobs:

> Textile industry gone you know. Nothing replace . . . People who have no job, they are very irresponsible people . . . People who could not achieve anything in school, and no jobs and the frustration there is . . . So this thing [rioting] can happen you know.

Having work brings responsibility as well as the camaraderie of other workers—he was himself a textile worker for nearly 30 years, a weaver, a spinner, a winder and a warper—and a trade unionist. And he has learnt that people need to fight for their rights without violence but through 'continuous struggle': 'people sacrificed themselves to get those rights'. The youth today are denied this political experience. Parents do not escape his criticism—they should know where their sons are and bring them up to respect and follow their religion.

# Limits to Peacemaking

The testimony of these varied parties to the events of 7–8 July 2001 suggests that the scope for peacemaking was lost in Centenary Square, not on Whetley Hill—and certainly by the time the riot reached its final stage only defensive actions were possible. A negative view of how the riot was policed is not limited to the rioters themselves, but shared with many others—the rally organisers, the Youth Service, the so-called mediators and the local community. Clumsy attempts to disperse the crowd, the early donning of what looked like 'riot gear', the cordoning off of the Square and the heavy deployment of horses, dogs and police video vans meant that the police immediately lost the confidence of all participants. It is not surprising that few believed their claims that the Far Right were no longer in the city, when those present could see some of them with their own eyes. Their half-hearted support of the Youth Service meant that any advice the latter might give about more conciliatory moves was ignored. And they do not appear to have been very welcoming to the later entry of so-called peacemakers aiming to mediate between them. By then they were locked into a battle which they could not win. In the end exhaustion all round seems to have brought the riot to an end.

It is easy to blame the rally organisers for their ineptitude and for providing a stage on which passions would be inflamed. But they could not have predicted the massive response from the Asian youth that transpired—and this was partly because they had no effective links with this section of the population. They saw themselves as protesting on behalf of victims, not fighting with them. Their capacity to control or marshal the crowd was infinitesimal.

Like the police, the putative peacemakers risked their lives to bring the violence to an end. And they suffered from finding themselves 'in between' the police and the rioters, with any authority they might have had with the latter undermined by their location behind police lines. It is also evident however that these so-called 'community leaders' had very little influence with the youth in class terms they are mostly the more affluent who are seen as using others for their own economic and social ascent. From this position they claim to represent 'the community', when they cannot speak in the name of alienated young men. It is worth noting however that class divides can lose their potency in the face of a common threat from the Far Right to people's ethnic and social existence.

Generational, class and ethnic divisions are exposed in some of these attempts at peacemaking. For example, it is no easy matter to relate to rebellious youth. They avoid the well-meaning who would represent them, such as the rally organisers. They have no time for the Imams or local political leaders. They spurn the hand of compassion extended to them from the devout. A Christian witness describes an encounter with young men: 'Last night I was walking to church and the word "priest" went out, followed by a banger—a very loud banger!' And they rebel against the older generation who would control them. A young man (not a rioter) sat in on the interview with the elderly Muslim and could not contain himself when greater parental controls were promoted as one solution to the unacceptable behaviour of the lads. He insisted that harsh parenting made for greater rebelliousness. 'But youth are sitting every night up to 1am, you know, in the road', protested the elder. 'Yeah, I know' said the young man, challengingly, 'I used to be one o' them boys, uncle, that's what I'm saying'. Leave us to find our own way is his message.

# 5

# WHY BRADFORD?
# LIFE AND LIVELIHOODS

*Textile industry gone, you know. Nothing replace. Because if these people, young, have a job—people who are working are good people you know, responsible people. People who have no job, they are very irresponsible . . . People who could not achieve anything in school, and no jobs and the frustration there is. So this thing [rioting] can happen you know.*
**(Muslim elder, ex-textile worker, trade unionist and political activist)**

Samuel Cunliffe Lister's 1873 elegant mill chimney, which still dominates the Bradford skyline, remains a memorial to the city's industrial significance. Lister, and his mill in the middle of Manningham, encapsulate the rise, decline and regeneration efforts of the city from the 19th to the 21st century. In the 19th century it was the symbol of Bradford's rise to global textile giant, a 'worstedopolis' (Firth, 1997). By 1992, it lay abandoned. Manningham, once an enclave of the wealthy surrounded by workers' houses, had become an enclave of the poor. In 2001 the mill was bought by Urban Splash and converted into flats, as Bradford made every effort to overcome an image of economic decline and show itself to be 'A Surprising Place'—an imaginative slogan dreamed up some years earlier by council marketing officers to attract visitors to the city.

Between the 19th and the 21st centuries, Bradford has seen much unrest as industrial expansion created wealth and poverty, uplift and exploitation. With industry's greed for labour both in expansion and contraction, it drew in migrant workers, initially from the countryside, later from Ireland, and eventually from the world. New communities of immigrant workers were continually melded into what made Bradfordians. Here we explore the changing nature of working lives and of community relations in Bradford. In the next chapter, we discuss the political and activist responses that accompanied them. This is the history lying behind the 2001 riot. Viewed in this way we can see the riot as more than the violence of angry young men. It suggests a collective failure—both local and national—to deal with the social legacy of economic decline within a multicultural urban setting.

# Making a Living in Bradford

## Boom and Bust

Lister's mill replaced an older mill destroyed by fire, which he had dedicated to the combing machine he invented with the help of others. The mechanisation of wool-combing enabled Bradford to consolidate its predominance in the worsted wool trade which had begun to distinguish it in the 18th century national economy. Firth describes the 'pushy wealthy Bradford master-manufacturers' who 'put out their wool at various stages of production to skilled artisans, the journeyman weavers and combers in their own homes' (1997:61). This had led to the production of lighter, more durable worsted cloth in Bradford. However, it was the mechanisation of this process which took Bradford onto the global stage. By 1850 worsted production was factory-based. The transition from rural to urban life, from hand-weaving to mechanisation, from home to factory was traumatic. Several men died in their resistance to mechanised combing at Horsefall's Mill in 1826 (ibid:69). Child labour, working 13 hours a day in harsh factory conditions, was one of the most exploitative practices in the history of working life in the city. The Clerk to the Bradford Poor Law Union, whose remit was wider than the inner city, estimated that the average age of death in Bradford between 1839 and 1841 was 18.69 years (James, 1990:87).

Bradford overtook Leeds in the worsted trade by mid-century and set up its own commercial centre. Bradford's worsted merchants increased from five in 1822 to 157 in 1861 (James, 1990:30). Lister got rich by patenting textile machinery and dedicated his rebuilt mill to his silk combing machine. It became the largest silk mill in Europe (Fieldhouse, 1987:152-53), employing at its height 11,000 men, women and children. Titus Salt, whose Saltaire mill, built in 1853, is another landmark for Bradford, built his fortune on combining Peruvian alpaca with other wool mixes. These and other local manufacturers dominated the economic, political and even social life of Bradford after 1850. Many historians record the 'paternalism' of the masters in relationship to their workforce. Titus Salt's dedicated mill community, where he carefully monitored the social morals of his 3,000 or so workers, is the most spectacular and best known example. In the mid 19th century many mill owners aimed to foster harmony between owners and workers by way of works trips, brass bands, cricket clubs and adult education (Jowitt, 1997:35).

In 1801 the townships of Bradford, Bowling, Horton and Manningham constituted the core of Bradford. The population expanded rapidly in the 19th century from 103,778 in 1851 to 279,767 by 1901. By then Bradford had also expanded to include Bolton, Allerton, Heaton, Thornbury, part of Tyersal, North Bierley, Tong, Thornton, Eccleshill and Idle (Duckett and Waddington-Feather, 2005:67). Clayton was not included until 1930. The last half of the 19th century constituted Bradford's 'golden age', but persistent poverty and squalor for working people also marked these years, alongside great fortunes for mill owners and gradual civic improvements in sanitation, water supply, urban infrastructure, transport and education. Bradford led the entire country in the provision of electricity, the appointment of the first Medical Officer for Health, the first Girls' Grammar School, the first technical classes, the first telephone service and other municipal provision (ibid:98). Bradford, which had been a borough, was designated as a city in 1897.

Employment gradually opened up in engineering, construction and transport, but Bradford remained the global centre of one industry, textiles. Historians have argued that dependence on a single industry and on unstable world markets was a key source of Bradford's later decline. A fall in demand for Bradford's mixed worsted fabrics as fashion changed, high tariffs from overseas' competitors and lack of investment in design, generated economic downturn in the industry. The late 1870s has been described as the 'first limited impact of de-industrialisation' (Jowitt, 1997:35). Manufacturers responded in a way which became a pattern for the future. They concentrated on cutting costs rather than on new investment, and selling semi-manufactures in the form of yarn and combed wool to foreign manufacturers. Machines were speeded up and workers were forced to work more machines. In the process, the paternalism of the industry broke down (ibid:36). As we shall see later, the seeds of Bradford's emergence as a centre for a new politics of labour were sown at that moment.

In the 20th century, the depression of the interwar years hit Bradford particularly hard. Unemployment rose to 20% in the 1930s. Other towns could turn to more diverse sources of employment. White collar jobs in finance and commerce did open up and a salaried middle class emerged. Historians point to mail-order business such as Grattans, and, in engineering, Jowett Cars, which in

Saturday Night and Sunday Morning

1935 employed 1,000 people, as examples of some diversification. But still by 1937, 38% of the working population were employed in textiles and 878 of the 1,003 members of the Chamber of Commerce were directly involved in the wool trade (James, 1990:138).

Bradford found new markets in the interwar years and benefitted from the abandonment of free trade after 1931 and the expansion of the domestic market. James, however, argues that industrial efficiency was held back by lack of investment in machinery and the workforce (1990:140). Too many small and middle-sized firms competed with each other, keeping profits down, while only combing and some stages of dyeing and finishing was done on a larger scale. Even as late as 1972, some 755 firms employed less than 33 people (ibid:174). Bradford remained in these years a low-wage city, with relatively high levels of female labour supplementing low male incomes.

J.B. Priestley captured the Bradford of these years in his *English Journey* (1934), revisiting the city where he grew up and had left in 1914:

> When I was a boy, we had certain wealthy families of manufacturers who came as near to forming an aristocracy as such a democratic community as ours would allow. Now they are gone, and their places have not been taken by other families. That chapter is closed. The main shopping streets have turned with the tide, and a glance at their windows shows that the shopkeepers are now trying to attract a much larger if poorer public. And of course, you no longer notice much difference between members of various classes. Clogs have disappeared, for though they were really very sensible footwear for work, being healthy, comfortable and cheap, they carried a bad social stigma on them, even when I was young. The working woman's shawl is disappearing too.

The industry underwent some restructuring after the Second World War. There was a labour shortage. Forty thousand fewer workers were available than in 1939 (James, 1990:173). Better-paid alternative jobs had appeared. Demand for textiles was high, but production of man-made fibres was also growing. The industry began to modernise and smaller firms disappeared. The 1,123 woollen and worsted mills of 1950 were reduced to 825 by 1967. By 1975, 15 companies controlled almost half of the large textile mills in the city (Duckett and Waddington-Feather, 2005:123). Management practices were updated. In order to finance investment and meet demand, a three shift, 24 hour day was introduced.

As women were not permitted to work nights, the need for labour became acute. Central and Eastern European migrants were employed at first, particularly Poles and Ukrainians, 14,000 of whom came from the refugee camps of Germany after 1945 (Fieldhouse

1978:200). In the 1940s, the first Asian settlers arrived from Azad Kashmir, mostly ex-seamen, to work in wartime industries in Bradford and Leeds. They were followed by small numbers from what was then known as the West Indies and in the early 1950s migrants from India and Pakistan. By 1969 migrant workers constituted 10% of the workforce in the woollen and worsted industry and they worked the unpleasant night shifts. They also staffed buses, making up a third of all bus crews by 1964 (ibid). Cheap and low-skilled South Asian migrants enabled the textile industry to operate at maximum capacity and remain profitable while it restructured (Ratcliffe, 1996:5).

This was not the first wave of migrants to the textile industry. Irish workers had arrived in large numbers in the 1820s to 1850s, settling where the rents were cheapest and working in the most ill-paid jobs. They were faced by 'widespread prejudice and social ostracism' for their Catholicism (James, 1990:84). However, the Irish came when the textile industry was expanding. South Asian migrants arrived to prop up a declining industry.

Although 16.6% of the town's employed population were still in textiles in 1971, some 24,170 workers, this was half the number in 1950. The industry was in terminal decline. By 1960, there were more workers in construction than male textile workers, and by 1971 twice as many people worked in the retail, banking, insurance and the professions than in textiles (James, 1990:175). Bradford was still a centre of manufacturing rather than services, but this now included a wider range of industries, particularly engineering and electrical engineering, such as Thorns Electrical in Lidget Green (James, 175).

As the 1970s wore on, a more profound recession hit the entire manufacturing sector in Bradford. Between 1978 and 1981, 23,000 Bradford workers were made redundant, 16,000 of them from textiles and engineering. Thorn Electrical and International Harvesters in Idle closed down. Nine thousand redundancies were notified between 1981 and 1984 (ibid). In 1984, 29,000 people, or one in seven of the labour force, were out of work (James, 1990: 175). Bradford 'was shedding its skilled labour' (Greenhalf, 1997:42). As working life was transformed, the city's sense of identity and confidence was put in question.

## Unmaking of the Working Class

Between 1975 and 1995, Bradford's economy shifted from manufacturing to services. Employment in manufacturing declined by 40% in those years, while services accounted for 75% of jobs by 2001, though the statistics now refer to an expanded Bradford Metropolitan District (Local Futures Group, 1998:20). Employment levels in manufacturing stabilised between 1993 and 1995 accounting for 50,000 jobs, still a significant number in national terms (ibid). At the same time, there was a 15% drop in the total stock of manufacturing firms. The most important remaining sectors were electronics, printing, packaging and food processing.

The underlying trends were towards more part-time work and self-employment. Eleven per cent of the economically active population aged between 16 and 74 were self-employed in the 2001 census. However, between the two censuses of 1991 and 2001, there was a marked increase of 12,092 in the number of economically inactive people. Most of this increase was amongst the male population. The proportion of employees working in skilled trades, such as process, plant and machine operatives, fell from 13% in 1991 to 10.9% in 2001, and the rise of part-time and service sector work favoured women, whose share of employment rose by 3.6% (http://www.bradfordinfo.com/census/elibrary.cfm).

The South Asian population was particularly hard hit by the collapse of the textile industry and their lack of transferable skills to other sectors. As mill work ceased to structure the working day of the male breadwinner, community life in Asian areas was transformed. The high levels of self-employment in Bradford's labour statistics reflect how some first and particularly second-generation Pakistani men found their way into traditional service sectors, such as taxi driving, newspaper agencies, small shops, takeaways and restaurants. Kalra (2000) sees this as a mix of entrepreneurial spirit and pragmatic necessity. In his study of Mirpuri workers in Oldham, Kalra describes how Mirpuri and Punjabi/Pakistani drivers confronted the racism of the taxi-driving market in Oldham and eventually took over taxi rank ownership. Although there is no comparable study of similar developments in Bradford, Kalra offers important insights for our story of labour and the labour market in the city. We see how the energies of redundant Pakistani mill workers facing the dole in the 1980s were directed towards self-employment and how extended family and kin structures were enlisted in the search for rebuilding a working life.

In December 1998 a report on the Bradford economy and its prospects by the Local Futures Group summed up the situation of the District in the years immediately before the 2001 riot. The report identified the failure of the service economy to compensate for major losses in manufacturing. Although unemployment had declined following the recession of the 1970s and 1980s, this masked 'profound structural weaknesses in the labour market, specifically the lack of quality job generation' (Local Futures Group, 1998:7). Rates of pay in the District in the mid-1990s were very low, below both national and regional averages, particularly amongst women, young people and ethnic minorities (1998:21). Low standards of education and a limited skills profile blighted the potential of the workforce. Over 35% of the population aged between 16 to 74 lacked qualifications in 2001 (http://www.bradfordinfo.com/census/elibrary.cfm). Youth (16–24 years) unemployment levels reached 21.6% according to a report by the city council in October 1993 (quoted in Bradford Commission Report, 1995:21), but with much higher levels amongst minority ethnic groups. This gave the District a very low purchasing power with knock-on effects for retail and consumer services.

## Young People in the Post Industrial Labour Market

Bradford's labour force was predicted to grow by 10,800 between 1996 and 2011, a great asset for the District's future. Expansion was greatest amongst the District's Pakistanis. The challenge was to prepare this population with skills and to generate the quality jobs to employ them. This challenge must be borne in mind when we look at the profiles of the young men involved in the riots (see chapter 2). Those who were employed were mostly in low status, low paid work, and amongst our sample very few had qualifications.

Unemployment affected young people in the inner city of Bradford much more than in the rest of the District by 1993, particularly young men of Pakistani and Bangladeshi origin (Ratcliffe, 1996:21). In his 1996 study, Ratcliffe found that half of Pakistani and Bangladeshi households contained no-one in full-time employment (at least 30 hours a week) (ibid:32). Following a major disturbance in Manningham in 1995, a Commission of enquiry estimated that 70% of the Asian population in Manningham was under 30 (Bradford Commission, 1996). Unemployment amongst young Asian men here (mainly of Pakistani origin) reached 45% by the early 1990s. This in itself did not explain violent behaviour, but it was highlighted by young men as a major concern, second only to resentment against the police. The authors of the report ask us to reflect on how unemployment impacts on:

> . . . what are traditionally seen as the masculine virtues of self-reliance, assertiveness and the ability to provide for one's family . . . This creates a situation where any employment is seen as better than none. It should not therefore come as a surprise that a hidden economy exists, including both lawful and criminal activities. It explains why unemployment is resented so profoundly, because it is not seen just as an economic misfortune. It strikes at the root of a man's perceived masculinity. It destroys his claim to be considered a meaningful part of his community (ibid:24-25).

Young men on white estates were also growing up with unemployed fathers who were unable to perform breadwinning roles. At the same time a creeping culture of consumerism was creating its own pressures on young people and their parents. A generation which had been happy to play football in Manningham streets had given way to youngsters:

> . . . hanging around outside the local shop, getting mobile phones, trying to be street trendy, [wanting to buy] expensive clothes. So [nowadays] there's this image thing for a male . . . whereas my brothers used to wear hand me downs, you know. It was no big problem not to have Nike and Adidas (a quote from a sister of one of the 2001 rioters).

Such consumption was out of the reach of the vast majority of young men in inner-city Bradford and propelled some into drug dealing. In 2010 and 2011, we again interviewed young men involved in the 2001 riot, some from our original sample and some not. One of the latter had been very involved in the drugs trade in the 1990s and spent time in prison over the next decade. He recalls his painful recognition that Pakistani lads like him were not expected to make it in the professions. Drug dealing became a route to easy money and the trappings of success and status which he could not achieve in any other way:

> Before I got kicked out [from school], I wanted to be a police officer . . . Then somewhere down the line the ambition's gone, I wanted flashy stuff, I didn't care how I got it. At the end of the day it's the streets where I can be someone. You don't need grades . . . This is what I want to do the rest of my life, earning more than a teacher. Even if I go to university, Asians don't get the jobs, colour of your skin, pal. That sticks to you.

In prison, a number of the rioters reflected on the differences between the generations around work: 'My dad told me about work, he had no education, he just worked 12 hours, my grandad did 16 hours a day and then walked home'. 'Our generation is different', acknowledged another, 'they were good honest people, working people. They came home every night. We went out to snooker, took drugs. My dad was very hard working. He comes from a poor family'.

The opportunity for drug dealing and use involved and impacted on youth from white, Asian and African-Caribbean communities. The heroin route through Afghanistan and Pakistan and the cocaine route through Jamaica undoubtedly gave market advantage to dealers with links to those regions. The police informed the Bradford Commission report into the 1995 disturbance that despite inner-city Toller ward being one of the smallest of the force's 17 divisions, arrests in connection with the possession or supply of heroin, cocaine and crack represented 19%, 25% and 23% of the total arrests for the West Yorkshire force during 1994 (1996:108). Serious drug crime increased in the 1990s alongside more petty crimes and theft and what was termed 'anti-social' behaviour. The Bradford Commission report found a rising incidence of such behaviour amongst youth in all communities. In Mohammed Taj's supplementary observations to that report, he referred to the 'growing popularity of the "gangsta" fashion affected by local youths as they adopt the clothing and attitude of disenchanted American youth gangs' (Taj, 1996:4). In the peer group interviews we commissioned, the lads boasted: '[We're] the Bronx. I'm from America. Oak Lane.'

By 2001 there were complaints across all communities that the police were not tackling criminality and bad behaviour robustly enough. When this involved Asian young men, it was attributed by some in the community to police fear of being labelled 'racist' (Ouseley, 2001:11). More commonly Asians were blamed for the burgeoning drug scene in the city, whereas it is far more pervasive. Lack of jobs and a sense that some jobs are 'not for the likes of us' was widely experienced by young people. When asked what young people do on Ravenscliffe Estate if they don't get jobs, a young man who participated in the disturbances there in 2001 replied simply: 'thieving, drugs, stuff like that'.

Inner-city young people who reached their volatile teenage years in the 1990s were probably the hardest hit by the impact of the 1980s' recession on families. These were the young adults of 2001— the average age of the rioters in our sample was 24. The only prospects for advancement and dignified incomes lay in skilling up, but most were ill-prepared, with evidence that the education system in the District was failing them. However, the picture was not uniform. Within a general context of disadvantage, some within the minority ethnic community did break out. Nationally, 'it was no longer salient to talk about patterns of advantage and disadvantage simply following race lines' (Philips, 1998:1685). Many have attributed racial disadvantage to residential segregation so it is useful to ask in what ways the relationship between neighbourhoods and 'communities' began to change in the 1990s.

## Life and Community in Bradford

A senior council officer interviewed in 2011, explained the complex overlapping of neighbourhoods and communities in Bradford and the attachments they carry:

> Bradford is not unlike a lot of other big cities in that it's grown up from lots of small villages and gradually become a large city, and the District itself is more than one place. We've got the Aire Valley and we've got the Wharfe Valley as well. Bradford is a lot of different places as a District and always has been. People from Bradford identify quite closely with the place they are from—whatever age, race, gender they are, they will talk about whether they are from Eccleshill or whether they are from Barkerend, they'll talk about their local place rather than Bradford quite often. People have always had and still have an affinity for their local area, and talk about it sometimes in a bit of a grumpy way, but feel quite attached to it . . . to the local bit . . . When you start to look at that along the lines of race for example, naturally people gather in groups around certain neighbourhoods, and they always have done. Whatever city you look at, people come in and they will go to places where they know people, or people who look like them, or where the services and shops look like the ones they want to use. You get congregations and aggregations of certain groups. It's much finer than Asians are here and whites are there. There are groups within groups, people from certain villages in Pakistan, you'll find those in certain places, and Bangladeshis in certain places. People have strong allegiances and the biraderi [clan] system is strong and people support each other.

As Bradford's collective working class identity slowly unravelled in the years before the 2001 riot, the impacts were experienced and overcome in diverse ways. The overall story is of a proud working class city losing what had held it together for so long: forms of solidarity and sociability based on the dignity of working life. However, when the heartlands of Bradford's industrial glory gradually became the symbols of industrial decline and social distress, the impacts on individuals, families and communities were profound.

Spatially, Bradford reflected the fortunes and misfortunes of its industrial rise and decline, with those who maintained a grip on regular employment moving up the hills or further along the valley. Nearing Ilkley, identification with Bradford grows less and less to this day. Meanwhile ethnic minority communities who had settled and remained in the inner city enjoyed networks and cultural resources less available to families where social bonds had been weakened. Working Men's clubs, Trade Unions and other forms of social and community life had taken a hit with the demise of manufacturing. Family breakdown had impacted on many. The 2001 census showed that the number of single parent households had doubled over the decade (http://www.bradfordinfo.com/census/elibrary.cfm).

## Inner and Outer City

At the end of the 19th century, some 40,000 back-to-back terraces housed two-thirds of the working people of Bradford (James, 1990:99-100). Manningham, at the centre of the industrial rise of the city, housed affluent elements, as its elegant Crescents and Squares of today still bear witness, but they were surrounded by small terrace houses. The wealthy left the area and today their grand houses are in multi-occupation by the poor. Other distinctive areas of housing emerged for the better-off, such as Heaton which had already become a 'good' address by the 1860s. As prosperity increased, new housing was built, particularly in Bowling and Manningham and the suburb of Girlington. The number of houses in the borough rose by 35% between 1881 and 1911. At the same time the semi-rural townships of Allerton, Heaton and Bolton expanded their population (ibid:101).

Fred Jowett, Socialist councillor and later MP for Bradford, campaigned at the turn of the century for slum clearance and the introduction of council housing in the face of rampant overcrowding, ill health and malnutrition in the working class streets of the inner city. After the First World War, local councils were encouraged to provide homes for the working class to rent. Under the Housing Act of 1919 almost half of the 23,000 homes built in Bradford between 1919 and 1939 were council houses. Slums in White Abbey, Wapping and Broomfields were demolished and people moved to new estates at Whetley Lane, Canterbury Avenue, Ravenscliffe, Swain House and Wibsey. The estates of Buttershaw, Woodside and Allerton were built after the war, and Thorpe Edge, Bierley and Holmewood in the 1950s and 1960s (Duckett and Waddington-Feather, 2005:116).

Bradford was transmuted from the status of an independent city in 1974 and recognised as the hub of a conurbation. The Bradford Metropolitan District was created under an Act of 1974, incorporating the borough of Keighley together with Ilkley, Silsden, Bingley, Baildon, Shipley, Queensbury, Cottingley, Haworth and Denholme, very reluctantly for many. Bradford today is around two-thirds rural, with concentrated populations in inner-city areas. According to the 2001 census the number of people per hectare was very high, at 12.8 compared to a national average of 3.4, and considerably higher in the inner city. Bradford citizens thus live in very diverse kinds of social space, with those in the highly populated inner city experiencing particular disadvantages. Perceptions, experiences and also life chances differ greatly, making the challenge of a shared and inclusive vision for the future very difficult to construct. Of course, people move. One of the great controversies in Bradford is when, why and where people move. Community fragmentation led to some people choosing to live amongst 'their own', while other evidence suggests that as long as incomes are rising people are happy to live in 'mixed' areas. The problem in Bradford is that incomes were mostly not rising. The inner city was an area of much deprivation by the 1990s. As most of our 2001 rioters came from the inner city, both in the main riot and the second smaller riot on Ravenscliffe, it is worth focussing on what life was like in these localities.

## Community in the Inner City

Council estates were dignified areas for working people to live until de-industrialisation. Coupled with the 'right to buy' policy of the early 1980s, social dynamics in these areas were transformed, particularly in the industrial heartlands of the north. In Bradford, many of the employed working class bought and then sold their houses, and moved out to the 'urban villages' on the hills around. Nationally, the proportion of social tenant householders in paid employment fell from 42% to 32% between 1981 and 2006 (Hills, 2007:2-3), while the national stock of council homes halved between 1979 and 2004 (Turnstall and Coulter, 2006:59). Social housing lettings came to focus on need, so that many families with high rates of disability, single parents and single people aged over 60 came to live on estates. In the early 1990s a series of urban hearings found that 30% of households on Ravenscliffe estate were headed by a lone parent, twice the District average (Bradford Metropolitan Faith in the City Forum: 18). Research on Scholemoor estate in 2010 found residents harking back to a time when community was a solid everyday experience. 'My fondest memories are of growing up in Scholemoor. It was a community. People didn't lock their doors. We were in and out of people's houses. Everybody knew everybody. And it's all gone now' (Pearce and Milne, 32). Bradford's older generation feel the change most strongly. The end of Bradford's relatively similar working class culture went side by side with the social and geographical fragmentation of many of its communities. Fragmentation fostered social distinctions and many estate residents came to see themselves as the 'lowest of the low' (ibid). That sense is conveyed by our 2003 interviews in Ravenscliffe, where feelings of neglect and losing out to other communities had grown.

The ethnic minority population—themselves also mainly working class—had meanwhile tended to concentrate in the inner-city areas of Bradford and Keighley. In 1971, they numbered around 20,000, 80% from Pakistan and India and the rest mostly from the Caribbean. Primary immigration from the Commonwealth had come to a virtual end due to restrictive anti-immigration legislation and only dependents, refugees, asylum seekers and special voucher-holders gained entry. This was the period when migrant workers began to build their own families and communities. While the first generation of migrants had intended to return home, gradually the decision was made to stay. Those born in Bradford or arriving as young children now saw the city as their home (Ahmed, 1997:86) though they still mostly returned to Pakistan to marry. In the 1970s and 1980s, families were reunited by the arrival of the wives of either existing male immigrants or their sons, often bringing children with them (Simpson, 1997:101). By 1987, fewer child immigrants were arriving in Bradford, but immigration of male adults continued as the European Court ruled that the UK could not discriminate in allowing wives but not husbands of British residents to immigrate. A cultural preference for cousin marriages is prevalent amongst the Pakistani community in Bradford. Between 1992 and 1994 around 700 immigrants arrived in Bradford each year. About 600 were South Asian immigrant spouses, about half of the total marriages in those communities (Simpson, 1997:104). Amongst our sample of rioters, 75% were born in the UK, mainly in Bradford, of parents predominantly born in Pakistan.

There is no single 'South Asian' community in Bradford. There are social, linguistic and religious distinctions between communities as well as caste and sect differences amongst them. Bradford Council statistics put the South Asian population at 94,250 in 2001 of which 73,900 were from Pakistan (Philips et al, 2002). The overwhelming majority of these were from Mirpur in politically-disputed Azad Kashmir. Others, the Pathans, came from the Attock District of the Northwest frontier with Afghanistan and speak Pushto. Most originated in rural areas, and were from peasant stock; a tiny minority came from Pakistan's urban centres with professional and middle class backgrounds.

Pioneer settlers from Pakistan arrived anxious to be accepted and some even took English names and had themselves photographed wearing bowler hats. They first congregated together irrespective of origins in region, caste or religious sect. In a study of minorities within the South Asian minorities (Blakey et al, 2006:35), local residents spoke of the importance of mutual interdependence to Mirpuri rural life and how this enabled the first cohort of male migrants to the mills to survive:

> You cannot be independent, you have to help out. And these were the values that these people brought with them when they came . . . when they came here, I heard stories of how 12 men used to live in this house and they all used to support each other. Some of them used

*Saturday Night and Sunday Morning*

to make lunch, go off to work and leave enough lunch for the other men coming back off. Some of them would make lunch in the evening and leave it for the night shift for when they came back.

East Pakistan became Bangladesh following secession in 1971. Migrants from Bangladesh share their religion with those from Pakistan but do not share a language. Most of Bradford's Bangladeshi population originate in Sylhet and speak Sylheti. Amongst the migrants of Indian origin, there are Punjabi Sikhs, Gujarati and Punjabi Hindus and Gujarati Muslims. Many Hindus came indirectly from East Africa in the 1970s.

Lewis reports that as numbers grew, ties of village-kinship and sectarian affiliation within Islam became more important as a basis for community (1994: 56). Over time, a religious distinction emerged in the 'labelling' of communities. Non-Pakistanis began to be distinguished as Hindus and Sikhs, so that Pakistanis became 'Muslims', even though there are also many distinctions to be made within Bradford's Muslim population. In our sample of rioters, 85% self-identified as 'British Pakistani' or 'British Asian', or 'British Muslim', hybrid identities reflecting a sense of dual belonging or evolving identities. Over time 'Pakistani' has come to be equated with religious belief, Islam, and with class position, 'working and poor', enhancing the complexity around identity. There is a Bradford story about belonging, rejection and affirmation in these changes to labelling and self-labelling, as a migrant community came to terms with a shifting sense of heritage and home.

In the 1990s Bradford Council's Principal Research Officer, Steven Simpson, pointed out that ethnic statistics are problematic because they try to categorise something which changes:

> over time, between cohorts, and when measured for the same person at different ages. These changes occur because of the way individuals see themselves and because of the way others see and categorise them . . . (Simpson, 1997:93).

They may also categorise themselves in different ways in different contexts.

In the early 1990s the undisputed common marker amongst the South Asian communities of Bradford was that they lived in areas of multiple stress, although there were signs that Indian families had begun to move into better areas and accommodation and a few Pakistani Asians had begun to follow them. A 1993 Bradford Council Study on Areas of Stress within Bradford concluded that:

> . . . three quarters of all Bradford's Bangladeshi residents live in areas of multiple stress, concentrated in the Cornwall Road area of Manningham and in inner Keighley. Other studies have also shown that Bangladeshi residents have much poorer living conditions than all

other groups. Nonetheless, over half of all residents of Pakistani origin and nearly half of the District's African-Caribbean residents also live in the areas of multiple stress. Indian residents have tended to become more spread out within the District and are not so concentrated within the same stress areas.

In fact a quarter of even the city's Indian population, as against 14.2% of whites, lived in the areas of multiple stress (Ratcliffe, 1996:17).

This data was brought up to date for 2000 by a team from Leeds led by Deborah Philips, whose interim study based on religious group classification indicated that over 80% of Muslims as well as 45–50% of Sikhs and Hindus were still living in 'struggling' areas. However, by now all groups were also found in smaller numbers in better neighbourhoods: 35% of Sikhs, 28% of Hindus and 10% of Muslims. Religious groups still retained some residential clustering as they moved out of the inner city. Other minorities should not be forgotten in this picture, notably, the African-Caribbean population, who felt ongoing resentment about how they were removed from Newby Square estate in Manningham in 1986, through the council's housing redevelopment scheme. Many felt they lost their sense of community when they were dispersed to other areas (Ratcliffe et al, 2001:47). Young African-Caribbeans had considered Lumb Lane in Manningham as the heart of their cultural and social life, from music to cannabis. However, by 1995 there were only two places left in Manningham where these young people could meet (Bradford Commission, 1996:82-83).

The issue of clustering by ethnic group is one of great contention in the District. In 2000, a Commission was set up under Sir Herman Ouseley to investigate race and community relations. Regeneration money from national government had led to competition amongst communities to present themselves as the most deprived in order to attract funding, fostering resentment. Two issues, a mechanism for ensuring race equality in the District and the state of community relationships, fed into the final brief of the Commission, which asked: 'Why is community fragmentation along social, cultural, ethnic and religious lines occurring in the Bradford District?' (Ouseley, 2001).

The 2001 riots took place a week before the presentation of the report, which highlighted a 'very worrying drift towards self-segregation', and spoke of retreat into '"comfort zones" across the District, made up of people like themselves' (ibid:16). Ouseley talked about communities preferring to live apart. His report also drew attention to '"white flight" and "middle class" people who were moving out of the city and leaving behind an underclass of relatively poor white people and visible minority ethnic communities' (ibid:9). Self-segregation, the report argued, was being 'driven by fear of others, the need for safety from harassment and violent crime and the belief that it is the only way to promote, retain and protect faith and cultural identity and affiliation'. In other words, for many, self-segregation was not a choice, but a response. These conclusions were welcomed by some for opening up debate around widely held prejudices (for example Singh, 2002:145), but strongly criticised by others who interpreted his conclusions to refer to the Asian population alone, particularly the Pakistani population, and moreover imputing 'blame' to them.

## 'Comfort Zones' Controversy

Bradford's evolution into a multicultural city has not been easy for some Bradfordians. Many have not understood the dynamics behind the settlement of Asians in the District. The initial clustering of the South Asian migrant community in the wards of Toller, University, Little Horton and Bradford Moor, reflected a range of driving forces. These included discriminatory practices by estate agents and property companies (sometimes called 'racial steering'), very localised searches for housing and the pooling of finance and interest-free loans from kin. In short, there was a mixture of limited options due to income and discrimination, but also influenced by preference and supportive community structures. Efforts to draw inferences from housing choice and neighbourhood demographics about the desire of ethnic groups to live apart are hotly disputed. The picture is more complex.

Ratcliffe's 1996 study shows that there were significant differences amongst the minority ethnic populations in terms of housing, with much lower levels of owner-occupation amongst African-Caribbean households, for example, and higher levels amongst all South Asian groups than the local white population (ibid:37). Again, caution is needed in assuming that this is preference, rather than perhaps ignorance about the accessibility and affordability of social housing.

The types of property in which South Asian people lived tell a powerful story. A third of Ratcliffe's Indian sample, mostly Hindus and Sikhs, accessed property built after 1919, while 88% of Pakistanis and 95% of Bangladeshis bought pre-1919 property. This latter kind of property was far more likely to be substandard. Ratcliffe's sample showed that a quarter of Pakistanis and around 30% of Bangladeshis lived in overcrowded conditions in properties with at least one major structural fault (ibid:43). Housing defects such as dampness, leaking roofs and condensation, affected the daily life and health of many more families. Just over 11% of Pakistani households contained someone suffering from respiratory problems connected with poor living conditions. Over 70% of Pakistani homes had no central heating and many that did, could not afford to turn it on. In addition, disability and long-term sickness meant that in a third of Pakistani households, at least one household member found it very difficult to get up and down stairs (ibid:59). Ratcliffe's study gives a shocking insight into the stressful housing conditions and health problems, particularly amongst Pakistani and Bangladeshi households of inner-city Bradford in the decade prior to the 2001 riot.

Ratcliffe (ibid:80) found that levels of overcrowding amongst Pakistani and Bangladeshi families in his sample were severe. However it was common for minority ethnic households to house extended family units under the same roof. The significance of 'overcrowding' is not necessarily the same for these families. Given the financial and social pressures faced by the minority ethnic community, there was an economic logic for generations to live together, as well as a cultural expectation that young people do not leave home before marriage. In a later study, entitled *Breaking the Barriers*, Ratcliffe et al (2001) found that many young Asians now wanted greater autonomy to set up their own households, but not too far away from their families. Proximity to community, shops and places of worship were important. Extended networks of kin and clan remained vital to community life.

Although many aspired to own their houses, they did not often have the money and Pakistani families were starting to look to the social housing sector. There were, however, many negative opinions about estates uncovered by this research team, including strong fears of racial harassment. Pakistanis would, for example, avoid Holmewood (because of drugs, dogs, racial harassment, isolation and insecurity), Thorpe Edge/Eccleshill (racist harassment risk), Ravenscliffe (too white, 'rough'), Queensbury (too white), Green Lane (declining, drugs, crime, neglected, council 'dump' people there), but would consider areas outside their traditional areas of BD1 or BD3, such as Heaton (though females expressed worries about drugs), north Bradford (Swain House, Shipley, Bolton), Odsal (would be more attractive if more Asians lived there) and Bradford 2 (Ratcliffe et al, 2001:57). Three of the Asian youth in our study lived in council houses.

The 2001 *Breaking the Barriers* team uncovered, like the Ouseley Commission, a 'lack of understanding and fear between communities' (ibid:85). Arguably the phrase 'comfort zone' is most pertinent in describing 'white flight' and the attitude of the wealthier outer city in distancing itself from the challenges facing the inner city. In reality, there were many external reasons why communities 'lived apart', alongside preferences rooted in community connections and customs. Some communities were expanding within inner-city wards, especially notable in the case of the Pakistani population which was growing due to birth rate and immigration. Ramindar Singh (2002) reminds us of the differences with Punjabi Sikhs and Hindus who gradually moved out from Thornbury, Laisterdyke, Bradford Moor and West Bowling, and the Muslims, who moved into their vacated houses from Manningham and Lumb Lane (2002:25).

Meanwhile three inner-city wards, Toller, Bradford Moor and Little Horton, lost between 20 and 25% of their white population through out-migration during the 1990s, though whether this is 'white' flight or 'middle class' flight has not been deeply researched. It matters a great deal whether people left because they became more affluent or because they did not want to live in areas where minority ethnic residents were the majority.

Manningham, with its large houses inherited from the early days of industrialism, had always been a 'first port of call' for migrants to Bradford as well as attracting a bohemian population of artists, activists and free-thinkers in the 1970s and 1980s. One local (white) shop keeper, whose family shop was set up in Manningham in 1973 but which he had run since 1978, recalled in a conversation with us how Italians, Poles and Ukrainians had come and gone from the area. He learnt some Italian and later some Urdu and Punjabi words. He and his wife became good at sign language. 'It was fun,' they said. But they described how in the late 1980s and 1990s non-Asian shopkeepers began to sell up and move out—the Polish meat shop, the Sikh chemist, the antique shop etc. They began to experience verbal abuse, and increasing vandalism from local youth. It did not make them abandon the area, and they put it down to exceptions rather than the community as a whole, but exceptions who were being looked upon as heroes by their younger brothers.

The 1995 disturbances in Manningham, which will be discussed in the next chapter, escalated tensions. The white-owned chemist shop was looted, a Sikh-owned supermarket extensively damaged and a white-owned DIY store and five BMW saloons destroyed in the forecourt of the white-owned garage in Oak Lane (which would be burnt down in 2001). Two windows in property owned by Asian Muslims were also damaged (Bradford Commission, 1996:46). The relevance of ownership identity to the targeting of these premises was not clear. As in 2001 it remained a matter of dispute.

Other former residents recall Manningham's gradual shift from its strong multicultural composition during the 1980s and 1990s towards an overwhelmingly Pakistani population. The reasons for this are mixed. The loss of Newby Square precipitated the dispersal of African-Caribbeans after 1986 as discussed previously. The bohemians moved out for a variety of reasons, though for some it became increasingly uncomfortable to be gay or lesbian in the area. An anti-prostitution campaign in 1995 also sparked controversy. Originally an outcome of community concern at the expansion of the Red Light District from Lumb Lane, vigilante patrols headed by young men led eventually to prostitutes abandoning the area. The Bradford Commission concluded that participation in anti-prostitution patrols had given young men a sense of empowerment through direct action (1996:44).

The 2001 census showed that Toller Ward was 63.8% Pakistani, compared to 14.5% in the District as a whole. Of this 4.6% are Indian compared to 2.7% for the District and 25.3% of the population white compared to 78.3% for the District as a whole. Those white people who did not move were often trapped by old age or lack of resources. In the 2000s, new Eastern European migrants arrived in Manningham, bringing a new white population to the area. However, equally there was evidence that some Asian families were moving out, confounding those who argued that residential dynamics were simply a question of self-segregation.

## Living Apart Together?
## Does Segregation Matter?

To most people segregation simply means separation, but statisticians measure something more precise—the proportion of one sort of people (however categorized) in a given area as compared to its proportion in another. Where this proportion is relatively high (though whether this is at ward or sub ward level can alter the figures), there can be said to be 'segregation'. A heated academic debate revolves around the question of whether the fact of segregation, which most acknowledge does exist to a greater or lesser extent, is the same as wilful self-segregation along ethnic and faith—or other—lines. More importantly, does this matter?

For some it matters because they object to claims by politicians and the media that ethnic minorities do not wish to integrate into British society. Given the ongoing efforts by the Far Right to rally 'British' society against the minority ethnic population, this is understandable. Ludi Simpson and others have tried to direct attention away from a focus on 'ethnic' separation, which elicits such fears and prejudices. They have pointed out that people cluster as much on the basis of economic position as they do by ethnicity.

Because economic disadvantage is concentrated amongst those who experienced the worst of Bradford's economic decline, race and class may coincide. The observer may see 'Asian Muslim ghettos' when these are also and potently reserves of the unemployed and the economically disadvantaged.

Simpson (2004) noted that the high birth rate and continuing immigration of South Asians into Bradford, combined with economic difficulties that make it hard for the poor to move, had exacerbated the clustering of Asians in certain parts of the city. This is not necessarily 'self-segregation'. Others, however, have seen it as a reluctance to mix.

Alan Carling (2008) points out that the South Asian population tended to expand into adjacent areas to those first settled ('comfort zones', in that they retained proximity to community), while the white population tended to move further out of the inner city, to areas such as the Worth Valley and Craven. He therefore concludes that: 'The mutual geographical segregation of the South Asian and white populations increased during the 1990s'. In 2001 the average South Asian lived in a ward with a South Asian proportion of 47%, while white residents were living on average in residential environments which were 87% white despite the ethnic diversity of the District (Carling, 2008:567). Nevertheless this still means that a substantial white population was living in wards where the South Asian population is high or predominant (Finney and Simpson, 2009:123).

No matter how we interpret the statistics, the question is, does segregation matter? Carling thinks that people choosing to associate with like others is not inevitably a 'bad' thing. It becomes problematic only when based on racial or ethnic lines involving antagonism towards other groups or leading to reduced contact between groups and the erosion of understanding and trust. Carling argues that there are dangers of polarisation between communities when this form of segregation grows.

Few academics would agree. Phillips and others (2002) insist that residential clustering is not the same as a desire to separate from others—people wanted to live together not to live apart, although it left an everyday sense of the 'racialisation of space'. Phillips (2006) found that continued association with people from a similar cultural and religious background is important to many Bradford Muslims. However, in her interviews many also voiced a desire for greater social interaction with people from other backgrounds and would consider living in other areas so long as they do not feel threatened, a point also made strongly in the Ouseley report (2006:37). She points out that evidence from her research 'suggests that the racialisation of space in Bradford speaks more loudly of white control and bounded choices, both past and present' (ibid). Simpson, Husband and Alam argue that growth of the Asian population will lead to greater mixing of ethnic groups no matter what, as there is limited capacity in the inner city to house them (2009:2000).

It is clear that choice and motivation do matter. A 2006 dissertation at the University of Bradford by Zafer Faqir took up the Simpson/Carling debate. He supplemented statistical data with interviews with his extended family in Keighley. He reported that statistically, segregation existed but was diminishing in Keighley. He also found that personal choice had a continuing impact on residential decisions and that people were strongly motivated to live near others like them.

> From my family interviews my findings support the view of Carling (2005) that self-segregation is a ubiquitous process of everyday life. It is something that has occurred within the wards of Keighley for many years and the reasons people self-segregate will vary between individuals as will the circumstances.

He also found that people maintain close and strong links with Pakistan which perpetuate these choices.

> Many people who have died in Keighley are returned to Pakistan for burial. Many friends including members of my own family return to Pakistan to be married or find partners. Economic and business ties are also strong. For many families or individuals English is a second language and many, especially women, do not speak English. A number of schools in the area are dominated by Pakistani children and English is treated as a secondary language. In some ways these represent the real roots of self-segregation . . . (Faqir:80).

A desire not to live in an all white area and to be connected with one's community is hardly a call for living only with one's own community. And in the end, this is probably as close as we can get to a conclusion. In the right circumstances people will live comfortably alongside others, but it needs a supportive environment. An appreciation of the contribution to community life from different cultures can and does happen. This needs to be a two-way street. Very few from the white middle class ever visit the inner city and lack the curiosity to get to know the histories and cultures of their fellow Bradfordians.

The demographic trend in Bradford will be towards more mixed communities. Better jobs, higher incomes and improved living conditions can make this work to a large extent. However, on the eve of the Bradford riot, inner-city communities remained in a considerable state of economic vulnerability and needed support from family and friends. In such contexts, socio-cultural affinities matter. This brings us to an important and highly complex and controversial discussion around the significance of 'culture' in community, and in particular, its relevance to the upbringing of the rioters.

## Culture, Gender and Generational Change

Whether you take Simpson's view that Bradford is on a trajectory of dispersal and upward mobility characteristic of migrant communities elsewhere, or Carling's argument that even when migration and natural change are accounted for, levels of segregation grew in the 1990s in Bradford, the fact is that on the eve of the riots, there were areas of Bradford where South Asian, particularly Pakistani, communities were concentrated. More important, these tended to be the most deprived wards in Bradford. To what extent did deprivation interact with cultural norms in explaining why Asian young men rioted in 2001?

'Culture' is an everyday term which refers to the human rather than natural or biological forms of our existence, one that gives us a history, not just a past. This is often forgotten and culture is seen as something we are born 'with' rather than 'into'. It is then used to account for essential differences between communities and groups, as if these are unchanging and unchangeable. Another approach to culture, however, recognises some ambiguity. On the one hand culture conveys a sense of stability, regularity and pattern, and on the other it conjures up creativity and innovation. It has been seen as both 'constraining' and 'enabling' (Baumann, 1999:xii). We can begin to see culture as something simultaneously about change and conservation. This helps us appreciate better how the South Asian, and particularly the Mirpuri majority population in the north of England, called upon cultural resources to deal with the upheavals in their lives as the mills closed. Culture was a source of the energy required to rebuild livelihoods, but at the same time it preserved an order which potentially constrained some of its young people, with different impacts for women and men.

Kalra's study of Mirpuri mill workers in Oldham as they faced redundancy is very helpful in enabling those of us outside that community to understand these responses better. Losing their jobs meant a profound lifestyle change, from 12 to 16 hour mill shifts to spending days at home. Kalra traces how religion, extended family— and for some involvement in community and political associations— became a source of 'work' for this generation of Asian men. Kalra argues that Islam provided a structure to time that replaced the discipline of the mills—the mosque in other words replaced the mill as a centre of activity (2000:148). Voluntary work at the mosque conferred status as well as consumed time, as did local party politics which gave influence in the local biraderi or clan structure and in turn, political clout to further the community's interests.

Similar dynamics seem to have occurred in Bradford during the collapse of textiles and unemployment in the 1980s and 1990s. Cultural resources to deal with the stress were vital to all those affected, but arguably were more available to the South Asian population with their strong family structures than to the white population, where statistics point to family breakdown and loss of identity previously provided by a shared working class culture. The majority Mirpuri community had resources from their extensive clan structure, the 'biraderi' or 'brotherhood', as well as religion—and for some, their origin in a disputed territory of Kashmir. Biraderi offered mutual well-being and emotional and material support. It is culture as enabling. Members of a clan (which may include several hundred people) trace their kinship through the father's line. Marrying one's father's brother's daughter helps maintain the boundaries of the clan and protect its resources. This is why cousin marriage is so important to the community. Faced with a sense that society is hostile or promotes values which clash with community-sustaining cultural norms, biraderi offers collective affirmation and protection.

The significance of culture to communities also helps to explain the persistence of links with place of origin. Some authors argue that the Mirpuri population in particular is a transcontinental community. Land as well as kin ties and religious practices (such as burials in Pakistan) have maintained the flow of visits and travel and ultimately a form of dual identity. Rather than see this as a reluctance to integrate, it should be seen as attachment to secure moorings in the face of uncertain futures and the need to preserve values and identities.

However, there is also a constraining side to the cultural requirements of community bonds. Cousin marriage, for instance, may carry health risks. Biraderi structures also reflect caste inequalities which have been imported to Bradford and which profoundly impact on status, power and access to decision-making. In the course of the 1980s and 1990s, Pakistani men drew on biraderi to access political opportunities. Struggles for recognition of cultural and religious norms empowered the community, but that power was concentrated in religious male leaders, supplanting younger, more secular and politicised actors who had struggled against racism in the 1970s. This story will be told in the next chapter and it includes the role of the local state, which supported the new forms of leadership in the Pakistani Muslim community.

Cultural norms also impact on language and learning. In 1993, 77% of South Asian births were to mothers born outside the UK according to Bradford Health Authority's birth records (Simpson,

1997:104). A language survey found that 1,800 pupils across age groups, spoke a language of the South Asian subcontinent for some of the time at home. Steve Simpson's research on demography and ethnicity in Bradford in the late 1990s from which these figures are drawn, was designed to highlight issues relating to the 'cultural preferences that impinge on public services and the need for specific support to allow all citizens to take equal part in public services' (1997:105).

The relationship of language to identity was highlighted by the Bradford Commission into the 1995 disturbances. They quote a Kashmiri parent who said: 'Children starting at school still can't speak English. People like me should have been pointing it out. Our children are not white, and don't feel British. The identity of our children is the crux. Language is important for that' (Bradford Commission, 1996:141). An Upper School Headmaster working in Manningham told the Commission that standard English acquisition had been 'soft pedalled':

> We have a sadly ironic situation whereby, in a laudable attempt not to appear too Eurocentric, Bradford's educational policy planners may well have increased inequality of opportunity by not emphasising the centrality of effective English acquisition, which I firmly believe is the key to helping Asian families prosper in England (ibid).

Mohammed Taj, who produced a Minority Report for the Commission, emphasised the 'heartfelt desire for educational success' amongst Bradford's Muslims and spoke of the danger of trapping children in a 'language ghetto' by the use of an Asian tongue as the sole domestic language (Taj, 1996:8). He also criticised Arabic rote teaching as the means to deliver Qur'anic education. Inculcating the high moral standards of Islam required guidance in an accessible language. It should be:

> provided with the interests of the child as paramount, all too often it is conducted at the convenience of the providers, during the school week, leaving pupils tired and unresponsive to their wider education.

Several of our sample of rioters also recounted experiences of physical punishment in the course of their Islamic education in the mosques. Parents sometimes saw this as a source of discipline for their sons but it may well have had other effects. One rioter recalled he had been so badly beaten that he had called the police, but then his mother persuaded him to drop the charges.

The Bradford Commission was at pains to point out that language difficulties were not a problem of ethnic minorities alone. Poor white lads as well as Asian lads were doing badly at school, so that not just culture, but gender as well as poverty have to be factored in. Bradford schools were failing in the national league tables in the

1990s. Council statistics for 1997 show that only 29% of Bradford pupils achieved five or more GCSE grade A-C passes compared to the national average of 45% (Macey, 1999:5). But at the same time, schools were facing many challenges. One of these was the way residential clustering impacted on segregation in schools, limiting the social mixing which often raises overall achievement.

While the Mirpuri community struggled to overcome financial worries and to build small businesses and other ways of earning a living, family life was put under huge pressure. Expectations around the role of women and young people are influenced by understandings of power and authority in communities, which amongst the Pakistani community is concentrated in male elders. Young men are not fully adult in the eyes of parents until they marry. The question of male dominance is a cross-cultural phenomenon, but in some cases strongly reinforced by religious values. Marie Macey has explored the importance of appropriate gender roles, arranged marriages, female dress, family authority and honour to Muslim families (Macey, 1999). The dominant role of husbands, fathers, brothers and sons over females in family life in the Muslim community is widely recognised. Our rioters were very protective of the women in their family. At the same time attitudes towards women were very paternalistic, and with lesser respect towards non-Pakistani women.

There is some evidence, nevertheless, that gendered role expectations limited young men more than young women. The weight upon young male shoulders of codes of honour and shame has been discussed in terms of the effects of low-paid or no jobs. However, the same codes made it impossible for young men to disclose their alcohol and drugs problems with their families or the wider community, given religious as well as social taboos. If families did become aware, sharing this with public bodies would be very problematic. Shame refers to dishonour in the public more than the private realm. Many of the families were genuinely unaware that their sons and brothers had serious problems of this nature when they went to prison (interviews Himmat: December 2004 and January 2011). There was a widespread sense that the young men had shamed the Muslim community by their behaviour in the riots.

We have seen in previous chapters that most of the young men were dismissive of efforts by community elders to mediate before and during the riot itself and positively angry with local politicians from their own community. Some interpret this as a generational gap, as youth grappled with a street culture of drugs and freedom which their elders wanted to protect them from but did not know how. Street culture was an exciting magnet for the young men, a source of status, pride and power unavailable within their own community. However, another way of looking at this, is that the young men felt totally unrepresented in the community and in the broader political realm. The biraderi network ensured that representation was limited by clan, caste, gender and age. Many younger people had no-one speaking for them and had not found their own voice. Although the younger generation also continued to visit Pakistan, some no longer felt comfortable there. The sister of a rioter we interviewed talked about visits back to Pakistan and laughed at how she and her brother:

> . . . were both dying to come back to England. Cause it was different . . . the lifestyle's different and that, you know, the houses and the way they live . . . The food and that as well for my brother and me, we missed our pizzas and that kind of stuff, living in the village it was a different lifestyle you know from the cities . . .

In 2006 a Manningham resident involved in a study on Minorities within Minorities in the South Asian community explained that whilst women suffered many restrictions, and levels of domestic violence were high, in many respects the pressures were greatest on young men: 'Surprisingly things have already changed for young women'. The reason for this was:

> because Imams and mosques have talked about women's roles in society and what Islam used to do in terms of women's roles, and the Prophet, and the roles of women in the Qur'an . . . and that has opened many people's minds . . . The power for women in terms of participation—of not being restricted to her neighbourhood—are now prevalent because it's been allowed that women can be allowed to drive. So major things in terms of women, but what do men have in terms of new things? So that's why I think the men feel more disheartened than the women at present. There are many other things that women have got—there doesn't need to be a woman present with them shopping . . . It's no longer the case that women should be at home before eight o'clock. Women shouldn't work—now it's acceptable. Her earnings should be shared among the family and taken importantly, seriously. So the women's role has become having power, of running the household, the whole of the mechanism—that wasn't the case years ago—men have taken, if you like, a drop in that side, and they are feeling isolated because the power doesn't allow them to get involved politically, they're suppressed on wealth . . .

A sister of one of our rioters confirmed that her life had begun to change, 'I noticed the changes, I think more girls are learning to drive than before. Because I don't remember before a lot of girls when I was younger that were driving or anything'.

Our interviews with the rioters suggest that expectations about being a man, which included a readiness to fight on the streets, played a part in the excitement of 'taking on the coppers' in White Abbey Road. It is evident from their interviews that this was influenced by film and television, by images of Rambo and James Bond, rather than drawing on local community values. Young men were creatively negotiating different cultures and cultural fusion is often taking place under the radar. Many young men had histories of fighting in the school playground, quite often around issues of race. They had not achieved their intellectual potential. The profile of our sample of rioters, discussed in chapter 2, shows that over half had not completed GCSEs and had dropped out of school by age 16 or before. Of those who did complete school, none had finished further study courses. Their sense of self involved little conscious 'political' interpretation of the world around them, but awareness of Far Right hatred—the very questioning of their right to live in Bradford and the UK—resonated with experiences of powerlessness in several areas of their lives. Low educational achievement does not mean lack of sensibility to the everyday politics of power and powerlessness. These were not young men with high self esteem but much bravado and pride.

Some of the rioters had started further study with the aim of continuing. Our random sample conveys a general picture but does not capture the differences at each end of the spectrum. At one end were those already involved in criminality for whom the riot seemed to be pure adrenalin. The young men at the other end were more aspirational. One rioter (not in our original sample) whom we interviewed in 2011 had been on a degree course at the time of the riot. He acknowledged that he felt different from other rioters in that he did not speak Punjabi or Urdu. He had gone to a Catholic school and his best friends were white. He had been brought up by a politically-aware and active mother and described himself as having a 'protecting, caring nature' and a passion for Bradford. When rung up by a friend in the early afternoon of 7 July, he made his way to Kirkgate and found himself drawn into the crowd and 'things took over'. The Far Right were bullies and he had always hated bullies. He also hated the way the police seemed to be pushing Asians back into their own areas. A sister of another rioter described her 30 year old brother as a 'family man' with three children.

> There's only about 10 months difference between me and him . . . We've grown up where we've had white friends, Sikh friends, black friends, we've not known racism. His reason for being in Centenary Square was to say to the BNPs—stay away from my home—stay away from my kids, keep your dirty ideas away from my kids. Because he knew that his kids were going to stay in this country.

Most of our rioters had not personally known organised racism nor had they experienced the politicisation of confronting it. The sister of the rioter quoted above was 28 or 29 when the 2001 riot happened. She insisted that:

> I had not experienced that kind of racism . . . That word never came into the dialogue I had with my parents, my friends, my teachers. I mean I was in Belle Vue Girls School, a predominantly Asian school, it was never mentioned. There was mentions of aspects of it, but it was always about the past—in the 1970s and 1960s when your parents came. It was never—now you will experience it as well.

The NF threat to march in 2001 was a shock to women as well as men. Tension mounted amongst the women in her neighbourhood as the rumours of the Far Right march spread, and the outcome shook the confidence of the community as a whole:

> Women were getting together and saying: Oh, the BNP are coming, the BNP are coming. It sounded like as if there was this mass invasion from outer space . . . I think people's image of the BNP was, you know, thugs with bomber jackets and skinheads and, you know, big Union Jack T-shirts, you know—rumper thumper type of thing, louts . . . The BNP whole ethos wasn't looked at—the impact it would have on Bradford. And I think what happened afterwards, I mean, the whole sense of community just went into oblivion. The B-N-P—those three letters just destroyed any faith in a community we would have.

This chapter has discussed life and livelihood in Bradford and how they became factors in the 2001 riot. It has stressed the complexity of the story. Deprivation alone does not explain the riot. However, our generation of rioters reached adolescence under the shadow of deindustrialisation. The social impacts were felt on all communities in the District in different ways. We have traced the effects on a cohort of young men growing up in a specific time and place, and in communities which had struggled to rebuild working lives, drawing on cultures of solidarity. Depressed, like young men from all communities without the stable job prospects of previous generations, they also knew that their fathers and grandfathers had experienced everyday disrespect and organised racism. Streetwise and angry, many seized the moment in 2001 to send a message. As one put it:

> What the message was? We're not taking no shit off no council, no NF and no police service. They've walked over us for long enough. They've walked over us for generations, but not this generation, man . . .

# 6

# WHY BRADFORD?
# POLITICS AND ACTIVISM

*That was my first recollection of a riot in Bradford basically, you know, where police cars were turned over, paint was thrown at them, and being chased by police on horseback, you know, and that was basically because they'd allowed the National Front, I think it was Martin Webster at the time, that came to Bradford to hold a meeting in a school in Manningham. You know, so that was, I suppose, the first real campaign that I can recollect of any kind which was about defending our homes and our community basically, because that's where most of us lived. I lived on Lumb Lane.*
**(Jani Rashid on the 1976 confrontation with the NF, quoted in Ramamurthy, 2000:14-15)**

Bradford has a lively political history of established politicians as well as contentious activists and community organisations. Most were caught by surprise by the 2001 riot, and we need to ask why. Part of the answer lies in the way capital and social class evolved in the District and the impact this had on forms of organising as well as what people organised for. Struggles over livelihoods became caught up in the politics of race and anti-racism, amongst both activists and the local state. The history of Far Right efforts to provoke violence in Bradford stands out as a continuous theme, with the National Front making constant appearances. Other themes are the role of left activists and the nature of political organising and representation amongst the ethnic minority population.

# From Paternalist Liberalism to Class Politics

During its golden years, Bradford had been a heartland of reform-minded Liberalism with a strong nonconformist individualism. However, towards the end of the 19<sup>th</sup> century, paternalism broke down under pressure of economic downturn and independent working class politics began to emerge. Bradford Trades Council was formed in 1872, but it was the Manningham Mills Strike of December 1890 to April 1891 which was the turning point for working class politics. Faced with US import tariffs, Lister decided to cut the wages of 1,100 workers by 25% and to lock out those who refused. Five thousand workers went on strike. Ben Tillet, leader of the London Dock Strike of 1889 came to address the strikers. At a meeting on 13 April 1891, the Durham Light Infantry were sent into the city, a riot ensued and the Riot Act was read. According to one account: 'Police and troops baton and bayonet-charged the meeting. The crowd threw knives and bricks. Demonstrators were driven out of the town centre but reformed in small groups in areas like Westgate' (Robinson, 2004:2).

Although the workers were forced back to work through hunger, socialist politics and the idea of political representation of the working class had been born. The Bradford Labour Union was set up and in 1892, Frederick Jowett became the first socialist to be elected to Bradford City Council. A few months later, in 1893, the Independent Labour Party was established in Bradford, transforming local and ultimately national politics. In 1904, Bradford became the first local authority in the country to provide free school meals and in 1906 Jowett won Bradford West.

Bradford's role in national labour history is a source of great pride in the District. Bradford's many Asian textile workers later became part of that history, joining trade unions and becoming part of the broader labour movement. The 1970s saw a number of strikes in the UK by Asian workers, such as Mansfield Hosiery in Loughborough, Imperial Typewriters in Leicester and Grunwick in London, as Asians woke up to discriminatory practice and low wages. Racist violence grew in the decade, and increasingly, young Asians looked to build their own organisations to resist and defend themselves. Anti-racist and anti-fascist struggles became major aspects of Bradford's political life over the next decade. The vocabulary of such struggles would be echoed in 2001.

2001: Police in Ivegate try to restrain an Asian youth
© rossparry.co.uk/syndication

2001: A white youth is helped by police after being stabbed by Asians behind Sunwin House
© rossparry.co.uk/syndication

2001: Police vans massed on White Abbey Road while rioters gather behind them
© rossparry.co.uk/syndication

2001: A burning car on White Abbey Road as the riot rages
© rossparry.co.uk/syndication

© rossparry.co.uk/syndication

© rossparry.co.uk/syndication

**Top left:** 2001: White Abbey Road becomes a battleground
**Top right:** 2001: Rioters throwing missiles on Whetley Hill
**Bottom:** 2001: A community leader (in blue shirt) pleads with youth on Whetley Hill

© rossparry.co.uk/syndication

2001: Burnt out cars outside the torched BMW garage on Oak Lane
© rossparry.co.uk/syndication

2001:Nora Stanton in her dressing gown is helped across
Whetley Hill Rd by 29 year old Tariq Mahmood in the wake of the riot
© rossparry.co.uk/syndication

2001: Burnt out cars being removed from White Abbey Road
© rossparry.co.uk/syndication

2010: Bradford City Centre with City Hall and its banner: 'Bradford Peaceful Together'

2010: EDL banner, Kent contingent, unfurled for passers-by
© rossparry.co.uk/syndication

2010: EDL demonstrator being
bussed into Bradford
© rossparry.co.uk/syndication

2010: Mounted police outside City Hall
© rossparry.co.uk/syndication

2010: EDL demonstrators surrounded by police in Bradford's Urban Garden
© rossparry.co.uk/syndication

2010: EDL demonstrator arrested by police
© rossparry.co.uk/syndication

2010: Bradford Women for Peace, City Centre

2010: Bradford Together rally at Jacobs Well, addressed by faith and political leaders

2010: Peace Celebration, Infirmary Fields

# Confronting Fascism: 'Hard' and 'Frilly' Left

Bradford's history of anti-racism and anti-fascism begins at the end of the 19<sup>th</sup> century with the founding in Westgate of the Irish Democratic League Club to organise resistance against attacks on Irish immigrants. In the 1930s, when the fascist leader Oswald Mosley tried to hold a public meeting in what is now the Odeon cinema, he met with strong local opposition from the trade union movement and a demonstration erupted. According to long-time anti-fascist campaigner, Geoff Robinson, demonstrators rolled 'the big old-fashioned iron man-hole covers down Godwin Street at the police lines, which they believed were protecting Mosley and the Blackshirts' (2004:2).

Bradford would become a focus again of Far Right activity in the early 1970s. Following Enoch Powell's 'Rivers of Blood' speech in 1968, a former Conservative Councillor, James Merrick, set up the Bradford Campaign to Stop Immigration, which became the Yorkshire and then the British Campaign to Stop Immigration (BCSI). They demanded the closure of Asian community centres and repatriation. Between 1971 and 1975 they also fielded dozens of district and county election candidates. Merrick himself stood for the BCSI in Bradford North and later joined the National Front. The Pickles Papers (Grogan, 1989: chapter 9) reveals the turmoil in the 1970s and 1980s amongst Bradford South and Bradford West Tories as they came to realise that around a third of their electorate were now Asian, yet significant numbers in the party held right-wing anti-immigrant views. The BCSI came together with other fascist groups to form a new group, the National Front, in 1974 (Robinson, 2003). The NF held St George's Day marches and rallies three times in Bradford between 1974 and 1976.

A challenge for those opposing fascism and racism was the differences amongst activists on tactics. Around 1974, an Ad Hoc Committee Against Fascism was set up in Bradford attended by 300 people, including members of the National Front! (Robinson, 2003). After a heated discussion they were expelled, and the demand, 'No Platform for Fascists' was created. However, implementing that demand in practice was the source of much contention. In the 1970s, the Bradford Trades Council coordinated and led the fight against the NF in the absence of an organised Asian and Black voice in the city. At this time new communities kept a low political profile. They did not challenge inequalities in service provision or expect that evidence of racial discrimination would be acted upon. The Bradford

Consultative Council for Commonwealth Immigrants (BCCCI) had been set up in 1966 to address problems arising from Black and Asian arrivals in the city, and this became the Bradford Community Relations Council in 1969. Singh's history of this organisation in Bradford reports the view that the CRCs were official tools to gloss over racism, although the NF smashed its windows 10 times during 1977 (2002:77). Nationally the CRC believed that the best way to deal with the National Front was to deny them publicity and ignore them (Ahmed, 1997:87). Various Marxist left parties supported the Trades Council, but did not always agree with each other either. In the meantime new political voices had emerged in inner-city Bradford.

As we have seen, in the 1970s Manningham became a bohemian quarter. In the revolutionary wake of 1968 a new politics opened up around culture, sexuality and forms of oppression. Politics was no longer based just on social class and livelihoods. One of the haunts of the new activist group was the Bavaria pub, run by a couple of gay men, and there were other venues where lesbians, prostitutes, activists and artists hung out together in an alternative demi-monde. This, said one of our interviewees, was a decade when the 'politics of below flourished'. Young people were exploring the politics in their personal relationships and politicising themselves through debate and argument. Bradford became a centre of cultural creativity, of vibrant street theatre. David Edgar, who went on to become a well-known left-wing playwright, was a Bradford journalist at the time and also worked with Bradford University Theatre. He would later write a play on the 2001 riot.

This new form of politics began to influence and divide the left. The International Socialists, later the Socialist Workers Party, expelled various members for wanting to open up gay and other sections. The General Will Theatre Company split when party socialists wanted to build a more didactic theatre capable of leading the masses while others wanted to allow processes to build up from the grass roots. One of the cultural activists of the time, interviewed for this book, parodied himself as a member of the 'frilly left' as compared to the 'hard left'. But he was equally committed to tackling racism and other forms of oppression.

At this time, a number of community and social organisations amongst the Asian and African-Caribbean population, such as the Indian Workers Association, the Bradford Black Collective and the Kashmir Welfare Association looked to the Trades Council for leadership on anti-racist issues. However, the fight against the National Front in the 1970s politicised the minority ethnic community, particularly the youth (Ahmed, 1997:87). This struggle took a serious turn when the NF announced its intention to hold an election meeting in Manningham Middle School on 24 April 1976 and march up Lumb Lane, with its mostly Asian and African-Caribbean population.

The anti-fascists could not agree on how to deal with the NF. The Trades Council and official Labour movement decided to march to a rally in the city centre, a mass counter demonstration which would not physically confront the NF but would mobilise big numbers against fascist ideas. A newly formed Manningham Defence Committee wanted local residents to stay and oppose the NF in Manningham:

> To some this meant sit downs and non-violent resistance, others planned to throw paint bombs, yet others had ideas about where there were stock-piles of bricks and a very small minority thought about how they could use the general mayhem to loot a couple of local shops (Robinson, 2003).

The radical left parties wanted to block off streets, many came from outside Bradford. The cultural activists describe how they used bicycles to take news to demonstrators of fascist movements, a reminder that this was the pre-mobile phone age. Over 5,000 local people joined the counter demonstration from Manningham Park to Bradford City Centre, while 200 tried to slow down the NF march (Ahmed, 1997:87). Robinson records that 'On the day, all three strategies overlapped and worked together' (ibid).

A white activist recalled how the situation escalated and how she and her mother got arrested along with at least 20 others:

> The Trades Council led the demonstration, met in Infirmary Fields and . . . went down to the city centre. They [the NF] started in the city centre, and marched up from the city centre to Manningham Lane. And the idea was that there wouldn't really be a confrontation, because the previous year . . . there'd been a lot of, I think, verbal abuse, and, it had been quite aggressive. So, that in '76 the West Yorkshire Constabulary, the police, decided to keep the two demonstrations apart . . . But on the way down into the city centre, down Westgate, there was a 'call to arms', really. People said, 'They're coming up Cheapside!' So, quite a lot of people decided to go and confront them . . . So, we went down one of those streets to Manningham Lane, and sort of encountered them at the top of Manor Row and marched, well, ran alongside them. And, there was people everywhere, throwing things. And, me and Mum . . . [and] a couple of friends were throwing paint at them. And, my Mum was there as well, because we lived with my mother, just along from Belle Vue School. And, she was outraged that they were marching in her backyard, really. And, she got arrested, and so, I tried to stop the police arresting her and got into an argument. He said 'A lot of police had spotted you before. Can you deny that?' . . . it was very scary. They [the National

Front] had lots of those long sticks with spikes on the top, flags, and sort of what looked like to me, when I was 18, sort of paramilitary uniform. It was terrifying. And [there were] a lot of the police between the National Front and the other people. So, I was arrested by what was the . . . the garage, opposite the Mecca (interview, 2011).

The NF did not return to Bradford until 2001. The British National Party which had split from the NF in 1982, had changed direction under its new leader, Nick Griffin, in 1999. The aim was to appear respectable and build electoral support. At the General Election in June 2001, Griffin secured 16.4% of the vote in Oldham West and Royton in the wake of disturbances there. John Brayshaw won 1,613 votes in Bradford North, a mere 4.6% of the vote, but they were marking ground. Griffin held a public meeting in Eccleshill in Bradford, the day before the riot. Anti-fascist campaigner, Paul Meszaros, suggested in an interview that they were expecting to pick up support in the wake of whatever kicked off the next day.

The Anti-Nazi League (which organised the 2001 rally) was formed nationally in 1977 by the Socialist Workers Party, but was not active in the 1990s. Bradford Left politics continued to be vibrant. The Bradford Resource Centre was set up to support trade union networks, women's groups and others through the recession of the 70s. As unemployment grew, Bradford's activists responded with humour as well as a hard edge. A newspaper, *Happy Days*, and a claimants' information service was set up, and 'clerk of the week' awards were made to highlight the treatment claimants got when they went to sign on in Textile Hall. An anarchist-oriented Claimants Union emerged to campaign for the low-waged and unemployed. It set up the 1 in 12 club in 1981 to ensure an accessible and affordable social venue for them. Its name derived from a government investigation into benefit fraud which found that '1 in 12' claimants were actively 'defrauding the state'. It was based on anarchist values of self-management, cooperation and mutual aid and operates to this day. These radical groups often faced harassment and assaults from Far Right *provocateurs*, such as David Appleyard who was in Bradford the day of the rally and riot. The rise of Black and Asian political activism marks the last part of this decade.

# Rise of Black and Asian Political Voice

The murder of a Sikh, Gurdip Singh Chaggar, in London in 1976 was the catalyst for the emergence of Asian Youth Movements in many UK cities, beginning with Southall in London. In Bradford, the Indian Progressive Youth Association was formed in 1977 but was renamed the Asian Youth Movement (AYM) the following year. The AYM was a secular and non-sectarian movement whose members saw themselves in terms of an inclusive black identity and willingness to embrace multiple identities. The Bradford Commission into the 1995 disturbances interviewed one inner-city resident about which communities he felt part of and he responded with the following list, depending on context and in no particular order: 'Black, Asian, Azad Kashmiri, Kashmiri, Mirpuri, Jat, Maril'ail, Kungriwalay, Pakistani, English, British, Yorkshireman, Bradfordian, from Bradford Moor' (1996:92). Notably he did not mention a religious identity.

The AYM focussed on the struggle for political equality, in the fields of education, employment and immigration as well as confronting police brutality and racist violence. It was a progressive movement in the widest sense, taking on traditionalists within their own communities as well as challenging Britain's colonial history and its legacy. The AYM proclaimed the right of self-defence of both the community and the individual against racist and fascist attack.

The year 1981 saw the Brixton riots. Police harassment and stop and search played a major role in those riots, alongside unemployment and discrimination. The Brixton riot took place on 11 July, but in the first week or so of July there was unrest in many parts of the UK, from Handsworth in Birmingham, to Toxteth in Liverpool and Moss Side in Manchester, all with a racial component. Smaller pockets of unrest took place in a number of other cities. There were various attacks on premises and people in Bradford that year, including the murder of Mohammed Arif, an Asian Taxi Driver, by a Far Right activist. Gary Whiting needed open heart surgery after being stabbed by a member of the NF in the centre of Bradford.

Tariq Mehmood recounted his feelings that year for the AYM oral history project (Ramamurthy, 2000:23):

> It was July the 11th, 1981 and that was the day where there were lots and lots of riots up and down the country, in lots of different places. And we heard rumours that the NF, or skinheads . . . the fascists were coming to Bradford and the police had gone round and said that, and they told everybody to stay indoors. Now we took the view that it's totally wrong. We're not going to stay indoors, we're going to get out and we're going to organise people.

The United Black Youth League, a more radical splinter group from the AYM, decided to make and store petrol bombs in anticipation of an NF return to Bradford. They had seen them used in Southall. They did not believe the police would protect them and they wanted to defend themselves. In the end, the fascists did not attack Bradford and Saeed Hussain recounts that they destroyed the bombs (ibid). Three weeks later 12 young Asians were arrested and charged with the very serious offences of conspiracy to make explosive substances and endanger life. These charges could have carried life imprisonment sentences. The central argument of what became known as the Bradford 12 was 'Self Defence is No Offence'. Ruth Bundy, a solicitor involved in the defence of six of the accused, recalled the response of Bradford's ethnic minority communities:

> Now the marvellous thing about the case was the support that it engendered from every section of the Bradford Asian community and indeed the Black community. In terms of age group, I remember going to one very, very early meeting when all the defendants . . . were locked up in Armley prison, and there were Sikhs in their seventies and eighties and elderly Muslim parents, a whole range of support saying, in a sense, these are our children, support them, defend them, and that's something that over the years I have never quite seen again (quoted in Ramamurthy, 2000:24).

In court the accused pleaded that they had been engaged in 'defending their community' and despite rumours that they would be made an example of, the jury acquittal of the Bradford 12 was a landmark moment in the history of anti-racist struggles.

# Anti-racism or Multiculturalism? Politics of Community

Jani Rashid of the AYM suggested that the organisation had some influence on the council's 'multicultural' policies which began to develop in the early eighties, but those policies did not reflect distinctions they would make between anti-racism and multiculturalism:

> These were issues about, sort of, acknowledging people's religious requirements, so they had to address religious issues, they had to address linguistic issues, they had to, sort of, have a better understanding of the modes of dress, for example, of children from different religious backgrounds, so, that, that was one of the things that we said that was important, but we never asked for multicultural education, and, and I'd have to say that I still don't believe in multicultural education. You know, what we were demanding was anti-racist education, in actual fact, but I don't think that the authorities were very comfortable with that, so they developed multicultural policies to address issues of racism in schools that we were complaining about, which we felt were more important than having segregated schools (quoted in Ramamurthy, 2000:26).

The riots of 1981 and the case of the Bradford 12 had shaken Bradford Council. In 1980, the Commission for Racial Equality (CRE) took on 185 employment cases involving racial discrimination in Bradford (Singh, 2002:80). That year, Labour took control of the council. The Council Management Team produced a report Turning Point: A Review of Race Relations in Bradford. According to Singh, the report was highly critical of the council's casual approach to race issues. There was no mechanism to monitor policy on racial matters, racial disadvantage was not seen as an issue in its own right and there was no procedure to ensure that the special needs of ethnic minorities were considered and met. A 12 point plan was produced in which it was recognised that Bradford was a 'multiracial, multicultural city and that every section of the community has an equal right to maintain its own identity, culture, language and customs' (quoted in Singh, 2002:3). The council also expressed its determination to be an equal opportunities employer and 'reflect in a detailed and practical way that Bradford is and will remain a multicultural community. We now require of all our managers that they take effective action to correct racial disadvantage' (ibid:116).

There was cross-party support for developing a race relations policy. An all-party sub-committee was set up: the Race Relations Advisory Group (RRAG). The RRAG reviewed action plans from each Directorate and sought to shape policy on the effects of racism and discrimination. Training on race issues and cultural awareness was introduced for council staff and elected members, a source of contention and resentment, but the number of ethnic minority employees increased during the 1980s from 1% to 6% (Mahoney, 2001). The council had broadly accepted multiculturalism, drawing on the Greater London Council template, argues Kenan Malik, who strongly opposed it. This had redefined racism not as 'the denial of equal rights but the denial of the right to be different'. In policy terms this meant that equality had to enable different communities to exercise their right to be different. This policy shift coincided with the time when Bradford's largest community of Pakistani Muslims were settling their families and rebuilding their livelihoods in the midst of unemployment and poverty. While a generation of young Pakistanis had been awakened to how racism explained their economic disadvantages, emergent community leaders were seeking opportunities for a political voice in the District.

In the 1960s recognition and respect for cultural and religious difference had led the Sikh population nationally, and in Bradford, to struggle for the right for bus drivers and conductors to wear turbans and for exemption from wearing crash helmets. The first turbaned Sikh conductor was appointed in Bradford in 1968 (Singh, 2002:29). Bradford's policies of dispersing migrant children through 'bussing' across the city was opposed in the 1970s by the Muslim Parents Association and the Indian Workers Association. They presented a petition in 1977 to the Local Education Authority, and in

1979 the policy was declared discriminatory and phased out. Although it had been introduced to ensure social mixing in Bradford's schools, the burden of it fell only on African-Caribbean and Asian children. Ethnic communities suspected that the goal was to distance children from their backgrounds (Bradford Commission, 1996:85). In 1983, the Muslim Parents Association and the Muslim Education Trust submitted an application to take over a number of local schools. Muslims were not united around this, however—most did not want separate educational provision and it was successfully opposed by the AYM and some within the newly formed Council of Mosques. They did want respect for their religious practices but this was not the same as a demand for separate education. The right to halal meat provision for children in schools rallied most Muslims and this campaign hit the headlines in 1984. Two demonstrations took place outside City Hall, of 1,000 and then 3,000 people, in favour of a proposal by the Education sub-committee to support provision. Muslim parents withdrew their children from school for a day, showing a growing collective spirit amongst the community. The provision was passed.

The Local Education Authority also issued a number of memoranda in 1982–83 aimed at developing a multicultural curriculum, the provision in schools of a Muslim prayer room and allowing Muslim children to leave school early to attend Friday prayers. Advice was given on how to recognise and address racism and head teachers and staff responsible for recruitment were told to go on five-day race training courses. Animosity over this training between the Labour's RRAG members and many head teachers 'smouldered', as the latter refused to attend without supply cover (Greenhalf, 2003:62). Head teachers, argues Greenhalf, 'objected to being lectured on slavery by ardent race workers and informed that white history implicated them as racists too' (ibid). The courses may have been implemented in a tactless manner (Samad, 1992:512), but racism remained widespread in schools across the District. Students at Wyke Manor School, many from West Bolling, remember when they walked out in 1985 after a supply teacher exposed the number of racist incidents and remarks by staff against Carlton Duncan, the school's black headmaster (interview 2011, West Bowling Youth Initiative).

By 1984, a backlash to these policies was underway. Local *T&A* journalist, Jim Greenhalf questioned the abandonment of integrationist approaches and warned of antagonising the 'white public' (2003:59). He argued that the latter would see these policies as forcing them to accommodate to ethnic minority interests rather than encouraging the ethnic minority to accept the culture of the society they had joined. A white employer can no longer pass on a job by word of mouth, he argued, but Asians can and do employ only Asian workers. He maintained that the council was giving in to threats of unrest: 'If West Indians riot and commit arson a Government Minister and millions of pounds are rushed to the scene. If whites riot on football terraces they are fined hundreds of pounds and called thugs' (ibid).

The council was pushing through change. It did not do enough to bring the 'white public' with it. The political risks were high and fear of urban unrest amongst the minority ethnic community was probably a priority in the minds of politicians. Right-wing opinion in this age of Thatcherism was strong, even though Labour had won control of the local authority. The 1980s was a decade of economic devastation for the District as a whole and many might be easily persuaded to blame the minority ethnic population for the squeeze they were feeling. A delicate balance across parties was maintained in favour of the new policy. Benefits included the South Asian vote. At the same time, as the policy environment oscillated between anti-racism and multiculturalism, some began to feel that the council was listening very selectively to 'representatives' of the minority ethnic communities.

The council had acknowledged how few contacts it had with the Asian community at the beginning of the decade. It opted to facilitate the formation of umbrella bodies based on religious identity, which would enable permanent dialogue with a few leaders from each community. In 1981, they helped set up and fund the Bradford Council of Mosques and, in 1984, the Federation of Sikh Organizations and the Vishwa Hindu Parishad were established. Checkpoint became a social focus for the African-Caribbean population with a council grant in 1983. The council also funded welfare projects. These centred around the mosque for the Muslim community and included advice workers, a service for women in clinics and hospitals and Muslim youth and community centres. Kenan Malik suggests that this enabled the council to 'define the needs of the Asian community without having to think about the political changes necessary to ensure real equality' (2009:75). He also suggests that council leaders and Muslim leaders essentially came together around a mutually beneficial agenda:

> By subcontracting its mandate for providing welfare services, the local authority expected the Council of Mosques not just to attend to the well-being of Muslims in the town but also to maintain peace and decorum within its community.

Religious leadership was institutionalised and strengthened over secular opponents (Samad, 1992:512). Council officials saw Islam, rather than any secular ideology or political policy, as the best way of 'keeping angry young men in check' (ibid). Community elders welcomed support to deal with their fears of exposure to 'Western' values on their youth. In the 1980s, these values were secular and political. The loss of both frameworks amongst young people without replacement by something with equal potency and meaning, would impact on the cohort of young people who came of age in the next decade and a number of whom participated in the 2001 riot.

Meanwhile, the so-called 'Honeyford Affair' erupted in 1984, bringing to an end the political consensus around tackling racism alongside the right to cultural difference. This affair demonstrated the danger of combining these two issues. On issues of cultural difference, Honeyford made some important points. He expressed concern about Muslim parents taking their children to Pakistan on long visits particularly during school term times. He was also critical of physical punishment meted out on children attending mosque schools and he emphasised the importance of English language proficiency. But Honeyford was also strongly opposed to the council's race relations policy and race awareness training. He spoke disparagingly of the patois of some minority ethnic children compared to 'pure' forms of the English language. He criticised Pakistan and the Pakistani community in ways which deeply upset Muslim parents in Manningham, especially when an Urdu translation by his opponents somewhat distorted his views (Samad, 1992:513). Having once described himself as a Marxist, he had become an enthusiast for right-wing philosopher Roger Scruton and submitted an article, 'Education and Race: An Alternative View' to his journal, *The Salisbury Review*. This was summarised in the *Yorkshire Post* and widely disseminated.

A Parents Action Committee was set up at Drummond Middle School where Honeyford was headmaster and eventually he negotiated a generous 'retirement' deal. Honeyford's intervention made it more difficult to talk about some of the substantive concerns around education in the inner city. It tapped into the sensitivities of the Pakistani Muslim community in deep and lasting ways. In the meantime, racial attacks and harassment escalated and the political consensus around race relations policy fell apart (Singh, 2002:37). Labour gained Asian voters and won Heaton Ward in 1986 and increased its vote in Toller ward, while Conservatives began to talk about the 'over concentration of resources' in the inner areas of Bradford (Singh, 2002:36). The difficulties Bradford has had in addressing its community relationships have their origins in this period in the first half of the 1980s. The need to build a robust anti-racist policy became entangled with recognition of cultural rights, while politics and power in the District played out beneath the surface.

The problem was that culture was understood as unchanging, natural and devoid of the power inequalities which run through society and all communities. Not everything in every culture is of equal value. Many women, in particular, do not gain from inequality which is defended in the name of 'culture'. It became all too easy for the media to exaggerate the significance of 'cultural conflicts', such as Sikh turbans, halal meat, and dress codes, which are relatively easily resolved, while issues of race, disadvantage and non-representation due to caste and clan, class and gender (which impact across communities) remain unresolved. Events such as the public burning in Bradford of Salmon Rushdie's book *The Satanic Verses* in 1989 attracted world-wide attention. But when, later that same year, 130 Pakistani youths armed with iron bars and cricket bats took to the streets in West Bowling to protect their neighbourhood from drunken white lads, it received little attention.

Kenan Malik has argued that the Rushdie affair 'was a turning point in the relationship between British society and its Muslim communities' (2009:xviii). Bradford's religious leadership was able to 'steal a march over their secular rivals' through their leadership of the campaign to ban Rushdie's book (Samad, 1992:518). The Bradford response was the most vociferous in the country and the only place where WH Smith was forced to withdraw the book due to threats. As the influence of the secular AYM declined, so the Bradford Council of Mosques, which played a leading role in the Rushdie Affair, attracted backing from Mirpuri youth, still nursing a 'lingering injury' from Honeyford's comments (Samad, 1992:516). The Gulf War of 1991 placed the issues facing Bradford's Muslims within a wider international context involving Muslim states and Western powers. However, Samad points out that there was no evidence of increased religiosity or reduction in alcohol consumption amongst the youth. Rather he argues, youth were 'resorting to Islamic idioms and metaphors to express their discontent against society which refused to accept them on an equal footing'. Political leadership had shifted amongst the Pakistani population in Bradford, and religion was integral to their politics. Moreover, the leadership which had come from more secular, non-sectarian and politicised elements linked into wider labour and left politics had been eclipsed, particularly amongst young people.

# Politics and Riot

*I personally really very committed you know, for democracy. But we should respect each other whatever we have . . . which party . . . So people come 'Oh we are Muslim, we support Muslim'. I dislike this idea. This is not democratic you know.*
**(Pakistani Elder from Manningham)**

Bradford's Pakistani Muslim population gained political representation in the course of the 1980s and 1990s. The first Asian councillor was elected in 1978 and in 1986 Bradford had its first Asian Mayor, Mohammed Ajeeb. In his 2002 review of the struggle for racial justice in Bradford, Ramindar Singh identified the major achievement of the council's Race Relations policy as 'the empowerment of ethnic minority communities'. However, fault lines developed 'within and between ethnic minority communities' as they competed for financial resources through community grants (ibid:119). With its weight of numbers, the Pakistani Muslim community became increasingly equated with minority ethnic needs in Bradford. Cooperation between religious groups and ethnic communities diminished. African-Caribbean groups, for instance, had become increasingly sceptical towards the Community Relations Council and felt unrepresented by it. Taj (1996:7) noted that factionalism was rife amongst Muslim communities, resulting in a plethora of community groups and centres: 'It is . . . a besetting sin of leading community figures wanting to be "big fish in small ponds" rather than mere contributors to a more unified representation'. There were growing complaints that the distribution of grants was made on political grounds. A report, The Riot Area Reviewed, produced in September following the April 1995 disturbance in Manningham, concluded that central government funding to urban programmes in the 1980s had been distributed according to community pressure and in a piecemeal fashion, while in the 1990s with less funds available, new groups found it difficult to access resources (quoted in Bradford Commission, 1996:191). This coincided with a shift in government funding away from the inner city and a curtailment of grant aid to private sector housing. This badly affected Asian families who owned their houses but lacked the resources to bring them up to standard.

Inner-city party politics increasingly reflected and exacerbated divisions within the Pakistani community. The Bradford West parliamentary seat was a particular source of competition after its incumbent hinted he would retire, as were inner-city council seats. The National Executive Committee of the Labour Party put a freeze on new members in Bradford West at one point, amidst rumours of corruption (Greenhalf, 2003:161). The Bradford Commission report described the local election campaign immediately prior to the 1995 disturbances:

> The campaign for the city council elections occurred shortly before the disorders of June 1995. For the first time in Toller Ward, which includes part of the area involved in the disorders, candidates were fielded by the two main political parties, who both emphasised and concentrated on loyalties within the Muslim community. The Conservative candidate was a Muslim from the Bains Clan, which had a much smaller presence in Toller Ward. Two of the existing Labour councillors were from the Jat Clan, which led to divided loyalties and conflict . . . During the local election campaign many Asian community divisions and loyalties were highlighted, and many young men roamed the streets for several weeks with the enthusiastic support of their elders. 'Jat or Bains' was the frequent cry on the streets. The whole election came to be seen as between warring clans. The Asian people in the area were subjected to immense conflicts of loyalty, whilst the white people felt marginalised and threatened by a conflict which they did not understand. Both political parties had released forces which the party hierarchies did not understand, and could not control (1996:88-89).

Political position in Bradford became linked to status and recognition in Pakistan. The transfer of clan battles and religious differences from the Asian sub-continent to inner-city Bradford were not acceptable to all Muslims in the District as the quote at the beginning of this section suggests.

In the meantime, pressing and urgent problems around race and disadvantage went unchecked. The Community Relations Council (CRC) itself became embroiled in many issues around representation and autonomy during the 1980s. The RRAG was abolished in 1990 and the CRC was reconstituted as the Bradford Racial Equality Council (BREC). The council had lost a number of cases of racial discrimination and was facing others. It then abandoned a race relations policy in favour of equal rights in accordance with national thinking, setting up an Equal Rights Sub-Committee with responsibility for race, gender and disability. In the midst of this, a major disturbance erupted in the middle of Manningham in the early summer of 1995.

The public disorder on the nights of 9–11 June that year became the subject of an in-depth report by the Bradford Commission and a minority set of comments and recommendations by one of the

Commissioners, Mohammed Taj. This account is taken mostly from the report which is the most systematic independent investigation. The 1995 disorder was not precipitated by Far Right groups or 'white' racists. It began when the police arrested four youngsters playing football in Garfield Avenue, Manningham. According to the police version of events, the lads were verbally abusive and one was a 'known trouble maker' (Bradford Commission, 1996:33). When one broke free, he was pursued into his house, where his sister and brother tried to stop the arrest. News spread and a hostile crowd of some 100 local people assembled. The rumour was that the police had manhandled the sister and her baby, a story which was gradually embellished. The police made no effort to explain their actions to the crowd, inflaming local residents' anger at what they saw as racial insensitivity. Trouble escalated on the Friday and Saturday evenings and into the Sunday, focusing initially on the Divisional Police Headquarters at Lawcroft House, locally nicknamed 'Fort Lawcroft'.

Around 60 men, mostly from the Pakistani community, arrived on the Friday evening and were joined by others. A range of ages were involved, and older men were particularly upset at the contempt shown to residents by the police, though not all had sympathy for the arrested youths. Seven further arrests were made that evening. The police made no distinctions between the protestors, fuelling the anger of residents who had come to protest against police behaviour rather than question the arrests per se. That night, shop windows in Oak Lane were smashed and bricks and bottles were thrown at police officers outside Lawcroft House. Officers put on protective equipment which looked like riot gear to the crowd. A more serious disorder took place in Oak Lane around midnight and a burning barricade was set up across it. A police video showed a car pulling up in the early hours of the morning with baseball bats and other weapons in the boot. Councillors tried to calm down the protestors the next day but their failure to secure the release of those arrested diminished their power in the eyes of young men.

The Bradford Racial Equality Council began talks with the police on the Saturday along with residents, but they broke down. On the Saturday night, a crowd gathered again, this time including young men from outside the Manningham area. Around 300 people gathered again outside Lawcroft House that evening and some broke up a wall and began to throw debris at the police. A group broke away into Manningham Lane and attacked a club, cars, a garage and the windows of public houses in Lumb Lane. A sub-group headed down Whetley Hill and set fire to cars in a garage forecourt, and into Westgate, attacking five out of six public houses.

There was looting of shops in Westgate, while another group attacked the BMW garage in Oak Lane. On the Sunday, representatives of the Council of Mosques and other community representatives had more success in discussions with the police, who became less confrontational, and the disorder calmed down. Mid-morning, four Asian women and four white women, members of Interfaith Women for Peace set up in 1994, carried candles and a makeshift banner saying 'Peace' in Urdu, English and Arabic.

Commissioner Mohammed Taj, of the Transport and General Workers Union, did not endorse the Commission Report. He maintained that it was overlong, did not give enough weight to police racism as a direct cause of the mistrust which led to the disorder and was also insufficiently critical of the Muslim community. Nevertheless it is a very thorough investigation into the background and events of that June. Overall, one is left with a strong sense that the police were out of touch with the local community at the very least, while prejudice and lack of respect also played a role. The Muslim magazine, *Trends*, entitled their report on the disturbance, 'Riot Police or Police Riot' (*Trends*, July/August 1995). At the same time, it is clear that Manningham's disaffected young men had become a force in their own right. Already young people were questioning their political and community leaders, though they did not generate a new politically-conscious leadership of their own. The report alludes to the anti-prostitution patrols, which gave some a sense of growing power on the street. On this occasion, there was a great deal of local sympathy for their anger towards the police, but quite a lot of shock at their violence. The police record that 102 premises were attacked, varying from a broken window to more substantial damage, mainly to white-owned businesses. Sixty-six vehicles were damaged, four of them owned by Asians, and 10 members of the public were personally attacked, all of whom were white. Nine policeman were injured but not seriously. Damage was estimated at a little over £0.5 million (Bradford Commission, 1995:67), though press reports put it at double that. More significantly, as compared to 2001, the Crown Prosecution Service decided that it was not in the public interest to prosecute most of those arrested.

The council published its response to the Commission report in March 1997, but it did not give firm commitments to addressing the concerns it identified (Singh, 2002:124). It did publish a Community Plan and a Community Consultation and Participation Strategy. 'Speak-Out' Citizen's panels were held in 1999 and a high-profile consultation event to feed into a '2020 Vision' for the District. The police set up a Minority Ethnic Communities' Liaison Committee in 1999 and appointed a Minority Ethnic Community Relations Officer at Inspector level. This officer worked hard to build relationships with community leaders. Issues such as forced marriage began to be discussed. The Committee, however, found itself under question for its reliance on certain community spokesmen. One of the few young members who joined it and whom we interviewed in 2006 said that 'the people of that committee weren't really there to serve the district where they came from, they were there because they thought it was a political position . . .' A Projects Officer was appointed to the police Community Involvement Unit to work with youth in the Oak Lane/Manningham area and individual officers began to gain the trust of some young people. Their own growing understanding of the young men did not, however, always feed back into the police hierarchy. In interviews, it was clear that community work was viewed as the 'soft side' of policing and not taken very seriously at an institutional level. Tensions continued with the lads around Bonfire Nights, for instance. On 5 November 1998, 80 youths set a garage on fire, destroyed a telephone box, burnt down a bargain shop, torched cars and launched missiles at police officers and the Lawcroft House Police Station (Singh, 2002:45).

A number of organisations emerged over the decade to work with youth and to help them build a future. The West Bowling Youth Initiative, for instance, was set up following the 1989 disturbances, to help youngsters in the neighbourhood find jobs and build esteem. The Manningham and Girlington Youth Partnership was set up with funding from the Single Regeneration Budget (SRB) after the 1995 disturbances, seeking to bring young people round the table and overcome the negative images the District had formed of inner-city youth. Frontline also came out of the 1995 disturbances, in recognition of the need to support African-Caribbean youth in Manningham. The Asian Women and Children's Centre in Keighley employed a multicultural staff and encouraged white as well as minority ethnic parents to use the centre and empower women across communities. The Quest for Economic Development Limited (QED) was set up in 1990 to support minority ethnic communities to engage in economic, social and public life. There were also organisations trying to work across the different communities. An Interfaith Education Centre was established in 1983 to provide information about world religions and issues of justice and peace. In 1986 it took up premises in Listerhills and came to employ 15 staff from across the District's communities (Thomson, 1997:110).

Despite these community-based efforts, Graham Mahoney, the council's Principal Race Relations Officer from 1984–1990 in his input to the Ouseley Commission in 2001 wrote that 'today finds Bradford with race relations at its lowest ebb' (Mahoney, 2001) The BREC collapsed in 1999 under a cloud of financial and other allegations. Communication and understanding between the council and its minority ethnic communities appeared to have got stuck. Mahoney felt that:

> The local authority has been either an ostrich or an apologist when issues have been raised which it either disagrees with or is fearful of the consequences. The local authority has never reached the stage where it will say to any section of the black or Asian community 'sorry, I disagree', 'I think you are wrong' or 'it is your responsibility to do something about this'. It has often created problems by refusing or failing to respond, thus demonstrating a lack of real respect for these communities (Mahoney, 2001:7).

A warning of the volatility of the inner city came in April 2001 in Lidget Green. Again this disturbance was not sparked by the Far Right, but did involve a racist incident. Around 30 'white' males from Clayton entered the Coach House pub on Legrams Lane—already drunk according to witnesses we interviewed—where an Indian Hindu wedding was taking place. Racist remarks sparked a fight which spilled into the street. The white men chased an Indian into the Bilal Pizza takeaway. He escaped but the shop windows were smashed. The group of white men were pointed out by Asian Muslim lads to the police who had arrived belatedly, but fights then broke out between the youth and the whites, some of whom had stepped off a bus taking them into the city centre. The police endeavoured to separate them, laying about with their batons, but their actions were misinterpreted, with Asian youth feeling that they were protecting the 'white' men. In a state of high adrenalin the Asian lads headed for the Second West pub to avenge earlier slights. In the past, the pub had put out provocative signs—in their eyes—in support of England against Pakistan in a cricket match. The youths attacked the pub with stones and bricks, and smashed up the premises. Customers huddled in a room upstairs. Other pubs in the area had their windows broken. Missiles were thrown at passing motorists and a brick put through the car window of a nurse who suffered serious facial injuries. The chemist shop of a prominent Hindu businessmen, believed by the youths to be anti-Muslim, was looted and burned. The young men had not escaped injury—they showed us their baton wounds. They were convinced that the police had focussed on them rather than on the men who had provoked the unrest. Anger lay very close to the surface for these young men. Many were troubled and torn between the legal and illegal economy, between their rejection of a world which did not accept them and their desire for acceptance by it.

Bradford leaders seemed unable to critically address the problems facing the District. Instead they came up with a raft of efforts to improve the District's image. *T&A* journalist, Jim Greenhalf, commented that Bradford was failing to confront its real problems:

> Time and again people were appointed to positions of authority from which they would repeat the same old formula: Bradford's central problem was its image; if the world's perception of Bradford's image could be improved then Bradford would surely prosper. It is as though Bradford Means Business, Bradford Hits Back, Bradford's Bouncing Back, Shout for Bradford, Bradford Breakthrough and Bradford Congress had never existed. Bradford has had more campaigns than Napolean, but fewer victories (Greenhalf, 2003:109).

The economic problems, the social problems and the problems of racism facing Bradford were interconnected and difficult to tackle separately. They required an overarching vision and leadership at a time when local authority powers were being eroded. Recognising this, the Bradford Commission report had argued that the council needed community partners. However, it called for leadership from the council itself:

> . . . the city council is constitutionally designed to sort out local priorities, and it should concentrate on this role as the organised 'centre', as a counterweight to the diffusions and confusions of separate geographical, social, ethnic, financial and operational forces of which presently it is a part (Bradford Commission, 1996:201).

In 2000, the local authority, and a new partnership body which became known as Bradford Vision, set up the Ouseley Commission. Its conclusions that Bradford communities were moving apart, were considered statements of the obvious by some, while others disputed this emphasis or whether it mattered.

One of the places and times when interaction between communities continued was the Bradford Festival or Mela. The Mela grew out of the Community Arts Movement of 1970s bohemian Manningham. The first Mela took place in 1988 with an attendance of around 10,000. By 1996 150,000 people were attending. The organisers, Alan Brack and Dusty Rhodes, wanted to build a vehicle for community self expression. 'It should not just belong to the city, it should belong to the people of the city', they argued (Rhodes, 1997:123). In keeping with its origins, the aim was to take 'community' in its broadest sense, from gay people to black people, from people with disabilities to stamp collectors and cyclists. The Mela became a showcase for Asian arts and culture but also for Bradford's Ukrainian, Polish, Hungarian, Latvian, Irish and Dominican communities. Rhodes wrote that:

> . . . the Mela is worth more than race awareness lectures and training. You take a white person and put them in an environment that is 70% Asian, in which they would normally feel intimidated, and you make

them feel relaxed because it's a fun event. You can't persuade people to feel that way unless they are actually exposed to the cultures. It's all about cultural understanding, about the very basic thing that says, 'I am safe in this situation, I do not feel threatened'. That is a fundamental lesson you can't teach in a classroom (Rhodes, 1997:126).

The Festival organisers had to persuade the police to allow the Mela to go ahead after the 1995 disturbances. They succeeded even in convincing them not to post police on horses with riot equipment at the gates, and to retain their contingency plans, but keep their presence low key. 'Let's say Bradford isn't just a few people burning tyres on Oak Lane', argued Rhodes. The Mela proceeded without trouble. In 2001, the Festival organisers made the same arguments. There needed to be cultural distraction, a celebratory moment which brought people together around something positive rather than police containment against the expectation of trouble. But this time they lost the argument. The finale of the Festival was cancelled. In our interview with him, Rhodes, who had participated in the anti-racist struggles of the 1970s, reflected on how he felt the night before the rally. 'I kept thinking, this is a terrible mistake. There did not seem to be the layers, those who knew each other, anti-fascists . . . it was a disorganised network of people. It really showed up . . .' On the day, he grabbed some friends and some sculptures and dressed as a fish, and as an 'anti-fishist', he weaved his way through the crowd.

## Bradford Riot: A Collective Failure?

*Bradford is today on a siding and there . . . it may remain till the crack of doom.*
**('The Through Train', quoted in the *Bradford Antiquary*, 1986:35-46 from the *Yorkshire Observer*, 19 November 1906)**

If Bradford was not in the 'grip of fear' it was not at ease with itself in 2001. What comes through is a sense of collective failure across the District to deal with the fall-out from de-industrialisation in a multicultural city. Failure does not lie just within Bradford. Failure, but also responsibility, lies with national policies, the interests they promote, and more impersonally but perhaps more potently, with the global logic of capital and its impacts on local labour markets and production. Bradford's entrepreneurs had responded to competition and downturn by cutting costs, and migrant labour prolonged the life of an industry already in decline. Bradford's mill owners had long rested on the laurels of the District's global reputation in worsted and textile machinery innovation. Railway historians suggest that their complacency even deprived Bradford of through trains at the end of the 19th century unlike all other UK provincial centres. Commercial interests and protection of water and land rights were allowed to hamper the plans of railway companies and eventually population build-up brought them to a halt. By 2001, it felt as if Bradford would indeed remain on a siding if a new vision did not turn the District round. In the riot, Bradford's Asian youth highlighted not only their own predicament, but also that of an urban metropolis full of potential but unable to realise it.

Migrant labour did not arrive in Bradford unwilling to integrate but nor to give up its religious beliefs and cultural norms. It faced hostile prejudice and the activities of racist and fascist movements throughout the 1970s. Everyday racism was pervasive and victims had no faith in the police's willingness to address it. A new generation of white radicals began to organise their own resistance and were joined by an increasingly politicised young Asian and African-Caribbean population. Those young people were applauded for defending their communities in the early 1980s. Two decades later, however, another cohort of young men were rejected by their communities when they made a similar plea to explain their riot.

As Bradford's fortunes declined, communities tapped into all the resources they could muster. There were signs of great stress across the inner city in the 1990s. When the National Front targeted the Pakistani community in 2001, pent-up frustrations were already high. Capacity to express these in political ways was limited. This was not the 1970s and 1980s. Alcohol and drugs were now props used by young people in all communities, and the Pakistani community was not immune from their effects. Drug dealing had also emerged as a short cut to status and income, but one which drew vulnerable young men into service for the sharks of the trade. The 1990s was a decade of economic decline in which a cohort of young men came of age who lacked the educational skills and political connections to help them interpret their condition in wider terms. Loyal to Bradford, they were also living in its poorest neighbourhoods. Petty crime brought many into regular conflicts with the police, a force which was still uncomfortable in policing multicultural urban settings and was ill-informed at best, racist at worse, towards minority ethnic communities. Community leaders competed for political clout using their extended clan networks but in the process closed avenues for wider representation, especially for young men and women. Religious leaders were fearful at the exposure of youth to the influences of modern Western society, but unable to connect with them. The District's political leadership had helped to marginalise the more secular and radical voices which had arisen in the anti-racist struggles of the 1970s and 1980s. Accumulated anger and frustration exploded on 7 July when the NF once again tried to destroy and divide communities.

Bradford has a history of riots, often fought out on the same streets, but each new generation makes its own riots, often imagining they are unique, knowing little or nothing of the history of riots that have gone before. And yet there are threads and connections. The police are always seen as protecting the other side. Young men from the bottom half of society nearly always predominate. At some points they fight bosses, at others their right to live and work in the city. Some are led by politically conscious elements and have an organised core to articulate their demands, others are more spontaneous and chaotic, appearing to come out of nowhere. And the battle-cries of one generation can be echoed in another, as we saw in 2001, when the rioters visualised their enemies as 'fascists', as had their forebears in 1930s Bradford. Then they were white and working class, fired up by threats to organised workers and to Jews. Now they are more likely to be Asian Muslims fighting to be heard against a threat to their existence. How did these struggles relate to the post industrial quest for a common Bradford identity?

Neither nationally nor locally was there a way of talking about communities and their connections and differences for such a wider Bradford identity. National policy pitted communities against each other in competition for regeneration funds. Locally the council reacted slowly to discrimination and racism and failed to develop meaningful dialogue across the District's communities. Anti-racism was confused with respect for cultural difference. The former needed robust intervention, the latter a light hand of sensitive policy. The Bradford Commission report and the Ouseley Commission picked up on anger about inequalities across all Bradford's communities, anger which needed to be exposed, debated and challenged if necessary. They both talked of community fears. Bradford's strong unifying working class culture, which was always multiethnic in some ways, was lost in the course of de-industrialisation leading to a sense of fragmentation across the District. This was visibly highlighted by residential settlement patterns. It would be wrong to take the riot of 2001 out of a time frame of the past or without a look towards the future. Looking back, we see a collective failure to take Bradford confidently out of the siding and give everyone a seat on the train to a promising future.

# 7

# THE AFTERMATH

*We thought this is it, we will put Bradford on the map.*
*We put Bradford on the map for the wrong reason.*
**(2001 rioter interviewed in 2011)**

The shadow of the 2001 riot hung over Bradford throughout the decade which followed. Two plays, David Edgar's *Playing with Fire* at the National Theatre and Neil Bisway's Channel 4 drama, *Bradford Riots*, and a BBC2 documentary, *Trouble Up North*, probed the event. In 2004, the BBC broadcast *The Secret Agent*, which exposed the activities of the BNP in Bradford through an undercover operation. One of those on film bragged about kicking an Asian outside a pub in Ivegate in 2001 and the pain he inflicted. Mostly, the national media turned to Bradford to highlight the District's problems and illustrate national ones.

2001 had immediate repercussions on the rioters and their families. We explored these with our original sample of rioters, and made a serious effort to retrace them in 2010–11. Sadly, one had died, some had moved, one, we were told, was back in prison, and a few did not wish to go over this part of their life again. We talked to four of them and to two more who were not in our initial sample and were able to explore their reflections as they looked back over the decade. In most cases, we were accompanied by a volunteer community researcher from the Asian community. We also draw on what we learnt from conducting workshops with a range of participants—the police, the Youth Service, the Local Strategic Partnership (known as Bradford Vision at the time) and interviews with those involved in the rioters' rehabilitation programme. We ourselves actively took part in a range of initiatives throughout the decade which sought new ways of thinking, talking and acting on the issues raised by the riot and subsequent events. Here we look at the creativity and limitations of local responses to the riot and at the national confusion around making sense of multi-ethnic Britain, echoed locally.

# Paying the Price

One of the 2001 rioters had argued that the point of a riot was 'to get police and council to listen to what people have to say'. However, it soon became clear that the state intended the young men to pay a high price for their actions on 7 July. Neither the police, who suffered so badly on the night, nor local or national politicians were in the mood for listening. By the end of July, Operation Wheel was set up, described by the Chief Constable as 'the biggest in the country for more than 20 years'. It involved 80 officers working from video footage and photographs. Their initial effort went into producing photo shots of all those who could be seen carrying out acts of violence, and asking the public to come forward with their names. Two hundred photos were on display in the press, on TV, in police stations and in public places. In response, the police reported receiving 'unprecedented support from the local community' (West Yorkshire Police, Chief Constable's Annual Report 2000–1).

## Penitence and Punishment: The Road to Prison

The majority of our sample handed themselves into the police voluntarily. Two were arrested during the riot, one went on the run and two were arrested as a consequence of other legal proceedings. In no case did they claim that their families handed them in, though they may not have wished to disclose this. Only one specific case of 'grassing' was mentioned. This had been done by a non-relative, a girlfriend's father with whom the young man in question had a fraught relationship. Their accounts of giving themselves in sound naively innocent, and they down-played the shock of seeing their pictures in the papers. One saw his mug shot in the *T&A* some months after the riot. He went to the Central Police Station and said 'I've come to hand meself in'. Another had gone to London on family business and claimed he did not hear he was wanted until his return nine months later. At that point he went into Lilycroft Police Station and said 'I'm here for t'riots'. Another was already in prison (on another charge) when he saw his face on television and later in the *T&A*. He rang his mother and asked her to contact the police and say it was him. Several implied that the decision to hand themselves in was motivated by dread of arrest at the family home and the shame that would bring. Others said they had given themselves up because they feared being arrested by force.

The majority of our sample of rioters admitted feeling remorse, but not all. Peer group interviews which took place very soon after the riots (and where we were not present as a possible restraint) suggest little remorse, though note that these were men who had not been caught or sentenced. Typically they revelled in what they had done and claimed enhanced self-esteem from their participation. 'I feel victory', said one, whilst another exulted that, 'I felt like, I felt proud of myself. When I look back to it, I feel proud. I like to tell people what I've done . . . Happy for the bricks and bottles that I threw'. Our sample were already in prison or had just served their time. Here there were more mixed feelings. Whilst reiterating that his sentence was unreasonable, one added, 'I apologise to all those coppers I hurt'. Others showed remorseful regret. 'I let meself down, me family down'. 'What I've done is stupid, yeah, I admit'. Some felt that they had made a point to racists by rioting but regretted the damage to innocents:

> The racists know now they can't hold the power, they can't intimidate, they can't bully or abuse Asian people. But on t'bad side, there was a lot of damage done to a lotta innocent people, businesses and things like that.

Those interviewed in 2010–11, having lost several years of their lives in prison, were more likely to feel they had done themselves a disservice: 'In my head I was doing right, protecting my community. I thought this was right for me, but in the end it wasn't right for me'. 'I made a mistake and I paid me price'. One remained adamant: 'No, I don't regret what I did, we were doing it for the right thing. Asians used to say "kill all coppers". We were doing it for everyone'. But he later admitted that 'Prison did change me. There are only four walls, you're locked up, you regret it then that you did the damage'. A number made distinctions between those who got caught and the hardline criminals who often did not and who covered their heads because they were more canny about CCTV and 'thought . . . while this is going on, we'll rob a garage'. This convicted rioter summed up what happened to those like him: 'First interest in what was going on, then crowd frenzy, and then caught up in a moment . . . most felt, why did we do this?'

The rioters rarely admitted their fear but their emotions come through when they talk of feeling 'anger and depression'. They were very concerned at the impact on their families—on mothers, in particular. One of the young men hid the picture from his mother, saying, 'It's killed her, ha'nt it?'—not literally, but she was devastated by the shock. A sister of one of the rioters recounted to us how she persuaded her brother to hand himself in:

> Well I did convince him to go, I said, you know, look, rather than someone telling over you, I think it might look good for you to go yourself, you know. Because you've done it and your picture's out in

the newspaper. So he went in the same day . . . He called his solicitor, he went 'I admit, I were there'. And he said, 'I were in the wrong, I cannot explain why I took part in it, I shouldn't have took part in it, but I were there'. So he handed himself in.

The shattering impact on families is vividly described in a second sister's story of how her brother was unmasked as a rioter and how the family responded:

As the sentencing started happening . . . every time I used to come home to Mum's, Mum would say, oh, they've sentenced another guy . . . I think it was in December, and his [her brother's] picture appeared in the *T&A*. [The corner shopkeeper pointed it out to her.] He goes, 'Your [brother's] picture's in there'. I said, 'Get away'. And I looked, I was shocked, I thought, my God, that's my brother. You know, it was a clear picture of him. I mean I couldn't say to anyone that wasn't him, because the bloody shopkeeper that he grew up with knew it was him . . . So I thought, right, OK, went home and I cried my eyes out, and I thought what the hell has he done? Was it one stone? Was it three stones? Was it a petrol bomb? What was it? What's this picture? The worst thing was, it said, 'The Most Wanted', and that didn't help. So I rang his wife up and said, 'Where is he?' She said he hadn't come home yet. I said, 'Wherever he is, get him home, I'm coming'. I waited for my husband to come, I said, 'Have you seen this?' He said, 'What the hell!' So all us brothers and sisters piled in the car and we went over to his house. I was crying my eyes out and I said, 'You're going to get sentenced'.

As indeed he eventually was. Some rioters were said to have fled to Pakistan, but others decided not to take that option:

If you've got to . . . do your time, go do it. They ran away and I had that choice, I couldha' gone, but I didn't take it. I'd rather do what I've got to do now, rather than face the music two years down the road . . . I know one of the lads who ran off to Pakistan. He got a six and a half year sentence for running . . . It didn't pay off.

They were also aware by then that they could not rely on the 'community' to cover up for them. 'A lotta people know yer. It's no use running'. Families and communities generally encouraged them to go to the police. No-one was aware of the implications. Some thought it would be 'a slap on the wrist like the '95 disturbances, nobody got arrested and nobody got done for it'. It is clear that the pictures in the *T&A* were very effective and the young men would not have handed themselves in without them. As one of our sample admitted: 'obviously if I could have got away with it I would have.' Two of our sample were charged with intimidating witnesses in order to resist arrest.

Even more shocks were to come. Many of the lads contracted local solicitors. The capacity of these solicitors to properly brief their clients varied greatly. The solicitors usually told them that they would be charged with violent disorder. However, it gradually became clear—and for some only in court—that this was the least likely of the charges to be brought by the Crown Prosecution Service. The main charge would be riot.

## The Riot Act

The original Riot Act dates from 1715 and was not repealed until 1967. Originally it was read out at disturbances involving more than 12 people, giving them one hour to disperse. Its last recorded reading in public was in 1919. It was read in Bradford in 1891 to the crowd of strikers outside Lister Mill. A Public Order Act was drawn up in 1936 following Oswald Mosely's fascist march in Cable Street. This was revised in 1986 in the wake of riots in Southall, Brixton and Toxteth. It applied only to England and Wales. It established four categories of offence: Riot, Violent Disorder, Affray and 'Threatening Behaviour'. The key paragraph which opens the Act reads:

> Where twelve or more persons who are present together use or threaten unlawful violence for a common purpose and the conduct of them (taken together) is such as would cause a person of reasonable firmness present at the scene to fear for his personal safety, each of the persons using unlawful violence for the common purpose is guilty of Riot (quoted in Carling, Davies and Fernandes-Bakshi, 2004:11).

Central to the charge of riot was the idea of 'common purpose' which could be inferred from action together with others, irrespective of individual behaviour. Throwing one stone as opposed to a petrol bomb might incur a lesser sentence, but it would nevertheless be a sentence within the framework of riot and therefore much longer than if the action was viewed in isolation. Conviction for Riot carries a maximum prison term of 10 years whereas Violent Disorder, which involves only 'three or more persons' carries a maximum term of five years for conviction on indictment (at the Crown Court), or six months on summary conviction (at the Magistrate's Court). The decision to bring charges for riot therefore had very serious implications. Stephen Gullick was appointed Senior Resident Circuit Judge in Bradford in July 2001. On 3 November 2001, he made a 'Tariff-Setting' Statement on the occasion of a 19 year old, the first rioter to be convicted:

> An examination of the events of July 7th, 2001 in parts of this city, reveals a clear picture of a long-lasting concerted attempt of very grave proportions by aggressive force of numbers to harm, if not to overpower, the police and to cause mindless damage and general mayhem . . . Those who choose to take part in activities of this type

must understand that they do so at their peril. It must be made equally clear, both to those who are apprehended and to those who might be tempted to behave in this way in the future, that the Court will have no hesitation in marking the seriousness of what has occurred and it will act in such a way in the present case as will, I hope, send out a clear and unambiguous message as to the consequences to the individual of participating in events such as were seen on July 7th. It is a message which I trust will deter others from engaging in this type of behaviour in the future (full text reproduced in Carling et al, 2004:49-51).

The Judge took mitigating circumstances into account, including the young man's guilty plea, lack of previous convictions, his expressions of remorse, letters of support, including one from his employer, and low risks of re-offending. He nevertheless sentenced him to five years in a young offenders' institution. Video evidence had shown him on the streets between 5.55pm and 8.20pm throwing missiles at police vans or police officers and encouraging others.

In 2002, Judge Gullick was awarded the exceptional civic honour of being appointed Bradford's first Honorary Recorder (*T&A*, 11 April 2002). Conservative Council Leader, Margaret Eaton, said she 'welcomed the transparent and clear sentencing framework' he had set and pursued and to award him the honour was 'the least we can do' (ibid). In 2008, Judge Gullick was asked to address a ceremony to reward several police officers for their bravery and professionalism, together with members of the fire and rescue service, the Crown Prosecution Service and all who had worked on 'Operation Wheel': 'which led to the identification and conviction of nearly 200 rioters' (*T&A*, 5 March 2008).

There was widespread cross-party political support for treating the riot severely and ignoring underlying 'causes'. At the time, the Home Secretary, David Blunkett, commended 'the police for their bravery and determination in the face of enormous provocation'. He also denied that the police were in any way to blame for the violent upheaval and in particular they were not 'institutionally racist' an analysis of police shortcomings dating back to the Scarman Report on riots in the 1980s (*T&A*, 9 July 2001). In 2002 in a speech to business leaders in Sheffield, he spoke of rioters' 'whining about their sentences': 'These maniacs actually burnt down their own businesses, their own job opportunities. They discouraged investment in their areas' (*Independent*, 6 Sept 2002). Local politicians rallied to condemn the rioters as criminals: 'It was nothing to do with deprivation, this was sheer criminality' said Marsha Singh MP, the first minority ethnic Labour MP for Bradford West (Allen, 2003:24). Terry Rooney, Labour MP for Bradford North, talked of 'mindless thuggery' and insisted that 'it was nothing to do with race or social problems, like it was in Oldham or Burnley. In Bradford it was a straightforward criminal act' (*T&A*, 10 June 2005).

Sir Herman Ouseley, however, spoke out against the sentences as 'undeniably unfair and possibly racist' (*The Guardian*, 31 Aug 2002) and Michael Mansfield QC described them as 'manifestly excessive' (Carling et al, 2004:6). Some of the mothers and sisters set up a 'Fair Justice' campaign in 2002, launched at a public meeting attended by 300 people on the first anniversary of the riot. Families and some employers submitted evidence for mitigating circumstances. A Leeds-based solicitor told us how she 'worked terribly, terribly hard on . . . mitigation'. One of the young men she worked for had once come across a young woman who had been raped, called the police, comforted her and agreed to be a prosecution witness. The Prosecution Service did not have records going back that far and it was only by luck that the young man found a letter from them in his attic telling him when he was expected in court. 'It was an absolute miracle, so that was absolutely accepted, because by that time Judge Gullick and the other Judges were starting to treat with some scepticism tales that so and so . . . even on the night, had helped so and so'. Imran Khan, a London solicitor well known for uncovering institutionalised racism in the police during the Stephen Lawrence enquiry, took on Appeal cases. Relatively few were successful. In the course of the Appeals, the Judges detailed the 'tariff' and the range of sentences, from 'ringleaders' (10 years), active and persistent participants who used petrol bombs (8 years), to stone throwers there for a number of hours (6–7 years) and stone throwers present for a 'significant period' (5 years) (*The Times*, 5 February 2003).

Comparisons were made by critics between these tariffs and the low sentences for continuous, sometimes called 'recreational', rioting in Northern Ireland, as well as sentencing for football hooliganism, or even the 1995 disturbances in Bradford. The 1986 Act did not cover Northern Ireland, and one solicitor we consulted noted that football violence had been treated more harshly in recent years with prison sentences. Comparisons were also made with other disturbances in England (Carling et al, 2004) and in particular the disturbances of Burnley, Oldham and Leeds which also took place in 2001. Only in Oldham was riot formally declared. Twelve white people were initially charged with riot but the Judge convicted them for the lesser offense of Affray. Around 50 Asians were charged with Riot in Oldham, and two thirds of them were sentenced for this to two to four years (Carling et al, 2004:27) In Ravenscliffe, seven were charged with Violent Disorder and sentenced to prison terms ranging from four to 36 months (ibid:26). There is clearly some discretion around when the charge of 'riot' is invoked. There are differences between Northern Ireland and the rest of the UK, and the Public Order Act has undergone a relatively recent evolution since the 1981 riots. This evolution did allow for 'exemplary' punishments to be made under the collective charge of 'riot', once a decision was made to invoke it. In Bradford, the 1995 disturbances hang over the sentencing. Only 16 people had been punished for offences arising from the 1995 disorder, only four received prison sentences (Bradford Commission, 1996:66; Carling, 2004:28). The Crown Prosecution Service had dismissed a number of cases and decided not to prosecute officers accused of heavy-handedness. The police were determined that in 2001 a message would be sent to the youth of inner-city Bradford that public disorder would not be tolerated again.

By 2004, some 256 people had been charged, 178 with riot. A total of 170 of these were convicted. The average sentence for the 110 imprisoned adult rioters was over four years and for the 12 imprisoned juveniles, a year and a half. Thirty six other young people were given Detention and Training Orders for Riot averaging 15 months (Carling et al, 2004:2). In the next couple of years the last few rioters were discovered and sentenced similarly. Sixteen Appeal cases were upheld out of 44 as of 2004 (Carling et al:57)]. Seventy-five per cent of our sample got sentences of four to five years; two received six to eight months, three got two years (one also got a further ten for armed robbery) and one got six years. The Bradford sentencing was indeed sending a harsh message. Many questioned whether it was also fair or proportional.

Particularly controversial were the sentences meted out to Far Right activists, for incidents which some argue were critical to the tipping of the rally into a riot. The first incident outside Addison's pub in Ivegate came to court after the incident involving the beating and stabbing of Paul Laurie in Sunbridge Road, which chronologically happened later. The Asian responsible for the stabbing was sentenced to eight years (*T&A*, 30 July 2002). Of eight others, most pleaded guilty to Affray. Three received community punishment orders. Three were jailed for six, nine and 15 months respectively for assault occasioning Actual Bodily Harm (ABH). One who had a previous conviction for racially-aggravated assault was jailed for nine months for ABH, the last got 12 months in a young offenders' institution. In summing up, Stephen Gullick told them: 'Your victim was a white youth, Paul Laurie, who may have been associated with, or perceived to be associated with a number of white youths who had far right-wing affiliations'. He acknowledged that Laurie may himself have been involved in confrontation with a group of men of Asian descent immediately prior to the attack on him:

Saturday Night and Sunday Morning

> I fully accept that feelings were running high in the city centre at this time. I fully accept that you found the presence of Paul Laurie, and those associated with him objectionable. However, we live in a democratic society where wide-ranging views of various types can be expressed within the law. We may from time to time encounter those for whom we have little time and no sympathy, but in a civilised and democratic society, violence cannot be used to respond to this. That road leads to anarchy (*T&A*, 10 June 2003).

The Ivegate incident involved five defendants, four of whom were tried together. Although Kasel Altaf had been attacked and injured by the other four, he had to stand together with three of them in the dock. The first of these was David Appleyard, widely known to have links to Combat 18, the NF and BNP and a resident of Scarborough. Three other white men, all Bradford residents, Paul and William Burnett and Richard Swift, were also indicted, although Swift failed to turn up in court and a warrant was issued for his arrest. Appleyard was well known to local Bradford activists. As one told us: 'He attacked, stalked and intimidated members of the 1 in 12 club, the Resource Centre and the Law Centre for several years'. On the day of the rally, activists had observed Appleyard and told police that he was there to 'start a riot'. They asked them to watch him closely and if possible arrest him, and provided the names of two police officers who would verify their claims.

The Crown described the beating up of Kasel Altaf as 'a revenge beating' (*Yorkshire Post*, 19 July 2003). It argued that Altaf had walked past the pub where a group of men were singing 'Rule Britannia'. Photos showed white men gesturing or giving salutes. Altaf was said to have led a group towards the pub shouting, according to the police 'let's kill the white bastard'. Swift accused Altaf of butting him in the chest. At 16.22pm, Altaf is photographed in the doorway being beaten up. It was hearing of this beating that incensed the young Asians in the crowd in Centenary Square and led many to charge up Ivegate to defend Altaf. Appleyard was also charged with Racially Aggravated Behaviour. Mohammed Amran, the Commissioner for Racial Equality at the time, was being interviewed by *Sky News* when Appleyard came up behind him shouting: 'You'll get no fucking calm you wog bastard. You'll get no fucking calm'. Appleyard then turned to some youths on the road opposite and was observed making gestures, possibly a Nazi salute. This led to another incident in which a young Asian male attacked him, cutting his head. Appleyard was then arrested for his earlier racist language.

Our account of the court hearing comes from two witness observations, press reports and Kasel Altaf's solicitor. All the accused, including Altaf, put in a plea of guilty for Affray. Altaf's solicitor explained that they had waited almost two years to the day from the events. Judge Scott who presided over the case, made clear, she said that 'he didn't consider this incident very serious', particularly set against the stabbing on Sunbridge Road. He also let it be known that anyone who pleaded 'guilty' would get a community penalty rather than imprisonment. All did so. With respect to Altaf's case he had commented: 'It seems to me that Mr Altaf was just a little silly'. Appleyard himself was already serving a custodial sentence for another offence. In Altaf's case, he had been unconscious for a while and his memory was unclear of what he had said in running into the pub. 'Why on earth would I do anything so suicidal as to run at a crowd in that way', he had told his solicitor, but he could not swear that he had not. During the trial, in response to a query about Altaf's injuries, the Judge admitted that he had not yet read the medical notes. These had to be dug out at the trial and confirmed that he had been knocked out and may have suffered concussion. One eye was black and his face was cut.

When the Defence pointed out that a police officer had witnessed Altaf being knocked unconscious before he was removed from the scene and that the markings on Altaf's face were consistent with a witness statement that he had been kicked, the Judge responded, 'it looks a lot worse than it is'. While he acknowledged that there was some photographic evidence that he had been kicked, there was no CCTV evidence, he said. Altaf, he argued, had been 'bent on some kind of violence'. In contrast, the Judge commented on Appleyard's behaviour during the day: 'you had been having a fairly diffuse day' and that in reviewing his police intelligence file, he felt that his record was long but 'not as bad as it looks'.

Appleyard got a six month sentence for the Racially Aggravated Behaviour charge and three months for the Affray, to run concurrently, minus 49 days he had already served. The two others got 60 and 90 hours community service, and Altaf 120 hours. It was argued in court that Altaf got the highest tariff of all defendants because he had had previous run-ins with the police and a conviction in May 2001 for assaulting a police officer, although no custodial sentence. 'I am concerned about you,' said the judge, 'you do not have a good record' and Altaf was 'the author of his own misfortune'.

The Judge did not accept that the incident in Ivegate was relevant to the riot that ensued. Contrary, to the rumour on the 'bush telegraph', he argued, 'this particular incident cannot be taken as the start of the Bradford riots'. Members of the Operation Wheel team similarly downplayed the importance of the incident. They told us that the men in Addison's pub were members of Bradford's Ointment football fan club, drinking in their usual haunt at their usual time. They were convinced that there was no justification for Altaf's behaviour. However, the presence of Appleyard and at least one other known member of the organised Right who spoke about kicking an Asian in the *Secret Agent* programme, confirms that he had indeed spotted Far Right activists when he ran at the pub. The trigger impact, from our evidence, was critical to the unfolding events of 7 July. By downplaying it, the police and judiciary were limiting claims that provocation by the Far Right played a role in tipping rally into riot. They were also minimising evidence of a racial component to the attack on Altaf. A solicitor we interviewed commented: 'What actually is more serious, picking up a stone in the heat of the moment . . . or stamping on somebody's head in a racial attack?'

## From Sentencing to Serving Time

Nearly half of our sample of rioters thought the system or the judges were racist and discriminatory: 'We're getting stitched because we're Asian . . . they're racist . . . they don't like us at all,' said one, whilst another damned the whole establishment: 'Any Asian ud 'ave got t'same sentence. It was fixed . . . it's freemasons innit . . . all the top people . . . they don't like people o' colour . . . Judges, top police, bleeding government an all that . . . it's racism.'

While some were philosophical, the majority thought the sentences were unfair and unjust. They knew they were being made an example of, 'but yer don't show an example in that way, it's too harsh'. 'Four years for throwing four bricks!'

Resentment over the sentencing has not diminished over the years. The rioters we re-interviewed still maintained the sentences were unjust and exceptional. 'If you look at other countries, Ireland, there are riots every month. But they made a big thing of Bradford. People who commit murder get a chance. They made an example of the Asian community'. 'I still feel very hard done by', said another, a view echoed by others.

> It's still in the back of my head, the sentences were handed out like that because we're all Asians . . . it was riot that we did but we didn't deserve those sentences. How come they have the football riots [but] the only people who have ever been sentenced that long is Bradford?

Only one man (who was not in our original sample) saw the sentences in terms of deterrence, to prevent people doing it again.

One of the first experiences that made some of them wish they had not been involved was being brought up before a court. For several this was not a first time, but given the notoriety of the case it was a very public exposure of their guilt. Although they all pleaded guilty on the advice of their solicitors, the outcomes were not at first a foregone conclusion and family members usually expected to attend to show their support. The lads had ambiguous feelings as it meant their families would observe their humiliation. One said, 'I didn't want no-one there'. In particular most were concerned that their mothers and sisters did not attend and others forbad their wives from attending. One said, 'I didn't want any women coming . . . [they would] probably start weeping'. His mother would have been distressed and so he only wanted 'all the blokes in the family'. They were concerned for the health and well-being of their families—'you don't want to put them through it'—but also with their own pride and not wanting to break down in front of them. A young man interviewed in 2011 who had never before been in trouble described the experience: 'we were broken as a family'. In his case everyone had come to court to support him. When he was sentenced he said, 'I had to lift my head up to stop my tears coming out . . . I couldn't say goodbye to my mum'.

The prison experience had been difficult for most, although it was not a first-time experience for all. One said that drink and drugs were available inside and that, 'Yer pad is like a bedsit, just chill out', whilst another said, 'prison's not so bad as they mekk out'. Most had a negative view of prison life—there were fights and they were in with people, 'who haven't had a good upbringing'. 'You're surrounded by badness'. Some had succumbed to depression and one was labelled a suicide risk. Another said, 'They've done our heads in mentally'. They experienced racism both from fellow prisoners and from some officers—though other officers were singled out as 'right good', not tolerating bullying or racism and willing to help with writing letters 'if you can't write'.

However, all the lads we interviewed in prison were anxious about separation from their families. For one his participation in the riot had led to a family rupture. 'My father was bitter. He didn't speak to me . . . I was alienated from them'. But this was rare. Mostly their families supported them, and they expected this—'yer family sticks by you'. Most received regular visits, though this was occasionally impossible if they were located far from home, and there were some who refused to let families—or sometimes just their wives or mothers—come to prison. The sense of shame was strong. One said that 'I don't want 'em to see this part of me yet'. A protective stance towards their families continued in prison. Some worried about their younger brothers, and were fearful that they were no longer around to guide them, others that the material support they provided to parents and wives was now cut off. The rioters we re-interviewed emphasised the importance of regaining the trust of their families. One had relied in the past on his friends rather than his family. He said. 'I've grown up now . . . and I wouldn't like to go with my friends and that, friends would put me in the wrong thing, like drinking'.

The saddest expressions were from those with children. One man reported that his wife and two small children did visit him, but they had told the children that they were seeing him 'at work'. Another said that his children had forgotten him and now called him 'uncle'. Families made up stories to tell children why their father was away: 'He's gone to work in a factory where they make light bulbs'! One man expressed his grief at his separation from his 18 month old child: 'I've got a beautiful daughter and I miss it all now . . . my only child'. He was especially close to this child after looking after her single-handedly for a month when his wife was in hospital. In this case, however, he had been encouraged to participate in a parenting scheme for fathers within the prison. Once a month or so his daughter spent a whole day with him under supervision, when they enjoyed 'games and making stuff, playing with toys'.

Five of those who were in prison were bitter that they had not been allowed out to attend the funerals of close family members, amongst whom were several grandparents and a father. One claimed that 'they let a few English lads go [to funerals]'—it was for them one more example of racism. Not only were these lads very committed to their families, they also saw them as security for the future. A third detailed their expectation that on release they would go into their family's business. The rest feared that now they had a record they would find difficulty in getting a job.

When we visited one of the prisons in which a sizeable cohort of the rioters were incarcerated we were told by the education officer that rioters were taking up chances for further study or training and seeing it as a 'second opportunity'. Two were studying for OU degrees, whilst three or four had become 'peer partners', supporting other prisoners (two of these turned up in our sample). Five had got reading champion awards for outstanding participation. When we asked the prisoners in our sample what courses they had done, they confirmed this picture, with nearly all having done courses of one kind or another. For a few this was basic literacy and numeracy, whilst several had taken part in life skills programmes—anger management, budgeting, citizenship or drugs rehabilitation. One however had done an Open University Access course, another an A level course. The majority had taken IT or computer skills courses, and a third had done GCSEs. An equal number had taken up industrial training, mostly in building and construction. A rioter we re-interviewed told us that one of the rioters from our original sample had reoffended and was back in prison. He had chosen not to take any courses, he said, and that made a real difference.

The rioters we re-interviewed were very honest about why they agreed to attend courses in anger management, victim awareness and alcohol and drug abuse. It was mostly to meet their mates and gain credits which could count towards parole. But they admit the courses influenced them. Much depended on the attitude of those teaching the courses: 'I met a tutor. I got on well. She was really nice. No anger like the officers. She was on my level . . . You need respect. Someone to see the goodness in you'. Another had been made to do 'alcoholics anonymous': 'It was to pass time', he said. But then someone came to the group and told lies. This eroded his trust in the sessions. He acknowledged that he did cut down on alcohol when he was released, but not altogether and was on a drink driving ban at the time of the conversation. One lad who had participated in the riot but gone to prison for drugs dealing admitted that victim awareness had changed him.

> I [was] doing drugs, but I'm not forcing it into his mouth, he's not my victim. I have no victims. Then they brought a mother of a user . . . My son could have been your victim. What if it was my brother? This affected me. I got nine years. I deserved it.

Many of our rioters sample rediscovered religion in prison, especially where many Muslims were together. This was due as much to the prison experience itself as international events. One rioter told us that in Armley, with 300 Asian prisoners, there was 'a real Muslim presence'. He had a brief phase of 'turning to religion' where there was a group keen on this, but then slid back. Around half of our sample said that they prayed more because there were no distractions and they regularly went to Friday prayers. One or two had grown beards or already had beards and they mention the visual impact of that on other prisoners 'they think beards—Paki, terrorist'. Prison officers were not always sympathetic either—it was claimed that one implied a young man was a 'Taliban', whilst another said he had been told to take down pictures of Mecca and Medina. The rioters we re-interviewed all highlighted the importance of this aspect of their prison experience. One read the Qur'an twice. Another learnt about the schools of thought within Islam from fellow prisoners. One lad admitted that in prison his 'prayer wasn't 100%', because he didn't know the Arabic words well enough. He traced this back to the way he had been taught:

> you know all Muslims are put through the [Qur'anic] schools . . . and at a young age you don't really understand what you're reading,

apart from you know . . . you've got to read it otherwise you're going to get beaten.

He had heard that some of those who grew beards in prison went totally off the rails and abandoned religion once they were released. He began to turn to his religion in a meaningful way through the support of an Imam who came into prison for Friday prayer, but also through the kindness of a priest who visited the prison every day. The young man told us the story of how one day when he couldn't reach his mum on the phone: 'I rebelled against the whole system, I climbed on top of a cage and I said, I'm not coming down until I get to speak to my mum'. It was the priest who talked him down and offered to ring his mum: 'that's what made me think, hey look at that, he's not even a Muslim, but he's ready to push'. Another spoke of his shock but appreciation when an Imam asked him to give the call to prayer in front of 130 inmates: 'It built my confidence'.

While the rioters were in prison, momentous events took place in the world outside. 'There has been trouble between Asian and non-Asian prisoners', we were told by a prison officer on one visit. 'September 11th created some ripples as Al Qaida literature went around and some spoke of a *jihad*'. A number of our rioters awakened to the politics around Islam while in prison, though this is most apparent amongst those we re-interviewed and who had therefore been out of prison for several years. One young man recalled the 7/7 train bombing and his steps to avoid an anti-Muslim backlash in prison:

> I remember when that happened in prison and I remember walkin' out and saying to people, you all know me, you've known me for a long time, yes I'm a Muslim, I'm proud of being a Muslim, but have I ever pushed my religion onto you? . . . They just looked at me funny and they say, what's wrong wi'you? I sez look, there's a lot of racism that's going to happen now with this and . . . you know, I just want to know that you are all with me than against me you know.

He remembered people shouting names like 'terrorist' from their cells and a lot of Muslims 'kicking off and demanding that they said these things to their face on the prison landing'. Awareness of religious identity grew in these confrontations, and a sensitivity to how Muslims are treated in the world: 'There is more attention on Muslims now', one told us, 'Bradford tried to blame the riots for September 11th, but September 11th happened afterwards. Riots was nothing about terror'. This former rioter admits that now he is 'more aware of politics. I am more alert now. My family says I should become a journalist. I watch the news, Muslims gettin' killed all over the world, no one gives a toss'. Another admitted his resentment towards white people after the riots, until he read a book about

Malcolm X and 'politically, I learnt to analyse more'. Several of the young men in our re-interviews, influenced by internet sites, believed that they had not been told the full story of September 11th and felt there was a 'bigger conspiracy'. However, they made very clear distinctions between these views and support for suicide bombings and the killing of civilians: 'I don't believe religion and violence go together'. Another said he had opposed the war in Iraq and Afghanistan, but:

> I was against the guys [Al Muhajiroun] wanting to march in Wootton Bassett. I thought, how dare you. I was against the war, but at the end of the day, they are soldiers dying for Britain. If you want to do it, do it outside Downing Street, not when families are gathered.

## Rehabilitation Programmes

Greater confidence is something that the majority of the former rioters we re-interviewed recognised as an outcome of the painful experience of prison. A thoughtful and systematic offender programme played a key role. An inter-agency group was convened, led by West Yorkshire Probation area and under the umbrella of Bradford Vision, which made the re-integration of offenders a part of its community cohesion plan. Others in the group were the police, Bradford Council, Job Centre Plus, (Developing Initiatives for Social Care in the Community DISC, which worked with the rioters in prison to assess their skill levels and job status prior to conviction and on release) and Himmat/Ummid. Himmat played a key role in bringing understanding of the local Asian community to their support for convicted rioters and their families. It had been set up in Halifax in the early 1990s and its sister organisation, Ummid, was established in Bradford in 1995 to help probation officers working with male and female Asian offenders (Cocker, 2005:266). Himmat started work for the Probation Service in October 2002.

We had two long conversations with the Director of Himmat in 2004 and 2011. We were able to check our own data on the rioters against theirs, confirming that our sample broadly corresponded with the profile of their much larger number of convicted rioters. They worked with around 90, those who had received sentences of four years or more. We also learnt how the organisation had gone about its work, beginning with a meeting in the Carlisle Business Centre in 2002 with anxious parents. Many were convinced that their sons were 'saints', Himmat told us, and were often in denial about their sons' drugs and alcohol abuse. Himmat had to bring these problems into the open so that the young men could get the help they needed. They befriended each rioter as well as their families, getting a sense of the rioter's entire situation in order to find solutions that fitted the problem. This included visiting families at home: 'we got families on board'. Gradually, some mothers opened up. One admitted that her son was a heroin user and had stolen her jewellery. With acknowledgement of the problem, Himmat could then help the lad with his drug problem. Most of the rioters were seen as low risk in terms of re-offending, but getting to know the lads revealed problems which might increase that risk. There was the car mechanic who loved driving but could not read or write and pass a theory test. He therefore drove without a licence and would be quickly back in prison if this problem was not resolved, which Himmat helped to do. There was the wife who could not get benefits because everything was in her husband's name; sorting this out eased the anxiety of her husband and helped him to adjust to prison life.

Himmat also helped the rioters to get jobs on their release. Housing was not a major problem for the young men. Most returned to the family homes they had left for prison. Jobs were a different matter. All the rioters we re-interviewed had found jobs, but it had not been easy. Some were reintegrated into working life through day release from prison. This had a big impact on one young man:

> I was a benefit advisor. There was an 80 year old woman who didn't understand her benefits, she struggled to pay bills, she just sat there sobbing. I asked are you ok? . . . She had a problem with bills, was getting court orders. I went through her expenditures. We went to a tribunal. I represented her! . . . She sent me £50 and some sweets. I put it in the charity box.

However, this was a difficult time in the young men's lives: 'Would a normal employer want you?', said one, 'Life's not easy for an ex-offender. Employers look at you in another way. In one interview, half way through I said, I have failed in my past, now I've changed. But then the interview was terminated'. However, the dedicated programme of support for the rioters was very successful. An academic evaluation of the programme in 2005 which contrasted the outcome with a similar but not equivalent, intake of prisoners, found that 70% of the riot sample were in employment after release compared to 44% of the comparison sample. There was also an increase by 73% from pre- to post-prison employment compared to only 33% for the comparison group (Cocker, 2005:14). Not only did the rioters improve their skills, but extra effort was put in by the reintegration project when employer unease was apparent. Rioters were asked to complete a 'pen picture' of themselves and matched with suitable job vacancies. As their programme wound down in 2007 and 2008, Himmat phoned all the rioters they knew. They failed to contact 12%, but another 12% were in college and 79%

were in employment. While some had reoffended, 81% had not (Himmat interview, February 2011). When we checked these figures with the final tally of the Probation Service, we found that 70% had found employment and only 6% had reoffended. The national average is 10 times higher.

## Closing a Chapter

> *But it's that closure . . . maybe I sound really biased here, but cos I work in the public sector . . . I know about funding that comes in . . . For example, we've got this regeneration going on in Bradford, and people are saying investors don't want to come to Bradford because of the riot. And you can't help thinking, when are you going to put that [aside] you know—the families have done it, the lads have done it, they've admitted it. When are you . . . ? I feel as if for the last decade or so or half that the lads have been out, the lads are constantly apologetic. They're apologising because apparently in the whole grand scheme of the point when Bradford was created and had its pitfalls, it doesn't matter, the mills stopped it doesn't matter. It's the rioters [who are to blame].*
> **(Rioter's sister re-interviewed, 2011)**

A mother and a sister of two rioters interviewed in 2011 both said their lads had never spoken about the prison experience to them, and they worried greatly about its psychological impact. The sister said:

> When he did come out there was naturally a celebration and everything. But he closed a chapter on it. 'I don't want to talk about it', 'it happened', 'it was stupid' . . . 'I don't want to go down that road' . . . But he had to, because it had implications in his life to come. Getting a job. They do the criminal checks now, saying do you have any previous criminal offences? Before, he ticked no, now he has to tick yes. I remember that letter he had to write to explain why he was ticking yes, the first one. It was difficult, it really was difficult, because, how do you say, I was stupid, I've paid my due? . . . Even though he closed the chapter, the book was on the table and we weren't allowed to go and look in it. He only gave us glimpses of how it affected him . . . His relations with his family, having an absent father. So much happens in two and a half years . . . For the first year and a bit he was just picking up pieces.

Amongst the rioters we re-interviewed, one was a taxi driver, one had a packing job and four were working with young people in

Bradford: 'I wanted to work with young people' said one, 'deter them from making the same mistakes I had. I had no role model to make me stay away from crime'. Three of them had played a role in preventing young people being provoked by the English Defence League in 2010 (see chapter 8). One had set up his own organisation to get ex-offenders into employment. They all had deep insights into the problems facing young people in the District, Asian and white. One former rioter (not in our original sample and amongst the more aspirational and educated of the riot participants) ended up working with some of the most disaffected and highest-risk lads in Bradford, all capable of violent offences. He told us:

> I tried to gain a bond with them. If you ever need me I am here, and I will do everything to help you and I will never let you down. No-one had ever said that to them . . . Lads from Thorpe Edge and Holmewood, they've got a very negative look on Asians . . . I want them to understand we're not all what we are portrayed . . . we're very good-hearted people . . . We had 30 young people . . . I offered them a family environment centred around love, care and affection, everything the young people didn't have . . . I tried to make them feel better about themselves . . . I try to divert their thoughts . . . they want to destroy because that's all they've seen round them . . . And then their facial expression changes, their body language changes . . . The only way I can make a difference is listening to them . . .

The rioters we re-interviewed did not think Bradford had changed much. Although one felt as 'much British as the next', he still maintained that Asians and blacks are not accepted in British society. They were also sceptical about the politics of their own community. Several were openly critical of the way caste influences social relationships and politics in the District, and offers of help come from candidates only if you give them your vote, and you are expected to vote for the person whatever the party or policy. The first question asked is 'so where you from then back home?' All but one mentioned their worries about the on-going drugs trade in Bradford and the way it was dragging in younger kids: 'We've [the rioters] all grown up . . . The problem is the new generation. I work with the new generation. They're a lot worse. We had a 12 year old who was pushing drugs. We never had that at my age'. This may be the nostalgic voice of a generation moving into maturity. However, fears for younger brothers and sons were expressed by nearly everyone. The problem was 'easy money' and no opportunities. Kids could not even afford the Cineworld complex, said one. The taxi driver was working six days a week from 7.00pm to 6.00am to pay boarding school fees that would keep his son out of trouble. He reckoned there were some 20 drug dealers in the five streets in his neighbourhood, but the police were only 'grabbing the small fish and leaving the big fish'.

Yet, this man would not move. He felt his family was generally safer in Bradford's Asian community than Leeds where, as an Asian taxi driver working nights, he felt vulnerable to racist attack:

> Basically, I'm away from home, but my family and kids are safe, you know. Slight bit of problem, me sister's two streets away, me cousin's down the street, all these neighbours, I've grown up with them. We've known each other for years. It makes me feel more secure with the family being there.

One young man felt there would always be a divide in Bradford, '[even] if we were living in the same area, like Ravenscliffe, people still would not mix . . . Frizinghall is all Asian and other parts are white'. Another admitted, however, he would like to move from the inner city to Haworth. He would like to 'get away from the Asians, they have so many kids'. But it would be difficult to move from the family, he said, 'I wouldn't know who would help if my wife got into trouble'. He argued that all communities stick together, even the English expatriates in Spain, but he preferred working with the English, he had a better laugh with them: 'Everyone must move forward. Not put racism into everything. I want a Bradford where people mix'.

## 'They Blamed Us': Local Responses to Riot

*The community, I don't know what I say about the community, so I got mixed feelings wi'em now, as it is yer know . . . on the riots. Just 'ave, it's hard to explain as it is . . . Yeah, they blamed us.*
**(2001 rioter)**

*When you look at the economic conditions we had from 19- probably 1996 actually, up to 2007, an 11 year period of constant [national] macro-economic growth and of economic stability . . . you think of what 2001 did to the Bradford economy over that period. Because it wasn't just the companies that left, it was the companies that didn't come . . . And . . . the human cost which was dreadful, the wasted, the human waste of, you know 200 young people going to jail . . . the impact, the devastating impact on their families and communities—the way that Bradford's perceived by the outside world . . .*
**(Senior Council Officer, interviewed 2011)**

The Asian community as a whole were deeply upset by the actions of the young men on 7 July. On 11 July, Asian Trades Link, representing 400 businesses, placed a £3,000 newspaper advertisement in the *Telegraph and Argus*, apologising: 'On behalf of the silent majority of law-abiding Asian citizens of Bradford, we would like to express our sincere sympathies to all those affected by the mindless destruction and violence of last weekend's events' (11 July 2001). On the other hand, Manawar Jan-Khan of the Manningham Residents' Association wrote in *The Guardian* on 12 July that:

> Bradford needs to wake up from its denial and pretence that there is harmony in the city—and employers, driving in their top automobiles to homes in the nice villages and suburbs, need to understand the reality of Manningham and what 'no hope' means.

The Ouseley report was launched on 12 July in Valley Parade to an audience of 300 and the world's media. Launching the report and his proposal for a 'Bradfordian People Programme', Lord Ouseley issued a strong plea to involve young people in the District from all backgrounds in solutions to its problems, to get them mixing in schools and the workplace, to make them 'feel proud of who they are and where they live' (*T&A*, 12 July 2001). The police also called a public meeting to discuss events with the inner-city community. The arrests and sentencing were not yet an issue in these early months, but the meeting was tense.

## Manningham in Bloom

Immediately after the riot, a local community activist met up with the Anglican Minister of Manningham to discuss how to heal the grief in the area. They wanted to give people a chance to air views and then encourage them to focus on the future. They got a leaflet printed inviting people to a meeting. It asked: 'People of Manningham—How do you see the Future?' The meeting was held on 14 July in the local church, because the activist argued that the mosque had no tradition of opening its doors for such an event. Later the Manningham Parish Team would write to the *T&A* recording their strong individual relationships with Muslims in the area but also the difficulty they faced in building constructive engagement with Manningham's mosque leaders (5 November 2001). Many Muslim residents and businessmen did turn up on 14 July and the former Asian Mayor, Mohammed Ajeeb, chaired a good mix of some 150 people. The Anti-Nazi League also arrived, but were asked to leave when they tried to politicise the discussion. The organisers encouraged people to talk about local issues, in particular the need for businesses to unite around the development of

Manningham, to organise better services for young people and to strengthen residents' interaction.

Even the owner of McCann's, the Oak Lane DIY shop, came, although his shop had been ram-raided and looted in the riot and he and his wife were in shock. The shop was a lifetime work and had just completed a year-long refurbishment. He could not afford to leave and he and his wife 'fought back' to rebuild the business (interview, 2010). They hung on in Manningham until 2008, by which time the long hours they had to stay open had begun to take its toll. But in 2001, the owner joined others on 14 July to see what could be done for Manningham. People were encouraged to express their feelings towards the destruction. We 'went through the shock and horror', one of the organisers told us. Some asked, 'where are the politicians?' But the meeting chose to focus on what Manningham people could do.

Both Asian and the remaining white-owned businesses were galvanised by the meeting and the first local business partnership was set up for Oak Lane to restore faith and confidence in the area. Security was improved, graffiti removed, a Crimestoppers campaign launched and gradually the dereliction on Oak Lane, where half the shops had lain empty after 2001, was turned around. Amidst fears that the regeneration of Manningham Mills as luxury accommodation would lead to a gated community, Urban Splash (the development company), were invited to explain how they would assist the local business community. Manningham Youth Action Group was another outcome of the meeting. It was not to be a traditional youth centre with its pool table, but to generate a 'positive view of life and society' one of its founders told us (interview, 2011), where training and skills would enable young people to benefit the community and gain self confidence. The organisation went on to build strong and lasting roots. Every year local youngsters are taken into the countryside, with fun days organised around health and education.

The third strand of the meeting was around Manningham residents, particularly the elderly, the middle-aged and people with families, mostly Asian but also white. The churches were faced with an ageing population of lonely white people who had roots in the area and could not get out—and who in some cases were subject to harassment from local youths who did not understand why elderly women and men should be living alone. For the churches this was 'a community which is not really a community'. St Mary's Residents Association was set up. The Association built a community garden on a piece of land left derelict for 20–25 years and campaigned to make the roads safer. Yorkshire in Bloom was a traditional garden competition focussed on 'nice areas', such as Esholt. The Residents Association decided to enter their Community Garden project and won a commendation even though they were aware that they could not compete with the immaculate gardens of wealthier areas. Later, Manningham residents organised their own garden competition, Manningham in Bloom, starting with workshops on planting containers and hanging baskets. The competition got stronger every year and involved schools, residents, and businesses in a range of gardening categories. Other neighbourhoods set up their own 'in bloom' events. Competitiveness is high, they tell us, but the benefits in physical and mental health have been great, as well as restoring pride to this epicentre of the riot.

## Fair Justice for All

The Fair Justice for All campaign was a different kind of community response, set up in 2002 to bring families together who wanted to appeal the sentences. The families had no idea what the charge of riot meant. Until the sentencing began, most expected fines or at most a year in prison. The campaign was set up with the support of Bradford-born singer and musician, Aki Nawaz, and the lawyer, Imran Khan, but local women played a prominent role. It 'was never a mass campaign'. The community 'thought it shameful to be in prison', said one of the two founder members we interviewed in 2011, part of a group of half a dozen men and women who constituted the informal organising committee. Families were scared, while some 'didn't know how to be active'. The women spoke of how hard it was to campaign while grieving for their sons and brothers who had gone to prison, sometimes facing hostility from their own community. Fridays they would gather at the court, a group of about 20 with their banners. 'It was always wet!'

One of the campaign's achievements was 'allowing women to come to the forefront—sisters who were at the time maybe too young to help their brothers or husbands, fathers'. Wives, mothers and sisters travelled to London to support Appeal cases. Although they had relatively few successful outcomes to celebrate with the 70 families they supported at appeals, the campaign served a broader purpose:

> The families were in touch with us constantly, protested as well, came down to London, [they] set up support networks amongst themselves. I think the families needed that, being ostracised by their community is hard enough . . . In a way we were almost like a self-help group for them as well. We seem to be the only group that were listening to them. People were saying, 'you're justifying the riot'. No, what we were trying to say is: God forbid if this ever happens again. These are the learning curves . . .

The events of 9/11 added a new dimension to the sentencing: 'a different sort of struggle was going on in the community . . . that didn't help, that equation being thrown in . . . you were not only being charged for the riot, but also for being Muslim'. 'We've got another demon after us, being a Muslim', said one mother, a woman of urban Punjabi origin, who had spent her life working across faiths and 'loved debating' and was palpably shocked at the backlash towards even educated and 'integrated' Muslims like herself. They were reluctant to blame 'Islamophobia', but could not make any other sense of the disproportionate sentencing.

Over time, parents were also learning about their sons' street life:

> The relationship between the rioting person and the family . . . a lot of home truths that came out. How well did we know our child? Because in the Appeal things came out that the families didn't even know. So when some said it was a first offence, but it wasn't, there were 'previouses', but the families didn't know about [them], because . . . [they covered up] a community sentence, a fine, you know [by saying], 'I'm off to my mates for a month' . . . That dampened some of the motivation for the families, 'Oh, some of my dirty laundry is out there which I didn't know existed'. That was really difficult.

However, facing the reality that the lads were going to serve time and would need support was the biggest challenge of all for the campaign. It meant dealing with probation officers and the police and anyone who could help get their children and brothers back into normal life when they came out of prison. The women at the centre of the campaign were not always comfortable with what more politicised campaign supporters expected of them:

> I was grateful for their help. But sometimes I felt there was more than met the eye. At one point people wanted to put us on a pedestal, at other times they wanted to put the campaign as a set of, you know, women who thought they could change the world, 'do-gooders'. But the reality is you're not, your kids aren't all that.

As the Appeals process came to an end, the families had to move beyond the issue of the disproportionate sentencing and 'get their lads sorted':

> At one point the campaign was very anti-police, anti-authority, anti-this . . . but actually, we needed them, which emerged when some of the families started talking about rehabilitation, reintroducing them . . . This is where the campaign disintegrated a bit . . . look we can't keep shutting them [the police] out . . . It got messy in the sense that people kept saying to us: 'you can't trust them you can trust me' . . . We're thinking, we're just normal people here, we're just families, we're concerned, our lads are still in there, we did a lot of soul-searching, we ate a lot of humble pie as well . . . This is reality and we did a lot of learning.

Political supporters of the campaign did not want to think about the reintegration of the lads, she says, 'Nobody wanted to join that bandwagon'. She recalls how the media approached the campaign every time new cases came to court, such as the burning of the Labour Club. They expected the 'same rant when the disproportionate sentencing was carrying on'. But she was clear that lives could have been lost in that incident and in the end she wanted to remind people that Fair Justice really stood for 'fair justice'. They had not questioned that the lads had done wrong and should be punished, they only questioned that the punishments did not fit the crime.

The campaign reached a 'comma', as one of its founders put it, as the Appeal process came to an end during 2004. She recognised that families wanted closure:

> I said to families, that closure I respect it, you choose when to shut that door, and if you want that door to stay shut you keep it shut. It was those kind of balances these families need, they need a form of normality.

Most recognised that the Probation Service 'really did work, they really were working with the lads, with the families'.

## Local State and Civic Responses

> *I was shocked by the institutional response. The fact that we sent to prison 200 people, wow . . . I still maintained that the institutional response had been too hard, we never learned from it, and that's a huge loss to the city. By not doing the learning, not having the stuff presented to the world, it reconfirmed the stereotypes we already have about young Asian people: they weren't to be trusted. It reconfirmed everything we knew, all the negative stereotypes, all the things we knew about young Asian men we had just reconfirmed by the institutional response and the lack of real information that said this is what they really are.*
> **(Interview: Liberal Democrat Leader, 2011)**

Although some may dismiss it as partisan, the Liberal Democrat analysis of the post-riot response amongst the local political leadership (where the Tories had just taken control) resonates with a widespread sense of political inertia in the wake of the riot. A Leaders' Steering Group met for six months after the riot, but was unable to build an agreement. The Local Strategic Partnership, formally constituted as Bradford Vision in April 2001, was charged with responding to Ouseley and producing an implementation plan supported by a council officer seconded for that purpose, but the plan was slow to materialise.

Ouseley's report set the tone for a new and highly contested debate on how to think about diverse communities and identities in contexts of poverty, inequality and discrimination. Its language of 'diversity' sought to remind people that discrimination persists in multiple forms. Ouseley underlined gender, race/ethnicity, language fluency, religion/faith, age, disability, sexual orientation, poverty/social status, homelessness, migration and unemployment (Ouseley, 2001:33). It drew attention to ignorance as well as prejudice in its multiple guises: Islamaphobia, racism, sexism and homophobia. Its Bradfordian People Programme rested on four concrete proposals: citizenship education in schools, a Centre for Diversity, Learning and Living, a behavioural competency framework for the workplace, and equality and diversity contract conditions. The aim was to work on ignorance and prejudice at the same time as underlining the explicit conditions for fostering equality outlined in the recently passed Race Relations (Amendment) Act of 2000 which imposed legal obligations on public bodies to eliminate racial discrimination.

Ouseley was as robust on race equality as on promoting community interaction and overcoming prejudice. But some argued that its emphasis on diverse forms of discrimination diminished attention to their key drivers, such as class, race and gender. Activists and organisations have spent decades fighting around the pre-eminence of one or other of these. In a submission to the Commission (2001) Mahoney had highlighted race and to some extent class, but did not mention how women differentially experience inequality under both categories:

> The issue of race is crucial. Given the demographic trends, Bradford as a whole cannot succeed unless its ethnic minority populations prosper. Some cities have demonstrated that they can succeed despite having a spatially segregated underclass. No city has succeeded when it has two spatially segregated underclasses: the poor Muslim communities in the inner city and the poor white communities on the peripheral estates— the real double whammy . . . In order to go forward Bradford must take a step backwards. It must establish structures and processes through which the voice of the ethnic minority communities and those white communities which are most affected are heard.

The emphasis on 'voice' and participation, particularly of young people, had also been stressed by Ouseley in his Bradfordian People's Programme. This still begs the questions: how do the voiceless gain voice and learn to be effective? Those who have not experienced society's prejudices often deride efforts to get them acknowledged as 'political correctness'. To listen is difficult. Do you confront or dialogue with the prejudiced? Do you make distinctions between gut prejudice, wilful ignorance and organised racism? Organised racists are a small minority, allowing many to deny that their own stereotyped views of others are actually 'racist'. And, how do you ensure that those who have experienced racism do not reproduce it against others? Some of our young rioters had pronounced anti-semitic views, whilst their apparent targeting of white businesses during the riot seemed to signal anti-white racism.

There was no agreement amongst Bradfordians on how to address these complex issues. Some believed that the answer lay only in economic progress, but such progress did not look promising in 2001. Chapter 5 described the dire situation in the city as the skills of its engineers and machine operators became irrelevant to the industries of the future. Yet Pace Micro Technology could not find local workers with adequate reading and writing skills for their factory conversion in Salt's Mill (Greenhalf, 2003:203). Most Asian businesses remained small-scale and family-oriented without the turnover to generate significant numbers of jobs in the District. One successful Asian businessman who had scaled up his enterprises was interviewed for our research in 2001. He employed 280 people in a range of businesses, but 96% of them were white, because he could not find technical and sales skills amongst local Asian youth. In January 2002, education in Bradford was handed over to a private international company, Serco, in recognition of the failure of education provision in the District. Informed debate on why many young men in poor white and Asian communities were failing to progress was lacking.

Time is needed to turn economy and skills around, coupled with strong measures to equalise the playing field and to maintain equity in the course of future growth. Economic prosperity for all would undoubtedly transform aspirations and mindsets. In the meantime, aspirations and/or mindsets were narrow amongst many of Bradford's communities, including the middle class white areas which denied their connection with the inner city. Should you work on these mindsets or wait for economic take-off? Did the mindsets themselves inhibit take-off through limiting openness to change?

The answer probably lay in tackling all these issues at the same time. However, Ouseley's proposals soon got sidelined in national debates arising from an Independent Review Team set up to investigate the northern disturbances. Their report (the Cantle report) was published at the end of 2001. Reports also came out on the Oldham and the Burnley disturbances (Ritchie, 2001, Clarke, 2002). The government's response to all of these was the Denham Report (2002). The concept of 'community cohesion' was born and rolled out as the new shape of policy in the field of multi-ethnic community relationships. Bradford District was now required to produce a 'Community Cohesion Plan'. An outline plan for consultation, was produced by Bradford Vision in August 2002 incorporating its response to Ouseley. The Bradford District Community Strategy, 'One Landscape Many Views' was published in October 2002. A Director of Community Cohesion was appointed the following year. A Bradford Youth Parliament was set up. There was considerable commitment and energy from officers and Vision partners, and a bid in 2008 (ultimately unsuccessful) for the European Capital of Culture represented an effort to mobilise people around a new image for Bradford.

But many felt that the real issues facing the District were not open for discussion. Community cohesion never went down well in Bradford as an idea. Ouseley's recommendations were disparaged as 'blaming' the minority ethnic communities for failing to integrate, which the national cohesion agenda seemed to require. His own African-Caribbean heritage and London-centred experience was said by some to imply lack of understanding of the Pakistani community. For others, his report merely stated the obvious: 'tell me something I don't know', one prominent politician told us. The issue of de facto segregated communities and segregated schools was sidelined if not suppressed, although it implicated all communities in the District and would change little while economic prosperity remained elusive. Positive and organic interactions between communities would have to evolve if horizons were to be lifted in the District amongst communities of all incomes and heritages. Only then could the multi-ethnic character of the District be acknowledged as integral to its future success and of benefit to the white majority as well as its ethnic minorities, removing any sense of competition for resources between them.

Although Bradford Vision's Community strategy placed much emphasis on enhancing the voice of citizens, in reality the local state, professionals and communities were disconnected. Political parties no longer attracted grass-roots campaigners who connected them to communities, if only at election time. This affected the Labour Party in particular, and its claim to represent the poorest. The Local Strategic Partnership (LSP) was there to bridge gaps in the decision-making structure of Bradford and other deprived areas of the country, but the statutory bodies round the table did not have deep roots in communities. Those working with communities were given representation at this strategic level for the first time, but their own roots were not as deep as in the past. Bradford's activists were now an older generation. The 'voluntary and community sector' which emerged during the 1980s and 1990s with state funding had transformed activism just as the UK shifted to a service-driven and de-industrialised economy. As one Bradford activist put it to us in 2011: 'As it [activism] became more organised, people began to see it more as a kind of life choice . . . Lots of us have ended up doing more mainstream things than we started off doing'.

Nevertheless, there was a lot of energy within Bradford. Many initiatives sprang up which aimed to build connections across communities. A notable example is the Schools Linking Network which began work with two primary schools just after the riots. This project spoke openly of the 'ghettoisation' of housing and schooling that meant that 'many pupils can spend their entire school lives mixing mainly with one sector of the wider community that makes up the city' (www.schoolslinkingnetwork.org.uk/pdf/ACKROY). Teachers felt ill-equipped to deal with tensions emerging from the riots. Many were concerned at the strong differences in performance of Pakistani boys and pupils from poorer English background which began to show as early as Key Stages 2 and 3 along with an increase in emotional and behavioural difficulties. The first Primary Schools Linking Project began in the autumn of 2001 between Eldwick, a primary school in a semi-rural setting and where all the pupils were learning in their first language and Girlington, an inner-city school where English was an additional language. By 2005, 61 primary and 12 secondary schools were taking part. A probing evaluation that year highlighted the serious commitment and detailed preparation required by teachers and other adults to generate positive and sustained learning outcomes from these encounters. It was not just 'a series of worthwhile activities' (Raw, 2005:61). Schools Linking went on to become a nationwide project.

The Intercultural Communication and Leadership School (ICLS) was launched in 2002 to bring emergent young actors together from all backgrounds and beliefs for five-day seminars. A generation of able young Bradfordians went through the ICLS school and built a connection with each other which has fed fresh approaches to challenges in the District. In the University, the Programme for a Peaceful City (PPC) set out to 'break silences' and organise spaces for safe discussion around the many sources of tension in the District (Cumming, 2006). It had been set up in May 2001 before the riot, responding to a sense of impending trouble. The University saw a large drop in applications as a result of the riots. One of the PPC's first events was to give impetus to Ouseley's recommendations for a Centre for Diversity, Learning and Living which would include a District-wide equality and fair treatment initiative for all public services and employers. The idea was under discussion in the council but slow in emerging. The PPC invited Herman Ouseley back to

Bradford and over 200 people came together in a bid to involve them in building the idea of a 'Diversity Exchange' and ensure it was a bottom-up initiative shaped by cross-District debate.

The meeting, on 8 April 2002, highlighted persistent disagreements on the very language of conversation around difference, diversity and equality, as well as the comparative value of time spent talking and time spent acting (Buhler and Pearce, 2002). But the idea that the Diversity Exchange should be flexible and open to community needs, rather than controlled and institutional was strongly voiced. A report to Bradford Vision following the Forum emphasised that it could be an:

> enabling mechanism, not a large institution or centre but a facilitating space for participation providing specialist facilities, expertise and resources to support the adoption of best practices across public, private and not-for-profit sectors in the pursuit of equality and diversity.

The Diversity Exchange was set up under Bradford Vision in 2002 amidst high expectations and limited resources. Navigating the tensions between institutional logics and facilitating process was not easy, however, and an evaluation in 2005 concluded that 'the projects have helped enable community-based exchange but this has been seen by some stakeholders as contrived linkages' (Meridienpure, 2005:7). The Diversity Exchange went independent in 2007.

Building connections and conversations reflecting natural dynamics was a major challenge in this post-riot aftermath. The PPC sought to use the idea of the University as a safe and neutral space to encourage this. It brought non-academics and academics together to discuss and debate the riots, young men, sentencing, cohesion, gender, Bradford politics, the decline of the pub, citizen education, the Iraq war, segregation (or not?), inequalities, regeneration, fascism, extremism, racism, multiculturalism and many of the 'analytical polarisations' (Cumming, 2006:19) facing the District. The government's emphasis on cohesion widened the differences between those demanding racial justice and inequalities and those wanting to bridge divides and connect communities. The PPC organised debates to probe assumptions on all sides. A parallel series of public lectures invited key thinkers such as Bikhu Parekh to Bradford to inform and progress discussion. Sectors of the Muslim community wanted fresh approaches. A series of visits to Bradford by Sheikh Hamza Yusuf, an American-born Muslim scholar with progressive views on human rights drew in audiences of thousands of local Muslims, with many young people present. The PPC worked with the Islamic Society of Britain to bring important Muslim intellectuals, such as Tariq Ramadan, to Bradford.

## From Culture to Religion:
## Bradford in the Global Context

Already, however, international events, notably the invasion of Iraq, were making debate difficult. The idea of 'safe space' which had framed the PPC's work from its inception, was itself problematic and the PPC began to reflect on this as much as organise debates. One person's reasonable comment is another person's offensive remark. Some differences are deep and fundamental, particularly when religious belief is invoked. How do we deal with the 'right' to be homophobic on the basis of religious belief? Such issues were becoming more complex as belief rather than race entered the debate around inequalities, although the latter emphasised unchangeable distinctions while belief was about choice and values.

The PPC managed to bring people round the table in the post-riot aftermath who would not normally have interacted. It enabled police, politicians and council officers to share ideas with community activists, residents and academics around difficult issues. Organisations with experience of working on dialogue and deliberation in complex environments were brought to Bradford, such as Community Dialogue and Mediation Northern Ireland. The thirst for conceptual ideas to help interpret the problems facing the District as well as practical tools was palpable and these encounters built relationships. They also had some practical impact. In 2003, when we did the interviewing for this book, the Iraq war was at its height. Around the country a movement to Stop the War was organising rallies and marches, including one of the first, which took place in Bradford in February 2003. Again there were hundreds on the streets, from all communities in Bradford, but with an especially high representation of Asian men. The march, from Lister Park to Centenary Square, ending with a rally, was lively, passionate and chaotic, but it was entirely peaceful. Although the grievance at issue was very different to the riotous events of July 2001, what was notable was the way it was policed. As one of the organisers of the Anti-Nazi League rally in 2001 commented, the police were 'virtually not there'. A discussion in the PPC prior to the rally had suggested that the police needed to express their support for the public's right to protest and the police had done this in the press, stating that their job was to facilitate peaceful assembly. On the day they played a low-key role—'they weren't in riot gear' and it was 'handled very differently', as some of our interviewees noted.

The Madrid bombing in 2004 led to a new initiative in the District as perceived risks took a new turn. Fears grew of a similar incident in London, whilst there was concern that Bradford remained vulnerable to the fall-out from such an event. In Madrid, the local state had given strong leadership to bring the city's residents together against an attempt to blame Muslims for a bomb from extremists. The Civic Network was established to connect civic actors across the District from all walks of life, faiths and non-faiths, to build resilience in the face of a future shock. The Network therefore had a practical purpose. It asked people from the local media, schools, colleges and university, the NHS, police, the community and voluntary sector, the Youth Service, business and labour unions and all faiths to think about what they would do in their 'sector' in the event of an outrage like the Madrid bombing. The aim was to encourage each sector to organise its own discussions, though that proved a slow process. Meetings were hosted by the Bishop of Bradford and enabled a varied stream of people to give vent to ongoing anxieties about the situation in the District. When the London bombing took place on 7 July 2005, press releases were ready and the Network was convened immediately to attend a scheduled but rapidly re-themed PPC Annual Meeting on the anniversary of the riots. The message that the District would rally to support and the police to protect the Muslim community against any effort to target them went out and reassured that community. At the same time, the debate was opened up about why the bomb went off in the name of Islam.

Bradford was facing the fallout from a new twist in the District's fate: its insertion into a wider set of issues around Islam and the West. Islam had played no role in the riot, but in the aftermath it entered public consciousness as a factor of difference, following 9/11 and US and UK action in Afghanistan and Iraq. Local problems around de-industrialisation and poverty and their differential social impacts across communities, the role of racism and youth disaffection were now caught up in a much wider web of global and national problems. Islam became a much stronger marker of difference in the District and also of identity and victimisation. The Civic Network met a few times after the London bombing, with Muslim women coming for the first time to express their worries and fears. The Council of Mosques hosted one of the meetings and gave an opportunity to women to speak, and explained their plans for a citizenship programme. But soon it became clear that many Muslims in Bradford had been put on the defensive and were withdrawing into their communities. Some felt unable to share spaces such as the Civic Network, hosted by an Anglican Bishop, and where they were very sensitive to being constructed as 'the problem'. The 'War on Terror', declared by President Bush in 2001, was perceived to be against them. Religion, not culture, was now the defining boundary of belonging and not belonging. As one of the Muslim women we interviewed in 2011 put it:

> The unique thing is that in 2001, if you were a Muslim you were not visible, you looked more Asian, more cultural, what has turned for us was that actually, you know . . . the appearance of Bradford was [now] very much Muslim, which added the dimension that if anybody's going to get angry with this, if anyone was going to attack Asians they were going to attack Islam . . .

# 8

# 'THE DRUMS STARTED BEATING'— THE EDL COMES TO BRADFORD

*I know we succeeded as a city . . . when EDL happened, when the drums started beating . . . telephone kind of trees started, I started talking . . . In the last ten years, through the campaign, we've built our networks, we've built partners. We can trust the police, we can trust the local authority, we can trust our local youth centre, we can trust certain representatives that were in the community, and we are going to start sending a message out and say 'stay home'.*
**(Muslim woman, co-founder of Fair Justice, interview 2011)**

On 28 August 2010, Bradford faced another threat from the Far Right. The English Defence League came to Bradford. Their message was different to that of other Far Right groups who had targeted the city. Now it was specifically Muslims that were targeted. That day, the energies of hundreds of Bradfordians from all communities, faiths and generations as well as politicians, council officers and the police came together to prevent another riot. Much effort focussed on young male British Muslims, a generation down from the rioters of 2001. We now use the term: 'British Muslim', in deference to the spread of this label (self and by others) in the course of the 2000s. It was young male British Muslims that the EDL intended to provoke into street violence with their protest, but instead many participated in preventing another riot. The success of this collective effort has hugely benefited the District and its community relationships. Bradford now faces its many challenges more confidently than before.

Bradfordians, old and new, share a liking for forthright, outspoken convictions. As one of our former rioters, re-interviewed

Saturday Night and Sunday Morning

in 2011 put it: 'I love saying I'm from Bradford, it has a reputation everywhere . . . it's a strong minded place'. A Conservative Councillor interviewed in 2011 described Bradfordians in similar terms as 'quirky and opinionated . . . a degree of self confidence without wishing to display it'. Listening to other views, changing one's mind and looking to the future not the past are not always easy for the strong minded. Despite this, Bradford's collective achievement in August 2010 was to forge unity of purpose against the EDL protest. Networking and communication at all levels, from politicians to police, from activists to angry young men generated that success. However, sustaining it remains an ongoing challenge.

# 'A Field of Fire and Failure'?: Bradford Braces Itself

*The last thing people wanted to see was cars going up in flames and the place being torched, because Bradford's regeneration [would be] over. The city would have . . . gone . . . what would the city be? Just a place to come and have race riots . . . it would just be a field of fire, of failure and everybody didn't want that to happen.*
**(Council Officer, 2011)**

*. . . I think I was mindful of the fact that Bradford has had this sort of shadow or a cloud over it since the 2001 riots. And it's always, sort of hung there. It's been one of those areas that people—locals—don't really want to talk about or go there, but national press and commentators are always referring back to 2001.*
**(Safer and Stronger Communities Officer, 2011)**

The 2001 riot was indeed the dark cloud hovering over attempts to prevent another riot in 2010. The Dean of the Cathedral, a relative newcomer to Bradford, noted that the 'level of fear and anxiety was acute amongst those who experienced the riots. Those of us who have come to the city since then have a . . . slightly broader perspective.' A number felt remorse that they had not done more in 2001. In 1995 a member of the Bradford Women for Peace group had joined Interfaith Women for Peace and carried a peace banner up Oak Lane:

> it had . . . somehow calmed things down. So . . . when the second
> [riot] was happening [2001] and the police said whatever you do stay

at home, don't go into town . . . I obeyed them and stayed at home, and then felt bad afterwards, that I hadn't been active. So when I heard about the EDL one, I was determined that something should happen.

A Chamber of Commerce officer remembered that in 2001, the police had given business leaders categorical assurances that they were in control of the situation around the proposed NF march. He acknowledged a 'rising sense of anxiety' in 2010:

> we had been reassured before, ten years ago, and that came to nothing. But we had to send out the messages that there was business as usual . . . but what we were saying in public was different to what we were feeling in private . . . I was really worried . . . I'd seen the police videos [of the 2001 riot] and it's really, really scary . . . Ten years ago we'd seen in the images the Asian elders trying to control the younger ones and it not working.

The Muslim community felt the pressure intensely. The overriding fear was how the young men might respond, it was 'about managing and containing the response from Asian men, young Asian men . . . because of 2001. And . . . I think that was the biggest fear', said a Muslim council officer involved in community cohesion and engagement. Community activists were picking up on varied responses in that community, as one Muslim woman recalled:

> . . . I remember some brothers were saying, the best thing we can do is ignore them . . . I'm not even going to go down there, that's what they [the EDL] want. These were scholars, people who were devout. But on the flip side, you heard some saying, 'let's give it to them like we gave it to them in 2001'.

A clear difference with 2001 was the specific targeting of Muslims by this new Far Right tendency. The Council of Mosques described the burden of having to display the positive contribution of Muslims:

> Hang on, with them coming here we've got to be stronger in ourselves, to show them the positive side of Muslims in Bradford, because we were actually targeted by them, just the Muslim community. So, therefore, we felt that we need to rise above their thoughts and their thinking . . . and, make sure that [nothing] happened with our youth . . . and we got the message out to the mosques and to the youth . . . that they need to play their role and show the positive side of us, rather than . . . [the] negative which is normally . . . sort of lumbered onto us by the media (interview, 2011).

## 'Learning Curves': From the NF to the BNP to the EDL

After 2001 the Far Right did not disappear from Bradford. The British National Party (BNP) was attempting to enter electoral and mainstream politics, and had a growing base in the city. Their

Saturday Night and Sunday Morning

presence in Eccleshill the night before the 2001 riot was no accident. This had once been a National Front power base. The BNP (in the eyes of an anti-fascist campaigner) was happy to let the NF 'do the spadework and take the political gain'. The National Front, however, had always been about street violence rather than serious politics. As soon as the Far Right entered mainstream politics anti-fascist tactics had to enter a 'learning curve'. They began to 'bring politics into anti-fascism and anti-fascism into politics'. But this strategy soon suffered a blow. The 'hammer on the head' was a surprise BNP victory in a bye-election in Mixenden, Halifax in 2003. The Trades Council had leafleted intensively to expose the thuggish behaviour of the candidate, but now began to question this negative campaigning. With support from the Joseph Rowntree Charitable Trust, research was commissioned which showed that women had hated the leaflets. They realised that they needed to be more positive and produce something people wanted to read and which addressed actual concerns and anxieties. Some anti-fascist campaigners began to 'march off in different directions to far left groups'. Others regrouped. Hope not Hate was born 'in a pub down the road', and formally set up in 2005 as a national politically non-aligned campaigning arm of *Searchlight*, the anti-racist and anti-fascist magazine. It emphasised localised campaigning and working 'within communities where organised racists are attracting their support' (http://www.hopenothate.org.uk/about-us/).

Meanwhile the Socialist Workers Party (SWP) was on another journey. The party shut down the Anti-Nazi League and argued that anti-fascism must be led by those directly threatened by fascism. The SWP was already strongly involved in the popular Stop the War coalition, and thereby won support particularly amongst more politically-minded Muslims. Unite Against Fascism (UAF) was another national organisation, set up in late 2003, which attracted a broad constituency of political support. Its joint secretaries were both from minority ethnic communities, and one was a member of the SWP. Some suspected it was a recruitment front for the SWP. The UAF argued for confronting the BNP and preventing it gaining an electoral foothold. It appealed to a range of political opinion anxious to halt the march of the far right, on the streets if necessary.

As anti-fascists diverged, the BNP was on the political rise in Bradford. In the 2004 council election, where all 90 seats were contested, they won four—at Keighley West, Wyke, Worth Valley and Wibsey (by seven votes). 'That was a desperate time', recalled one anti-fascist campaigner. In July that year, the *Secret Agent* was screened, based on the experience of a former BNP member from Eccleshill who had defected to the anti-fascist campaign but remained undercover. Campaigners had intended it to come out before the election. The programme exposed BNP activists discussing firebombing vehicles, bombing mosques and shooting Muslims. A Bradford BNP councillor was heard urging party workers to change their behaviour: 'We do not want knuckle scrapers, piercings and baseball bats. Anything like that will not win votes' (*T&A*, 27 August 2004). Two men from Bradford and two from Keighley were arrested shortly after the film was screened.

In 2005, the leader of the BNP, Nick Griffin, stood as parliamentary candidate in Keighley. This time the campaign against him emphasised talking to local people about their anxieties. Leaflets were tailored to each locality. Anti-fascist campaigners undertook 'proper, old-fashioned community development work', organising discussions with local people. Some participants admitted they had voted BNP, but that was set aside. The sessions explored people's likes and dislikes about their area, listing each on flipcharts. The things they liked far outnumbered what they did not. One campaigner described a discussion on the predominantly white Braithwaite estate in Keighley. 'They started off . . . "Well the Pakis get all the money"'. He was ready with his response:

> What are the facts? Well they do! The SRB [Single Regeneration Budget, funding for deprived neighbourhoods] area was drawn around the Asian area . . . [but] the EDs [sub-ward Enumeration Districts] with the greatest deprivation were the 'white' bits at the side. Actually they were right! We think it's unfortunate how some of this regeneration money is doled out. However, are there some bigger pictures here? A million pounds on an SRB, how does that adequately deal with 25 years of de-industrialisation? . . . How does a million pound SRB work as a plaster over that? Across the road, they have been better organised, they have lobbied and they have played the regeneration game better than you, they've played the 'ugly contest' . . . you've got to prove that your area is shitty to attract some money. How destructive and soul-destroying is that? At the end of the sessions, it were about . . . what residents think they need most, how do we organise effectively to attract what we need? It may not always be money. It might be self organisation that we can build up that can improve where we live . . . The subtext of all that is that the BNP can't provide any of this and actually, for Keighley we need to be working with the [Asian] people who've got the SRB, because they'll have got the experience, knowledge and knowhow we need to tap into. And there was a dawning understanding that Braithwaite doesn't exist in isolation and neither does Keighley and that another world is possible.

This kind of political work succeeded. Mothers from the local Surestart, who had all voted BNP at the last election, turned the tide. Griffin lost, though with 4,240 votes, 9.2% of the total.

Increasingly the target of BNP activists became 'Muslims' rather than 'immigrants'. Here they capitalised on rising anti-Muslim feeling following 9/11 and the London bombing in 2005. Nick Griffin conceded their cynical ploy—to 'take advantage for our own political ends of the growing wave of public hostility to Islam currently being whipped up by the mass media' (BNP website, 21 March 2006 http://en.wikipedia.org/wiki/British_National_Party). In 2006, they lost three councillors in Bradford and gained only one in Queensbury. However, they polled an unprecedented number of votes in eight other wards, winning 25.9% of the vote in the District. A local pharmaceutical company manager, Dr Mohammed Iqbal, expressed his concern at this outcome in the *T&A* (22 May 2006), but added that:

> Despite the anxieties and stress caused by the BNP successes, I would still rather live in this beautiful city and in Britain than in any Muslim country. Undoubtedly, Nick Griffin, and others in the BNP are extremists and intolerant of people from other faiths and cultures— but I can equally point to a great many Muslim Imams and Muslims in the UK and elsewhere who are intolerant of other faiths and cultures that do not think or do as they insist. However, these Imams and Muslims have nothing to do with Islam, and the BNP has very little to do with the Greatness of Britain.

The BNP now appeared to have reached its peak in Bradford. Its share of the vote dropped to 19.2% in 2007 (http://www.hopenothate.org.uk/2007/). It hung on only to its two Queensbury councillors, and began to fragment. In national elections however, the BNP more than doubled its vote between 2001 and 2010, from 192,000 to 563,000, but this was much less than their peak of nearly one million in the European elections of 2009, at the height of public hostility over MPs' expenses. The BNP's heartlands remain the Pennines, Leicestershire and Essex (Biggs and Knauss, 2011:4). In 2010, the BNP had not deepened its vote in these areas, although there was evidence of some widening of votes to other areas of the country (ICOCO:18). In 2011, researchers used a leaked BNP membership list to analyse factors which explain attraction to this party. It concluded: that the BNP only thrives where there is little interaction between whites and non-whites (particularly south Asians or Muslims) rather than where whites have a substantial proportion of non-white neighbours. Close contact among neighbours breaks down racial prejudice. They conclude, 'segregation aids the BNP' (Biggs and Knauss, 2011:11). De facto segregation remained an issue in Bradford throughout the 2000s, even though Asians of Pakistani heritage were moving into traditionally 'white' estates and some to more affluent areas. There were fewer 'white' dominated neighbourhoods, but overall, the white population remained concentrated in areas of least diversity.

Support for the BNP, both nationally and in Bradford, remained associated with a racial, nationalist subculture and represented an older, male, working class politics around race and immigration (Goodwin, 2010:187). In the meantime, a new debate focussed on the value of 'Britishness', amidst fears amongst 'white' working class people that newcomers would further threaten their livelihoods and heritage. Ideas for defending 'white' British culture began to find fertile ground amongst people who would never associate themselves with the Far Right (Ford, 2010:150). As the Welsh, Northern Irish and Scots found political expression of their own in Assemblies and the Scottish Parliament, attention narrowed further around an elusive idea of 'Englishness'. However, 'Englishness' was usually defined against two groups in particular: immigrants and Muslims (Ford, 2010:151). Polls revealed that a significant minority of British voters would deny legal migrants the same rights as British citizens and believed British Muslims were more loyal to Muslims abroad than to non-Muslim Britons (ibid).

In 2011 the Searchlight Educational Trust commissioned a large-scale survey across the country in order to investigate attitudes towards English identity, faith and race. The survey confirmed deep resentment about immigration—a resentment shared amongst established Black and Asian minority groups. Although they considered ethnicity and religion more important to their own identity than nationality, the Asians polled were quite relaxed about displays of English patriotism and nearly as proud of flying the St George's flag as the 'white' population (Lowles and Painter, 2011:25). Minority ethnic groups shared majority fears about the impact of immigration on their personal economic situation. In Bradford tensions grew in the 2000s between Asian residents and new Eastern European migrants.

The survey also showed that the vast majority of British people reject political violence and view white anti-Muslim extremists as being as bad as Muslim extremists. However, it also showed 'popular' support for a 'sanitised, non-violent and non-racist English nationalist political party' (ibid:10). At the same time, 60% of those polled supported positive approaches—education, community organising and using key communal movers and shakers to defeat local extremism. The picture is therefore ambiguous—a new awareness of 'Englishness' but little support for an extremist party to assert this. There is scepticism towards multiculturalism but majority support for a campaigning approach to oppose political extremism and bring communities together (ibid:11).

The English Defence League (EDL) was set up in 2009, following a demonstration by Al-Muhajiroun in Wootton Basset, the small

English town which had begun to organise tributes to 'fallen heroes' from the Afghan war. The EDL hoped to channel the emergence of 'English' national sentiment amongst working class people into mobilisation specifically against Muslims. It sought to distinguish itself from the Far Right, showing itself to be liberal on gay rights and recognising the contribution from others to 'English' culture. However, 'this does not give license to policy makers to deliberately undermine our culture and impose non-English cultures on the English people in their own land', it argued in its mission statement (quoted in ICCO, 2011:21). The hard core of the EDL was football supporters and 'hooligans'. It built on 'firms' associated with major clubs, now overriding their rivalries to defend 'England'. Thugs known for football violence were picked out at the protests the EDL began to organise in cities across the country. Although the BNP distanced itself from the EDL, known Far Right activists were spotted at EDL protests. Thirteen took place before they came to Bradford in August 2010. EDL tactics were to instigate street level confrontations, mobilising support with dire warnings about Muslim extremism using internet social network sites. In Bradford, they knew there was a large population of inner-city Muslim youth and billed their protest there as the 'Big One'. Bradford's Muslim youth had been provoked into violence once. They had paid the price, not the Far Right. The EDL provocation in 2010 would test how far the District had come since 2001 in building resilience against the Far Right.

# 'New Shoots and Hopes': Bradford against the EDL 2010

> *It had to be this one colour. It was conceptual . . . because it was the colour of vibrancy, of fresh new ideas and growth . . . the growth of optimism, of positivity against the negativity of hatred from the EDL, new shoots and hopes . . . It packed a punch [but was] neutral politically and religiously. It had a message intrinsically, in its vibrancy.*
> **(Bradford Women for Peace activist, on the 'green ribbon', symbol of Bradford's stance against the EDL)**

The EDL declared their intention to come to Bradford in May 2010 but then cancelled their plan. They turned up unexpectedly in the city centre on 25 June at the 3rd Yorks Battalion Homecoming

Parade. An estimated 100–150 members appeared and marched behind the army. Some shouted 'Muslim bombers off our streets'. Their T-shirts showed that they were almost all from outside Bradford. Observers we interviewed reported that around 40 incensed Asian lads had to be restrained. Anti-fascist campaigners were angry that the police had let the EDL 'march' in the city at all, though the police argued that it was not a march and they could not stop them supporting the troops. When the EDL finally confirmed they would march in Bradford on 28 August, a bank holiday in the middle of Ramadan, anxieties were high. However, the advance warning proved invaluable. When the EDL came, the District was prepared. The contrast with 2001 could not be starker.

Hope not Hate called for a ban on the march and for 'business as usual' in Bradford. They were backed by the council. A ban the march petition, supported by the *Telegraph and Argus*, gathered 10,000 signatures. West Yorkshire police, treading a tightrope between the right to protest and the threat to public safety posed by the EDL, secured the ban. This did not prevent the EDL from organising a static protest. But the petition sent an important early message that Bradfordians opposed the EDL protest, though it was soon clear that they were divided about how to express their opposition. A local group, 'We are Bradford', affiliated to the national organisation, Unite Against Fascism (UAF), wanted a political counter protest. The UAF had already organised demonstrations against the EDL and this had sometimes led to violent clashes. Some feared that the national body was insensitive to the risks of such an outcome in Bradford. These concerns led a third group, 'Be Bradford: Peaceful Together', to organise a multicultural celebration in Infirmary Fields, on the route of the 2001 riots, for those who neither wanted to stay at home, nor to confront the EDL. Bradford Women For Peace, a group of local and professional women, Asian and white, provided the District with a symbol of unity amongst these distinct and sometimes acrimonious positions—the green ribbon.

A group of young women festooned as much of the city centre as they could with the ribbons before the event. On the Friday morning, 27 August, the day before the EDL protest, Bradford Women for Peace gathered in a small square at the bottom of Ivegate. They set up a 'tree' at one side on which people could post messages of peace. There was a table with green ribbons and cards to take away with the message: 'women standing together in peace, unity and solidarity for a peaceful Bradford'. Women of all ethnicities and faiths attended, some dressed in green, some with green sashes. They formed a circle singing a peace song and weaving

Saturday Night and Sunday Morning

a web with their green ribbons. Soon all kinds of people were seen around the town, wearing the ribbons, tying them to pushchairs and bags. A senior council officer told us later that he felt the women 'set the mood in the city for the whole weekend and it was immensely powerful'. He also acknowledged how, like many, he had been taken by surprise:

> Actually it challenged me and made me give myself a bit of a telling-off for being so sceptical about the role that women play in dealing with . . . potential conflict. It set a very peaceful, but stoically determined mood that resonated.

Around 5.30pm, a peace vigil was organised by Hope not Hate outside the council offices in Jacobs Well. There were speakers from all the faiths as well as trade unionists and activists and they sang: 'We shall overcome'. The atmosphere was tense and expectant.

The green ribbon seemed to weave its way through the city centre over the next 24 hours. On the day of the EDL protest, taxi drivers tied ribbons to their car aerials, and as we walked through Manningham to join the peace celebration early on that day, Asian shopkeepers came out to greet us when they saw them. 'It was like capturing a wave' suggested one of the women peace activists:

> it was like surfing, we caught the wave . . . the timing, you know. If we'd had another couple of weeks it might have tipped over, we might have lost it . . . For me it was the most visually powerful, purely activist thing that I've been involved in. It was effective because there were no words on the ribbon, because people had conversations because there were no words on the ribbon . . . We could dress buildings, there was a huge piece of green cloth to dress the Cathedral. It was just a piece of green cloth. There were no words on it, but it tied in. It was all resonating . . . Everyone was driven on by their conviction that the most important thing was to rescue Bradford from the clutches of the EDL, everyone was powered on by that . . .

The following day, several hundred EDL supporters were bussed into the city and corralled into Bradford's Urban Garden. The EDL knew that their very presence, even under tight police control, would be a provocation to Muslim youth. The police aim was to prevent the EDL from appearing to march, even from the buses to the garden. Now fenced off, this was a city centre space earmarked for the retail regeneration of the city which had stalled. At least 1,400 police officers were on hand to keep the peace in an operation which cost around a million pounds. Many shops stayed open to give a sense of normality. Curious shoppers mixed with crowds gathered in nearby streets to observe and, in some cases, to protest the arrival of the EDL. In the course of the noisy protest, three weddings took place in the city centre. As the EDL got off the buses, a group of youths (some Asian, some white) began chanting 'Fascist Scum! Off our streets!' The police moved them back onto the other side of the road so there was no close confrontation. Members of the EDL were 'chanting vile anti-Islamic abuse' (*T&A*, 30 August 2010). They carried banners saying 'Stop Sharia Law', 'No More Mosques', 'Keep Paedophiles Off Our Estates'. A couple of hundred members of the UAF from in and outside Bradford, protested outside the law courts, out of sight of the EDL, as they had agreed in their negotiations with the police. The celebration event attracted similar numbers of mostly local people in Infirmary Fields.

Two moments of drama were quickly brought under control at the Urban Garden. Just after 2pm the EDL started throwing smoke bombs, glass bottles, cans and stones, and there was a surge from the EDL against the barrier of police bodies. There were brawls amongst those in the Garden. A second surge around 3.30pm led to a group of EDL supporters getting over the barrier fences, storming past Foster Square Station and erupting amongst bystanders on Cheapside and Manor Row. A small mob of Asian youngsters gathered immediately, geared up for trouble, but the EDL thugs were soon rounded up. In addition to the EDL, members of a group calling itself the Muslim Defence League, mainly from outside Bradford, made its appearance on the day and were seen racing up and down Cheapside after the EDL broke out, but the police ensured that neither they nor local youth got near the breakaway group. Agencies and individuals were in constant communication with young men ready to 'kick off', calming them down and dealing with scare stories picked up from the social networking site, Twitter. Police were there ready to control the situation. At 5.30pm, the last EDL coaches left the city and once the news that they had left was communicated to the young men they and the crowds dispersed. As we shall see, many lads had been taken out of the city or enticed into snooker halls to remove them from potential trouble-making. The prevention of violence on the day was the outcome of months of preparation, in which many local actors applied learning from the 2001 riot. Those closely involved in the operation admit to some anxiety as EDL supporters clambered over the barrier fence. They held their nerve. Trouble was avoided but only thanks to an immense collective effort.

# The Ghost of 2001 Laid to Rest

*There were senior politicians, both local and MPs who were vehement in saying 'you cannot bring the EDL here. Bradford can't take this. We'll have a riot. A riot is the inevitable consequence'. And . . . [we] were saying to them, 'No, actually, we've got to be more confident in our city'. And actually, the message, if we say they can't come here at all, what we're saying is our city is not a normal place, and our city cannot cope with freedom of speech, and our city can't be resilient in the future to those outcomes. Yes . . . at the start of this process, we're a bit scared about the consequences of all of this, but we will front that up. We'll deal with it, and we've got to manage this situation. We've got to get those people in and out of our city without derailing the city, and let the people get on with their lives and do it confidently, so we enhance Bradford and diminish the EDL. If we do that, Bradford will take a big step forward.*
**(Senior Council Officer, 2011)**

*. . . the most important aspect is that people who really cared about Bradford, who actually have had lots of abuse about the regeneration of the city and things not happening . . . boy oh boy did they pull out their fingers and get everything done. They phenomenally worked. They worked hard every day . . . I remember being in the emergency planning room about 9 o'clock on the Friday evening, and it was myself and the emergency planner who was in charge. We were so knackered, we ate half a chocolate cake, it was massive. I've never seen slices like it. We each had one, just sitting there drinking tea and looking at the screens, thinking, I ought to go to bed . . .*
**(Another Senior Council Officer, 2011)**

### Planning, Partnerships and Policing

Unlike 2001, there was real leadership from politicians in 2010. The council was hung as it had been throughout the 2000s. The largest party since May 2010 was Labour, with close connections to the inner city. Its leader was proud to trace his family back 500 years in

Bradford. He understood the Asian as well as white working class communities. The Deputy Leader, an Asian councillor, came himself from the inner-city Asian community. He was a member of the generation who had rioted in 2001. He led the community engagement strategy for the council, working closely with 14 to 19 year old lads in the community to strengthen the messages of self restraint against EDL provocation. He urged them, against the instincts of many, to trust the police this time. The Liberal Democrats, who held the balance of power, wanted to turn the Bradford response to the EDL into something positive for the District, not to simply wait for the 'storm' to pass, but to harness it to fundamental change. The leader of the party saw her role as to 'open as many doors as possible. To allow as many people to do what they wanted to do, but to have a close connection to the institutional plans and policies and make sure that we weren't stepping over on too many toes'. The Conservatives, with their stronger connections to the urban villages, were less willing to get engaged. However, some did. One stood out amongst his colleagues in calling for a more honest and open debate in the District:

> Well, I hope the recognition that we've got to live together whether we like it or not . . . I mean . . . I've always felt that there's two imperatives that drive it: one is moral—that people should be more equal . . . or they should have more equal opportunities and they should respect each other . . . and have some self respect and self pride. And then, the other is just the imperative of sheer common sense—that you can't live in Wharfedale if the inner city is in flames.

On the morning of 28 August, all party leaders toured the city centre in a demonstration of anti-EDL unity. A senior council officer described:

> the collective leadership . . . and the atmosphere it created in the city, and the determination not to go back to 2001 . . . people put their political agendas to one side for the good of Bradford, and you know, I'd thank them for that, quite frankly.

Partnerships between statutory bodies and council officers and attention to detail stand out as Bradford's key institutions prepared for the EDL. The city centre was a regeneration building site in 2010. The opportunities for makeshift weapons were everywhere. Preparing the city centre was a massive operation:

> We poured vast amounts of concrete, loads of steel, bolted all the fencing . . . took away all the bins and anything at all that could be thrown in that whole area . . . we blocked off big chunks of the city so it couldn't move. We also designed a structure that meant that the fencing couldn't be rushed—so that none of the fencing could be taken up and used as ramming barriers. So we did some overnight

engineering and came up with a structure and then bolted that all the way through. It wasn't until probably 7 o'clock on Friday night . . . I was still out there, with a team bolting them together, and at this stage, I had done nothing other than this for two weeks (senior Council Officer).

The police were the lynchpin of a multi-agency operation, with a markedly different approach to 2001. We interviewed police at a range of levels and ranks once again in 2011. They had learnt a great deal from 2001, done that 'radical rethinking' and were very open about this in conversations with us. One senior commander who had not been around in 2001 but had reflected a great deal on the police operation at the time, acknowledged that the police had not then been 'good firefighters' as the trigger events in Ivegate and Sunbridge Road erupted:

relationships had got to such a fraught stage at that point and the police's understanding of their role was quite remote . . . it wasn't proactive, it wasn't focussed on neighbourhood policing, it wasn't actually understanding its role in the build-up of community tensions and its role with other partners and the likes of the local authority and other agencies to try and defuse that tension, that sense of distrust and lack of understanding from different communities. All those things that we do now as a matter of course, as a matter of fact, community impact assessments, community tension reports, information gathering from the Neighbourhood Policing Teams (NPTs) constantly being assessed . . . none of that was happening [in 2001]. So when it went off, it went off big style . . . and the police was often reactive to dealing with that . . . this was spontaneous combustion and in terms of the danger and the risk of that combustion in a public order sense, we weren't good firefighters, you know, because the training, the equipment, the command structure . . . we're much stronger today because we've learnt from that.

As in 2001, police officers we interviewed acknowledged their own passion for the city most of them grew up in, and how much they personally felt the threat posed by the EDL. This time, they had wider and deeper connections to all communities and understood much better the impact of Far Right hatred. Most were also sceptical about the intentions of the UAF. The police also recognised the changing nature of protest and counter protest: 'We understood that the community would want to do something. We understood, looking nationally, that there was likely to be a counter protest . . .' explained a senior member of the police community engagement team. They had to facilitate peaceful protest, while acknowledging local anger about the EDL being allowed to come to Bradford. They grappled with differences amongst activists about how to express their anger and with those who wanted the EDL simply to be refused access. They spent a lot of time explaining the limits to police powers and organised a meeting on human rights for key actors in the city so that everyone understood the arguments around policing protest. The EDL had wanted to march down Manchester Road, in the heart of the Asian community. Protesters do not have the right to choose their location, and a specialised team began protracted negotiations with the EDL and the UAF over where their static protests would be held. The police request for a government ban on the march won them confidence amongst communities. In the end most accepted that the EDL could not be prevented from organising a static protest, but some felt that the campaign for the ban had delayed preparing for the protest at the grass roots level.

The police attribute much of the effectiveness of the approach to the EDL to a shift to neighbourhood policing: 'Community engagement is the rock on which any operation is built'. They acknowledge the importance of talking to everyone in everyday contexts rather than a few spokespeople in emergency situations—not 'parachuting in to have a conversation when they want one'. Since 2001 they have invested a huge amount of time in building relationships and trust, getting to know the local issues and understanding why communities feel under threat. This enabled them to play a key role in bringing people together in the community with local authority and other agencies in preparation for the EDL protest. Through the command structure and the communications strategy, they were able to ensure a flow of information, damp down rumours and constantly monitor tension points. Findings were fed rapidly back to community and operational actors, and the latter reciprocated. The information flow was critical to calming tensions, and rested on the relationships between police and council and between these and the community.

The council's communication team worked with the police to ensure coordinated responses to rumours, which everyone knew had stirred passions in 2001: 'The most important thing is that people got the right information. Because when these situations escalate it's often because of rumour and people are reacting to rumour', the leader of the team told us in 2011. They monitored the social networking site, Twitter, throughout the day, a means of instant communication which made the mobile phone of 2001 seem almost old-fashioned. These more organised communication flows were complemented by the personal contacts of many actors committed to keep the peace in the city that day. From a vantage point in one of the operation centres, council community engagement staff kept a look out for danger. They checked rumours against the police log and then got on their mobiles and texted or phoned people in the city centre to quash them. When they saw young Asians on their video screens gathering in Cheapside after the EDL breakout, they

Saturday Night and Sunday Morning

located people they knew in the crowd and rang them up. As one of the team vividly recalled:

> I got a message—this guy's telling people things are kicking off . . . I rang up [the guy] . . . I've had a message that quite a few people near where you are now, are telling people things are kicking off and that they should come down here . . . can you see anyone doing that? Can you just make sure that anyone around you, that you have influence over, says no? . . . The police need to move people on . . . The best case for us is if you and other[s] there can encourage people to move away because, if the police come it looks different . . . Are you fasting? . . . God and I are going to hold you responsible if anything goes wrong in Bradford today.

In this way, risks of police interventions which might have heightened tensions were pre-empted.

The Youth Service also buried some ghosts of 2001: 'We are very clear from the 2001 experience, that it is not the youth workers' role to be on the street trying to mediate', they told us. This compromises the relationships they build up with young people. Their role is to do the 'underpinning' work: 'what we can do, what's been very successful and we've proven that on this EDL, is that we can utilise our relationships and our ability to engage with [young] people on the margins . . . ' They spent the post-riot decade trying to work on all kinds of prejudice expressed by young people—racism, sexism, homophobia. The EDL was for them a kind of test of how far their work had prepared young people to resist provocation. A small card, the 'Consequences Card', played an important role in communicating the risks to the youngsters in the weeks before the EDL protest. The Card began 'In the [2001] Bradford riots, 191 people were given prison sentences totalling more than 510 years. This could be you if . . . ' The Youth Service educated the young people they worked with, many of them the brothers, sons and nephews of those involved in the 2001 riot, about what the law could do, alerted them that the police would film and could trace mobile phone numbers. They used the Card to start conversations in a natural way. The trust of communities and solid relationships with young people built up over time, helped a great deal. They did not engage in 'targeting problem individuals' but reached as many young people as possible. This ground work enabled them to build a momentum leading up to August 2010.

They also built better working relationships with the police: 'The police have tried to definitely change the way they approach young people, communities . . . there has been a definite progression over the last ten years'. On the day, the Youth Service organised diversionary activities, taking around 1,000 kids out of the city to events, such as a Manchester United football game, that most could never otherwise have dreamed of attending. Youth workers were on high alert throughout the day, with detached workers intercepting youngsters in the city centre who looked as if they might cause trouble. They judged that most young people, whether 'white' or Asian, had come together against those trying to disrupt their city: 'Although we have got pockets of racism, we have pockets of stuff around the EDL and National Front . . . there was a sense of they have no right to do this. They are not doing this to us' (interview with Youth Service manager, 2011).

## 'We as a Community Have Moved on': The Fabric of Resilience

The Youth Service were not the only ones working with young people in the lead up to the EDL protest. The Council of Mosques liaised closely with the Youth Service and the police to send out messages to parents and their children: a youth worker said:

> We were writing to mosques saying: 'This is what we would like you to do . . . disseminate information. Give the information to parents and families that they need to make sure that they keep their children safe . . .' Also, we were asking mosques . . . can they do some alternative activities with these young people? And we were saying the same to community centres . . . There were also a number of public meetings . . . There were some difficult times as well, where we had to justify why our stand is the way [it is].

The Council of Mosques had brought out its own Community Engagement strategy in 2009 (Ahmed and Reid, 2009). Their active involvement in the Muslim community's response to the EDL as well as with Bradford's response as a whole was an important moment for the District. They talked to us of how impressive it was to watch young people, actively working to keep the peace alongside elders, police officers and politicians: 'here were the young people making a statement, they were taking responsibility for the city. And, that's something, you know, that says that: We as a community have moved on' (Council of Mosques staff member, interviewed 2011).

A number of former rioters warned younger lads not to get involved. Some did so through the mosques, and some informally, alerting their younger brothers, sons and nephews to the dangers. One had set up an organisation to help young people into jobs. He and others played an important role on the day, getting lads free sessions in a city centre snooker hall. He had close contacts with 'hard to reach' kids, those most vulnerable to provocation. He had picked up Facebook conversations where they looked back to what their elder brothers did in 2001: 'It's our turn now', they were saying. He spent time quashing rumours and reminding the lads of what

Saturday Night and Sunday Morning

would happen if they got involved. These lads thrive on the 'respect' they get from Bradford's tough reputation, he told us. He had to remind them of the cost of the last riot and what could have been done with the money, and the higher house and car insurance that residents paid afterwards. The message resonated with a car-loving youth. There were many other youth and community organisations in the inner city who took part in activities with young people to keep them off the streets on 28 August—organisations like the West Bowling Youth Initiative, with over two decades experience of working with such young people.

Two well-connected and committed Muslim women at the centre of the community engagement work in the council's Safer and Stronger Communities team, played a particularly active role in bringing people together in the often fraught weeks before the protest day. They disseminated information, sowed the seeds for 'Women for Peace' and strengthened partnerships with faith groups and community and voluntary sector organisations. They facilitated a lot of difficult conversations when people felt that the council leadership were not doing enough or were not accessible or visible enough.

Churches as well as mosques contributed, appealing to their congregations to sign the ban petition. Bradford District Faiths Forum, set up in 2006, brought all the religious organisations in the District together, and was a key player in the EDL planning and preparation. At the University, the Programme for a Peaceful City facilitated 'keep it calm' workshops with the council and helped activists have conversations with decision makers, encouraging everyone to think through the pros and cons of different approaches. They used their own connections, built up over many years, to keep in touch with people who had street level influence. Amongst others they worked with 'graduates' from the Inter-Cultural Leadership School (ICLS), as part of a 'Stop it Kicking Off Network' on the day. The information they transmitted was trusted and was another means by which rumours could be discounted. Just West Yorkshire, set up in 2003 by the Joseph Rowntree Charitable Trust, focussed on racial justice and raised critical questions around policing and civil liberties in the lead up to 28 August. It supported Bradford Women for Peace, along with the community organisation group, Changemakers, set up in 2009 and the Joseph Rowntree Foundation's Bradford Programme set up in 2004 to research social problems in Bradford.

Multiple individual as well as professional and community relationships were at the heart of the responses 'from below' to the EDL. There were tensions and differences in the way people thought about efforts to prevent disturbances. Whilst policy makers made efforts to disseminate information and ensure communication at all levels, not everyone was 'in the loop'. Some disagreed politically with the strategy, others simply wanted to 'do something' and felt bypassed by the power holders in the District. Varied motivations complicated the panorama. However, the fabric of resilience lay in the connections people had built since 2001, which did not reveal how robust they were until the EDL forced people to draw on them. Nevertheless, the outcome of the day was never guaranteed. Hierarchical structures and the instinct to control remained obstacles to truly fluid relationships between those acting 'from below' with those making decisions 'from above'. Young men known to be at risk had been taken out of the city, but many 'unreachable' by agencies remained. Whilst there was a remarkable attention to all possible eventualities and a sense of relief that peace was maintained, there had been some dangerous moments.

# 9

# CONCLUSION:
# BRADFORD JOURNEY

*I think we've come a long way. I think what we have now is a different narrative . . . we can actually say: 'The EDL came last time and couldn't destabilise us, because we're a strong city' . . . And I think there's a sense of confidence . . . a new sense of pride . . . I think those relationships and those networks are still there, you know for us to utilise. And people feel that . . . they have played a part . . . maybe in 2001, there was a sense of guilt. I think we've moved away to a sense of achievement, and that's a good thing for Bradford.*
**(Safer and Stronger Communities Officer, 2011)**

## 'A Different Narrative':
## Overcoming the 'Bradford Syndrome'?

The years since the London bombing of 2005 had been particularly hard for the District. The idea of 'community cohesion' sat uneasily alongside 'counter terrorism' and the government's 'Prevent' agenda (Husband and Alam, 2011). Many Muslims felt that they were under scrutiny—by state institutions, the media and the Far Right—simply for being 'Muslim'. The District's underlying socio-economic situation remained very fragile, and was further weakened by the banking crisis and recession of 2008. City centre regeneration had not materialised in the time frame expected. Bradfordians were disgruntled by the endless building works in the city centre. The council marketing team acknowledged in an interview in 2011 that the constant invention of new positive images of the District had made Bradfordians more negative about their future:

> . . . so many massive mistakes in marketing . . . it just bred cynicism . . . the problem with Bradford is there's been a lot of publicity, a lot of hype and a lot of expectation raised that's not been delivered. That's why people are so cynical. So what we do now, is we don't hype, we don't use language like 'first class' and 'iconic', nothing's iconic till people see it and experience it . . . There's been a lot of expensive and over-the-top marketing which hasn't been appropriate to the nature of Bradford.

On the other hand, many Bradfordians were unwilling to recognise the strengths of the District. They spoke highly of their particular locality and neighbourhood, but not of the 'whole'. A former *Telegraph and Argus* journalist who had returned to Bradford in 2001 just after the riot identified what she called, the 'Bradford Syndrome':

> It's a strange condition, betraying a sense of lost pride, an inability to hold fast to the bright nuggets that still single out Bradford among other post-industrial Northern cities: its thriving annual arts festival, its inventiveness in marketing its combination of Bronte moors, curries and Hockney gallery to tourists, its range of expertise—from the university's world-renowned Peace Studies department to the royal infirmary's groundbreaking research into burns plastic surgery (Lucy Ward, *The Guardian,* 23 July 2001).

The response to the EDL provided the grounds for a different 'narrative', because of a real collective achievement. But would it be grasped by Bradfordians in the outlying hills and valleys as well as the inner city? Greater self confidence in the District's future could encourage innovation and investment. Here we reflect on three key areas vital to this future: the economy, social issues around identity and belonging, and the ongoing search for an overarching political practice of inclusion and equality.

## Economic Futures

In 2010, a 'State of the District' summary of evidence was produced for the second phase of the District's Sustainable Community Strategy, simply entitled: Big Plan II: 2011-2014 (Bradford Metropolitan District Council, 2010). Based on a commissioned study by Local Futures, the plan painted a realistic picture of the prospects and problems facing Bradford.

It showed that the District's economy is the third largest in Yorkshire and Humberside region, and remains the seventh largest manufacturing centre in Great Britain. The fall in manufacturing jobs described in chapter 5 continued over the decade, and 15,000 jobs were lost between 1998 and 2008, a fall of 35% in manufacturing employment. Nevertheless, Bradford still had a higher proportion of manufacturing jobs than the regional average in 2010. Engineering remained one of the strongest sectors. However, only 4% of manufacturing jobs were in high tech industries. The District remained low-wage and low-skilled, with most (83%) businesses employing 10 or less people. Although Bradford's high levels of self-employment suggests an entrepreneurial culture, the forecast decline in lower-skilled sectors of manufacturing is of concern to a District with a growing population of young people. One in three people of working age in Bradford remained out of work, with female unemployment particularly high. The proportion of working-age residents with high skills (NVQ 4 or above) was below average relative to regional and national levels and the share of lowly-qualified working-age residents (below NVQ 2) was above average by national standards. Almost 18% of Bradford's working age population lacked qualifications compared to 12% for England. The proportion of the working age population qualified to level 2 or higher was still only 63.4% in 2009–10 against a target of 66%. The recession of 2008 and beyond saw a further growth in youth unemployment, with 9,500 young people out of work in April 2010. Black and minority ethnic communities, lone parents, people over 50 and those with disabilities were most likely to be out of work. High levels of inter-generational unemployment blighted deprived areas of the District.

The highest concentrations of unemployment were in the inner city and the outlying estates, such as Holmewood, Buttershaw, Allerton and Windhill. Spatially, economic activity centred on the city area, with new growth areas close to the M606 and M62 and the corridor from Shipley to Bingley and Keighley. Inequalities continued to deepen. Whereas 16% of households in Bradford had an average income of £50,000 or more, 44% had a combined income of less than £20,000 a year. The gap between the most and the least deprived areas in Bradford was the largest in the country in 2010. Two of Bradford District's 30 wards were ranked in the 15% *least* deprived in the country (Wharfedale and Ilkley), while Manningham and Bradford Moor fall within the 5% *most* deprived. Manningham had one of the lowest average household incomes in Yorkshire and the Humber. A total of 35% of households in the ward had incomes of less than £15,000. Bradford was the 32nd most deprived of 354 local authorities according to 2007 Multiple Deprivation Indices. In 2010, 42% of the district's population of 501,700 lived in the 20% most deprived areas in the country. Some 5% (25,085 people) lived in the 1% most deprived. Bradford had the highest infant mortality rate in England in 2010, although it has declined since 1999. Bradford also has the highest number of children living in poverty in

West Yorkshire. Another fracture line was between urban and rural areas. Access to housing, shops and services is poor in parts of the Worth Valley, Queensbury and Tong and even Wharfedale (Big Plan, 2008:16). A groundbreaking research project, Born in Bradford, has been following the lives of around 13,000 Bradford babies over 20 years with the aim of improving the health of Bradford people and others. Its data will provide vital evidence-based insights into poverty in the District and ways of addressing it (http://www.borninbradford.nhs.uk/).

Compared to 2001, this snapshot of the social and economic profile of Bradford in 2010 does not show much progress. And this is just at a time when the District faces large public sector cuts. Educational improvement remained a huge issue in Bradford. Its schools did progress in the course of the decade, with 25 judged 'outstanding' by Ofsted inspectors in 2008. The proportion of young people achieving five or more GCSEs at A*–C level, including English and Maths (41%) increased at a faster rate than nationally and closed the gap somewhat. But still, in academic year 2008 to 2009, this compared to 50% nationally. Progress at the foundational stage of education had been good compared with regional and national figures, but still only 47% of children reached a good level of development at the end of reception year in 2009 compared with 50% in Yorkshire and the Humber and 52% in England overall. The relationship between educational attainment and deprivation remained strong. Segregation along ethnic lines remained high in Bradford schools as evidenced by an Economic and Social Science Research Council study on the ethnic make-up of primary and secondary schools in England between 2002 and 2008 (ESRC, 2011). Education was scheduled to come back under the local authority in 2011 following a 10 year experiment with the private sector provider, Serco.

Education is key to the District's future, given the great asset of its growing population of economically-active young people, unlike the rest of Britain. The broad brush and statistical averages do not convey the nuances of progress in Bradford. Segregation is not necessarily an obstacle to educational achievement, although it presents serious problems in other ways. An influential head teacher told us in 2011 that deprivation is a far more significant factor than ethnicity. The important issue is how to make young people value the difference that education can make to them. Young people from Pakistani backgrounds have some advantages over youngsters from deprived 'white' backgrounds. Pakistani families have tended to stay together, and there is a community as well as family value to education which is sometimes lacking in contexts of family breakdown more common in poor 'white' families. Research on Bradford's traditionally 'white' estates highlighted the struggles of single mothers, the low esteem and intergenerational worklessness that blights lives there (Illingworth, 2008, Milne and Pearce, 2010). The main challenge facing Pakistani children as they enter school is poor English language skills. However, a number of Bradford's secondary schools have transformed aspirations and attainment. In one school, the number of young men of Pakistani heritage going to university has more than doubled since 2001 and GCSE achievement is far ahead of the District average. Pakistani young girls get even better results than young males in the school. The head teacher we interviewed puts the achievements of his own school down to an increase in resources in real terms, enabling the school to focus on the particular needs of young people growing up in serious poverty. 'Coherence' is vital, he told us, in the way the school works with its young people. Teachers may do fantastic things in the classroom, but this cannot compensate for poor aspirations and motivation. He and his staff 'tune in' to their pupils, get to know why some are achieving less than others and offer quality support and mentoring. In a school of 90% Pakistani heritage, and most of those of Mirpuri background, the level of attainment has been transformed. Here, the importance of Islam is recognised as integral to the students' learning, and although the school staff does not mirror its pupil intake, the role of faith and understanding all faiths and worldviews is part of school life. Students are taken on trips to widen horizons and link them with other schools. When asked about responses in the school to the EDL protest, he did not pick up tensions but a sense of the pupils wanting to be 'part of a community that could handle it'.

In 2011, the much delayed City Park in the heart of Bradford, with its mirror pool to reflect the Grade 1-listed City Hall, was scheduled for completion in the year, a centre-piece for the District's regeneration and critical to the drive to bring in investment and jobs and revitalise the city centre. Post-EDL, the private sector displayed new confidence in the District, and launched 'Positive Bradford' to shine a lens on its achievements and potential. A government award in 2006 had channelled resources to the 3% most deprived communities in the District. The programme, known as Streets Ahead, involved residents as well as councillors and all the voluntary and council services, in an innovative cooperative endeavour. It improved residents' well-being in those areas and showed the effectiveness of more equitable ways of delivering services (Bradford Metropolitan District Council, 2010:55).

At the macro-policy level, there was honest acknowledgement by one senior council officer of 'inherent weaknesses in this city because of bad planning and poor decisions . . . going back over decades . . . it was almost systemic'. He included here 'systemic failure in education . . . over twenty years which has led to a . . . lower skilled workforce than we should have had'. A very male leadership and council culture was beginning—just—to recognise the importance of its female population: 'I think the empowerment of women in Bradford will fundamentally change the way we [and] the outside world views this city . . . and the biggest opportunity for Bradford is to create the mechanisms that will allow women to empower themselves', one senior council officer suggested. A new openness was accompanied by fresh energy and vision based on an understanding of global as well as national and local dynamics. The vision was strengthened greatly by the huge collective effort to overcome the legacy of 2001. A similar unity of purpose was required to shape the District's economic future.

## 'A Cosmopolitan City'?

> Bradford hasn't been able to create a cosmopolitan vision of itself . . . even though, when you look at the stats and figures, we should be a cosmopolitan city. You know, we've got over 68 different languages spoken in the area, in the city. There's a lot more diversity. It's increasing in all hosts of way. And yet, we are still not able to fully embrace that somehow (Muslim Council Officer, 2011).

Bradford became even more diverse in the course of the decade under discussion. It had a net gain of 3,900 people through international migration between 1998 and 2008—and a net loss of 2,600 people through migration within the UK (Bradford Metropolitan District, 2010:21). There were an estimated 1,200 new migrants from Africa by 2006, amongst them refugees and asylum seekers, many of them well educated but unable to find good jobs (Mellor and Kingston, 2006). Another wave of migrants came to the District from Poland, Slovakia and the Czech Republic as new countries joined the European Union. Around 1,000 Filipinos also came to Bradford to work in local hospitals and the care sector (ibid). These newcomers settled in the inner-city areas of Bradford with its cheap housing and history of migrant populations. Bradford Vision's Communities of Interest Working Group identified 29 'communities of interest' in the District in 2006, including these new migrants as well as established Asian, African-Caribbean and Eastern and Central European groups. However, it also included groups which cross-cut all ethnicities and backgrounds to reflect needs rather than identity based divisions, such as adults with disabilities, children vulnerable to abuse, the deaf community, homeless people,

people with mental health issues and older people. Over a quarter of the projected population growth in the District to 2031 would be older people, a group of people with special needs in all communities (Bradford Metropolitan District, 2010:20).

The same population projection showed that another quarter of growth would be amongst children and young people. This bucked the national trend. This is accounted for by a higher than national average birth rate. People will move out of inner-city wards, but natural growth will mean that the population of inner-city areas will grow. This young, economically active population will be Bradford's great asset as it grows its economy. It will be mostly, though not entirely, Pakistani Asian.

Bradford had the third largest proportion of black and minority ethnic people outside of London boroughs and just behind Manchester and Birmingham in 2010. Its non-white residents accounted for 25.89% of the population in 2010, with the proportion of people of Asian heritage at 21.09%. Population projections to 2031 show that the Asian population will be the largest growing population, and will account for more than half the population by then. Bradford's challenge is to build an inclusive and equitable cosmopolitanism.

Through the decade, the plight of poverty amongst Bradford's white communities as well as those of south Asian heritage gained greater recognition. Studies on the District's traditionally 'white' estates show that prejudice against others often reflects a sense of being subjected to prejudice themselves (Milne and Pearce, 2010). Estate residents invented the term 'estatism' to capture the way they feel society looks down on them. In the meantime, the Muslim community has gained in esteem and confidence. Despite the picture of poverty and deprivation in Bradford's inner-city mostly Asian areas, there are many more textures to the picture than can be seen from a distance.

Islam, for some, has become a badge of pride, which has nothing to do with religious extremism and much more to do with the search for self worth. A new politics around Muslim identity has borrowed from anti-racism and feminism and put religious identity at the heart of struggles for equality for some young Muslims (Modood, 2005). New and articulate voices emerged in Bradford's Muslim community in the decade after the riots, particularly as educational attainment improved and a cohort of professional and successful young Muslims reached maturity. A number have published novels and histories of their experiences in Bradford (Alam, 2002, Mehmood, 2003, Malik, 2010). Many have entered the debate on identity and misrepresentation, such as Alam's powerful interviews with Pakistani young men (Alam, 2008). 'A few years ago' argued Alam in an interview in 2002 (http://www.route-online.com/read/m-y-alam-talks-about-kilo.html/7):

> . . . it was difficult for some white people to even walk up Oak Lane [in Manningham], which is the beginning of a largely Pakistani area . . . the people who were doing the barring of these permeable boundaries were of a minority group: young, Pakistani men. But that's not all, some of these idiots were just that: idiots who messed anybody around—young, old, black, white, Asian, male, female. That kind of thing leads me to suggest race or ethnicity was one factor, not the be all and end all—it wasn't that young Pakistani men hated white people—they hated everyone.

The difference in 2011, is that young Pakistani men are beginning to find a voice, gain self esteem and engage more confidently with the wider world. Many are still left behind, and therein lies danger. However, the new-found esteem of some is arguably the best way of influencing the expectations and aspirations of others. Some have become activists for change within their own communities. Many young Muslims challenge the traditional religious leadership of the mosques. In a conversation with us in 2011, one questioned whether Islam needs to fear a loss of identity and integrity. Returning to the principles of Islam is compatible with a more cosmopolitan world outlook, he argued. Others have worked hard to engage with issues of extremism while simultaneously challenging the exclusive focus on Islam. One Girlington young Muslim conducted his own intensive research in 2011 on the multiple and varied faces of extremism.

The Bradford Muslim Women's Council was set up in 2011 and together with the Islamic Society of Britain organised the first national residential conference on 'Muslim women critically thinking the past, present and future' in May. In 2004 Bradford elected its first female British Pakistani councillor, Naveeda Ikram, and had four Asian women councillors by 2011, still an under-representation, but evidence of progress. In 2011, Naveeda became the first Muslim woman Lord Mayor for Bradford. The Council of Mosques's Community Engagement strategy (Ahmed and Reid, 2009) made 'an official commitment to enhancing and empowering women in their roles in accordance with Islamic law and teaching' and argued that 'Each Masjid [Friday mosque] needs safe spaces for women to meet, share and take forward their needs and issues' (ibid:17). The same document called for an acknowledgement of the diversity within Islam and affirmed 'the importance of building ever stronger relationships with non-Muslims and non-Muslim organisations in order to seek the common good in Bradford' (ibid:18). A more confident community has begun to embrace change. The first mosque in Bradford was established in June 1958 in an inner-city terraced house. The District now has 85 mosques and madrasas (Muslim faith schools). The community is established and rooted.

A number of Bradford figures have challenged the Muslim community on social issues of forced marriage, under-age sex and beating children in madrasas as well as the health implications of cousin marriages. Ann Cryer, former Keighley MP, risked the wrath of elders in her inner-city electorate to raise these issues. The media hones in on such problems and creates an image of the Muslim community which is real but very partial. The problems are more difficult to address when the community feels under attack. Others have played an important role in enhancing understanding of Islam and the Muslim community. Philip Lewis, in particular, has emphasised religious literacy and encouraged non-Muslims to understand the varied expressions of Islam in Bradford. He has challenged popular stereotypes of an unchanging religion that overrides all other identities. Muslims share most identities with fellow citizens (Lewis, 2007:xiii). Many young Muslims tell us they do not wish to be forever defined only by their religion, however important religion is to them. While some Muslim women want to wear the hijab, others prefer Western dress.

Bradfordians in general still have to be persuaded that better understanding of each other has benefits for everyone. This cannot await the economic take-off which will undoubtedly accelerate interaction. People need opportunities to learn from and about each other without being accused of racism, Islamophobia or refusal to integrate. In turn, people need to be ready to acknowledge, at least, what they do not know about each other. A Muslim council employee feels that appearance still matters in the workplace, and many colleagues are unaware of why they see some as more competent than others. As we argued before, racism needs robust intervention but culture a light touch. Some argue that the shift to a politics centred on identity, culture and religion has not been helpful, either in confronting racism and inequality or to cultural understanding. Cultures and beliefs are not unchanging, nor are religious institutions—they are creatively adapted to new generations and contexts. Culture can also continue to play its equally important role of conserving what is valuable to people and providing safety nets during harsh times. The complex debate on multiculturalism and community cohesion—even Bradford's local variant of 'shared futures' which emerged in 2007—remains unresolved at a national level. There are dangers in 2011 that a new national discourse on 'integration' might shake the fragile progress at the local level in Bradford, as its different communities edge tentatively forward together.

Bradford has a strong history of activism and community organising as we saw in chapter 6. The State of the District report recorded 1,264 voluntary groups by ward in 2010 (Bradford Metropolitan District Council, 2010:32), while there were an estimated total of over 3,000 voluntary and community organisations as of 2006, providing advice, education, training, care, counselling and facilitating networks across communities and cultures (Mellor and Kingston, 2006:92). Umbrella organisations such as Keighley Voluntary Services (KVS) and Bradford and District Community Empowerment Network (C-Net) have played an important role in connecting these many efforts and building bridges between decision makers and community activists. Bradford Vision, the Local Strategic Partnership, when independent from the council, greatly emphasised participation at the grass roots through Neighbourhood Action Planning and experiments with Participatory Budgeting (Pearce, 2010). Bradford Partnership, as it is now known, continues to bring key actors in the District around the table with the council to build coherent and consistent approaches. But that focus on connections deep into the communities of the District and upwards to decision makers, needs strengthening to promote the communication, collaborations and community mobilisations which were so effective when the EDL came to Bradford. Activists and communities will differ in their goals, but their autonomy encourages participation and the council's task is to manage, not control, that energy. Not everyone wishes to participate, whilst communal politics based on caste and clan continue to limit the extent of participation in an otherwise participant Pakistani community. Amongst the poor 'white' community, the disconnect from formal politics is greater, but the aspiration to participate in shaping their future remains strong. There are many talents to be tapped in Bradford.

Deepening democracy and participation in Bradford is a key to tapping these and building a cosmopolitan city which overcomes particularism, based on communal or nationalist identities. Looking outwards towards the world paid off handsomely for the District in its days of industrial glory. However, real prosperity was confined to the few who became millionaires. The next phase of Bradford's global history must be inclusive and equitable. Those presently without power and voice within all communities must gain it so that they can see the worth of playing a role in shaping the District's future. Gaining a voice must include listening to the voices of others and acknowledging the complex trade-offs in decision making, especially when so many needs remain unmet across the District.

*Saturday Night and Sunday Morning*

# Bradford Journey

This book has taken us on a journey. We started out with the voices of participants in the events on Saturday night and Sunday morning of 7 and 8 July 2001. We asked the rioters to tell us why they think they rioted, the police to tell us how they endured the unending violence, and 'peacemakers' to describe their efforts to halt the mayhem. We travelled back in time to ask, 'Why Bradford?' and why these particular young men rioted. We contemplated the collective failure to prevent social tensions in the District—caused by de-industrialisation, deprivation and Far Right provocation—from erupting into violence. We journeyed forward to look at what happened after the riot, both to the rioters and to Bradford District. Our final destination was the collective effort in 2010 to successfully avoid another riot when the EDL came to Bradford, intent on provoking one.

The rioters of 2001, it must be recalled, lacked the means to express their frustrations and the place to express them. They did not feel represented by political or community leaders and they felt oppressed by the police. It is now clear that riots do not erupt spontaneously from 'mindless mobs'. They are rooted in a deep sense of injustice, in contexts where historic inequalities render futures insecure. In Bradford in 2001 their violent expression came both from Pakistani Muslim youth and from white youth on deprived estates. Both faced diminished prospects through the collapse of Bradford's economy. The violence of Asian youth was embedded for most in an endeavour to protect families and communities from racist attack, even though this was expressed through the bravado, destructiveness and heartlessness of young men, themselves marginalised in their communities. A distorted sense of even greater marginalisation was expressed in Ravenscliffe through racist projection onto those same Asians, seen as getting more than they deserved. Listening to those behind both disturbances it is possible to detect underlying grievances, though both groups lacked the models for political organisation. Such models (represented by political parties, trade unions and organised protest groups) have themselves been undermined by the decline of working class solidarities in Bradford. Their diminished legitimacy and strength meant that they failed to include new populations of young people in struggles to resist racism, inequality and oppression in all its forms. By 2010 they had wrested back some of their legitimacy and were even making efforts to bridge ethnic divides.

In the decade since the riots, collective effort has opened up a more inclusive role for young men and it is notable that Bradford

Conclusion: Bradford Journey

has not generated terrorist cells or homegrown suicide bombers and that it found a peaceful way of objecting to the war in Iraq. Those young people—and they now include more women—who have found a voice are now active in the District preventing later generations from responding to anger through violence and destruction and challenging political leaders to listen. Change can happen. This is one of the key lessons of the Bradford riot and through listening to the rioters over the decade we can learn it. The police definitely learnt lessons from 2001 and they put these very successfully into effect in 2010. A large part of that success is to be put down to their acknowledging the fears of Far Right incursions in a multi-ethnic urban setting and by including young people and a resurgent civil society in their planning. This is not to say that the strategy which averted another riot in 2010 would necessarily work in future. There are still many difficult issues around policing protest. Bradford still needs to strengthen and sustain the connections forced against the EDL in 2010 and turn them into a collective effort to build a cosmopolitan and equitable city.

## Bradford Narratives

Many writers and journalists have been attracted to Bradford. Hanif Kureishi visited in 1986. He felt it:

> was a place I had to see for myself, because it seemed that so many important issues, of race, culture, nationalism, and education, were evident in an extremely concentrated way . . . Bradford seemed to be a microcosm of a larger British society that was struggling to find a sense of itself, even as it was undergoing radical change (Kureishi, 1986:151).

Bradfordians find it hard to be the goldfish bowl for so much well-intentioned and some not so well-intentioned media and literary interest. Yet, our book does confirm Kureishi's hunch. While the South of England is today the heartland of the country's economic success, the opposite was once true. Bradford challenges the South to recognise the volatility generated by global markets and which have hit the north of England so hard. Understanding the process by which migrant workers become citizens is relevant to many other towns and cities of Britain and Northern Ireland. Building a sense of belonging with, rather than against, new neighbours is vital to future peace and prosperity.

In 1933, Bradford-born writer, J.B. Priestley, famously travelled across England, and his book, *English Journey* was published a year later. On that journey, he identified three Englands: The first, the 'Old England' of cathedrals, manor houses and quaint highways and byways. The second, that of the Midlands and the North, 19th century industrial England of coal, iron, steel, cotton, wool, railways, back-to-back houses, clogs, fish and chip shops and public houses with 'red blinds'. This England has 'not been added to and has no new life poured into it', he wrote. Thirdly he identifies a post-First World War England (whose birthplace was really America) of by-pass roads, filling stations and factories that look like exhibition buildings, bungalows with tiny garages, Woolworths, and everything given away for cigarette coupons. It is fitting that a son of Bradford should shine a light on the country as a whole. Priestley embraced social justice, rejected imperialism and the greed of industrialists and advocated a welcome to foreigners.

Other writers now come to Bradford to shine a light on England. Two writers, both Muslim and Asian, saw somewhat different Bradfords. Zaiba Malik had left what she calls 'Bradistan' in 1989, stifled by the 'community' she grew up in, though returning often to visit her family. In 2010, this is the Bradford she saw:

> Leaving the city's bus station on my way to Umejee's house, I pass the solid bronze statue of J.B. Priestley, who once said that 'the England admired throughout the world is the England that keeps open house', and 'History has shown that the countries that have opened their doors have gained'. And I wonder what he would think of this place now, where just under 20 per cent of the population is Pakistani . . . For years Bradford has been seen as a city of discord, a city of racial and religious tension. Various reports have pointed to long-standing problems of 'racial self-segregation and cultural lives' and suggested that the 'complete separation of communities will lead to the growth of fear and conflict'. Too late. We've had segregation in this city for as long as I can remember . . . I have no doubt that there are many Pakistani families in Bradford who do not live near, go to school with, work with or even ever speak to white people. And of course the reverse is also true. Still Bradistan thrives (Malik, 2010:6).

Luton-born writer, Sarfraz Manzoor, on the other hand, found a Bradford sprouting the seeds of synthesis, of new encounters and relationships amongst the young of the city:

> I began my journey standing by the statue of J.B. Priestley wondering what he would have made of his city and country. Coming to Bradford it is easy to be blinded by the changes and to believe that England today is an utterly different country than in Priestley's day. But Englishness is more resilient than we suspect, changing out of all recognition and yet remaining the same. As I walked to the train station I saw a young black girl with her arms around a white boy. Minutes later I saw an Asian girl, in a short summer skirt and body-hugging T-shirt, holding hands with her white boyfriend. There is [Priestley] . . . standing in the centre of Bradford guarding the past, as all around him the young are busy writing the future (Sarfraz Manzoor, *The Observer*, 5 July 2009).

In 2009, Martin Wainwright reported in *The Guardian*, that Bradford had been declared:

> . . . one of the three most 'English' places in England for patriots to spend St George's Day. The Yorkshire manufacturing, tourism and university centre comes second only to the coastal town of Scarborough and the Cornish district of Penwith for traditional English activities per head of population. Curries may win it more headlines, but Bradford has one of the country's highest ratios of fish and chip shops to people, and an astonishing number of cricket clubs and leagues. It also scores exceptionally well for Morris dancing troupes, tea rooms and . . . centres for children and families in the district's outlying areas around the Bronte village of Haworth and Ilkley Moor (23 April 2009).

Bradford is many places depending on where you look from and where you look to. Some continue to look back. This is true of all communities. A letter in the *T&A* of 12 December 2008 looked back to a Bradford of the 1980s:

> Recently, a friend loaned me a copy of the *Telegraph & Argus* dated June 3, 1983. What a difference in just 25 years. Local shops and stores regularly carried adverts: Woods Music Shop, Negas, YEB, Sunwin House had three in this edition while Rackhams—affectionately still known as Brown and Muffs, had two. Hillards, a local supermarket group, swallowed up by Tesco, has two full page spreads announcing the opening of a new store in Ilkley . . . All these shops have now gone, part of the memory.

It is completely human to hang on to memories. But our conclusion is about journeys, change and the wider world. We need sensitivity to the impacts. We need participation in managing it. We need to ensure we are all aboard. Now is the time to move on from the 2001 riot, embrace the success in averting a second one in 2010 and use the learning to inform the on-going national debate on our multi-ethnic society.

# REFERENCES

Ackroyd, C., Grant, Pl., Kersaw, J. and Kotter, A. *Building Bridges—Making Links: Bradford's Linking School's Project*, 2001-2004 www.schoolslinkingnetwork.org.uk/pdf/ACKROY downloaded 22 April 2011

Ahmed, I. (1997), The Quest for Racial Justice on Bradford, in Rank. C. (ed.), *City of Peace: Bradford's Story,* Bradford: Bradford Libraries, pp. 85-94

Ahmed, I. and Reid, H. (2009), *A Call for Engagement: Report of the Masjid Engagement Project,* Bradford: Bradford Council for Mosques

Alam, M.Y. (2008), *Made in Bradford,* Pontefract: Route

Alam, M.Y. (2002), *Kilo,* Glasshoughton: Route

Allen, C. (2003), *Fair Justice: The Bradford Disturbances, The Sentencing and the Impact,* London:Forum Against Islamophobia and Racism: FAIR

Baumann, Z. (1999), *Culture as Praxis, London*: Sage Publications

Biggs, M. and Knauss, S. (2011), Explaining Membership in the British National Party: A Multilevel Analysis of Contact and Threat, European Sociological Review, 3 May 2011, www.esr.oxfordjournals.org. downloaded 5 May 2011

Bradford and District Future (1998), a Strategy for Sustainable Economic Development, Local Futures Group

Bradford Antiquary (1986), 'All Change' Bradford's Through Railway Schemes available from www.Bradfordhistorical.org.uk/antiquary/third/vol02/allchange.html downloaded 5 May 2010

Bradford District Community Strategy (2002), *One Landscape Many Views,* Bradford: Bradford Metropolitan District Council, October

Bradford Metropolitan District Council (2010), *The State of the District: Bradford District's Intelligence and Evidence Base*, Version 1, 17 September, http://www.bradford.gov.uk/bmdc/BDP/Key+Documents downloaded 15 May 2011

Bradford Metropolitan District Council (2008), *The Big Plan (Sustainable Community Strategy) 2008-2011* http://www.bradford.gov.uk/bmdc/BDP/the_big_plan/Big+Plan+I downloaded 15 May 2011

Bradford Metropolitan Faith in the City Forum (1995), *Powerful Whispers. The Report of the Bradford Urban Hearings*, mimeo

Bradford Vision (2002), *Bradford District Outline Community Cohesion Plan,* Bradford: Bradford Metropolitan District Council, August

Buhler, U. and Pearce J. (2002), *Bradford Distict-Wide Forum: Towards a Diversity Exchange. Beyond the Soundbites: Report of the Outcomes of the Forum and Suggestions for Further Discussion*, mimeo

Burlet, S. and Reid, H. (1998), *A Gendered Uprising: Political Representation and Minority Ethnic Communities, Ethnic and Racial Studies,* Vol. 21, No. 2 1 March, pp. 270-287

Cantle (2001), *Community Cohesion: A Report of the Independent Review Team,* London: Home Office

Carling, A. (2008), 'The Curious Case of the Mis-claimed Myth Claims:Ethnic Segregation, Polarisation and the Future of Bradford', *Urban Studies,* Vol. 45, No. 3, pp. 553-589

Carling, A. Davies, D., Fernandes-Bakshi, A. (2004), *The Response of the Criminal Justice System to the Bradford Disturbances of July 2001, Bradford*: Joseph Rowntree Charitable Trust

Clarke, T. (2002), *Report of the Burnley Task Force,* Burnley: Burnley Task Force

Cocker, S. (2005), Re-integrating the Bradford rioters: Lessons for NOMS and the future of resettlement, *Probation Journal,* Vol. 52, pp. 259-276

Copley, N. (2010), *Challenging Our Country and Our Values of Social Inclusion, Fairness and Equality* Faith Matters www.faith-matters.org downloaded 5 May 2011

Cumming, L. (2006), *Programme for a Peaceful City: Systematising an Experience 2001-2006,* ICPS Working Paper 6, mimeo

Denham, J. (2002), *Building Cohesive Communities: A Report of the Ministerial Group on Public Order and Community Cohesion,* London: The Home Office

Duckett, B. and Waddington-Feather, J. (2005), *Bradford: History and Guide,* Stroud, Gloucestershire: Tempus Publishing

ESRC (2011), http://www.measuringdiversity.org.uk/ downloaded 15 May 2011

Faqir, Z. (2006), *Ethnicity, Segregation and the Planning System in Bradford District,* Unpublished Dissertation, Department of Geography & Environmental Sciences; University of Bradford

Fieldhouse, J. (1972, third edition 1978), *Bradford,* Bradford: Watmoughs Financial Print

Firth, G. (1997), *A History of Bradford,* Chichester: Phillimore & Co.

Finney, N. and Simpson, L. (2009), *Sleepwalking to Segregation? Challenging Myths about Race and Migration,* Bristol: Policy Press

Ford, R. (2010), 'Who might vote for the BNP?', in Eatwell, R. and Goodwin, M., *The New Extremism in 21st Century Britain,* London: Routledge, pp. 145-168

Greenhalf, J. (2003), *It's a Mean Old Scene,* Bradford: Redbeck Press

Grogan, T. (1989), *The Pickles Papers* 1in12 Publications http://www.1in12.com/publications/library/pickles/pickles.htm downloaded 24 March 2011

ICoCo (2011), *Far Right Electoral and Other Activity: The Challenge for Community Cohesion Institute of Community Cohesion* http://www.cohesioninstitute.org.uk/Resources/Publications downloaded 15 May 2011

Jowitt, J.A. (1997), 'Bradford and Peace 1800-1918', in Rank, C. (Ed.), op.cit., pp. 31-43

Honeyford, R. (2006), Education and Race: An Alternative View. Reprinted *The Telegraph* http://www.telegraph.co.uk/culture/3654888/Education-and-Race-an-Alternative-View.html downloaded 24 March 2011

Illingworth, H. (2008), *Findings from the Holmewood Development Project 2007-2008,* York: Joseph Rowntree Foundation

James, D. (1990), *Bradford,* Halifax: Ryburn Publishing

Kureishi, H. (1986), 'Bradford', in *In Trouble Again,* Granta 20, Winter 1986 pp. 147-170

Lewis, P. (1994), *Islamic Britain: Religion, Politics and Identity among British Muslims,* London: I.B.Tauris

Lewis, P. (2007), *Young, British and Muslim,* London: Continuum

Lowles, N. and Painter, A. (2011), *Fear and Hope: The New Politics of Identity*, London: Searchlight Educational Trust

Macey, M. (1999), 'Class, Gender and Religious Influences on Changing Patterns of Pakistani Muslim Male Violence in Bradford', *Ethnic and Racial Studies*, Vol. 22

Mahoney, G. (2001), Race Relations in Bradford www.bradford2020.com/pride/docs/Section1.doc) downloaded 24 March 2011

Malik, Z. (2010), *We Are a Muslim Please,* London: Heinemann

Malik, Z. (2010), *Bradistan,* Granta, 2 November, http//www.granta.com/Onlinke-Only/Bradistan downloaded 15 May 2010

Manawar, Jan-Khan (2003), 'The Right to Riot?', *Community Development Journal,* Vol. 38, No. 1, pp. 32-42

Mehmood, T. (2003), *While There is Light,* Manchester: Comma Press

Mellor, P. and Kingston, S. (2006), *The Silent Majority: Listening to Communities of Interest,* Bradford: Bradford Vision

Meridienpure (2005), *Bradford Vision Evaluation of Community Cohesion Projects, Final Draft Report,* mimeo

Milne, E. and Pearce, J. (2010), *Participation and Community on Bradford's Traditionally 'White' Estates,* York: Joseph Rowntree Foundation

Modood, T. (2005), 'The Emergence of Muslim Identity Politics', in Bunting, M., *Islam, Race and Being British,* London: Guardian and Barrow Cadbury rust, pp. 19-23

Ouseley, H. (2001), *Community Pride not Prejudice,* Bradford: Bradford Vision

Pearce J. (ed.) (2010), *Participation and Democracy in the 21st Century City*, London: Palgrave Macmillan

Philips, D., Butt, F. and Davis, C. (2002), 'The Racialisation of Space in Bradford', *The Regional Review,* July 9-9-10

Philips, D. (1998), 'Black Minority Ethnic Concentration, Segregation and Dispersal', in *Britain Urban Studies*, Vol. 35, No. 10, pp. 1681-1702

Philips, D. (2006), 'Parallel Lives? Challenging Discourses of British Muslim Self-Segregation Environment and Planning', *Society and Space*, Vol. 24, pp. 25-40

Priestley, J.B. (1977, first published 1934), *English Journey,* Harmondworth: Penguin Books

Rank, C. (ed.) (1997), *City of Peace: Bradford's Story,* Bradford: Bradford Libraries

Ratcliffe, P. (1996), *'Race' and Housing in Bradford*, Bradford: Bradford Housing Forum The Bradford Congress

Ratcliffe, P. (2001), with Harrison, M., Hogg, R., Line, B., Phillips, D. and Tomlins, R., *Breaking Down the Barriers: Improved Asian Access to Social Rented Housing*, Coventry: Chartered Institute of Housing

Ramamurthy, A. (2000), *Kala Tara: A History of the Asian Youth Movements in Britain*, www.tandana,org downloaded March 2011

Raw, A. (2005), *Education in Bradford: Schools Linking Project 2005–06 Full Final Evaluation Report* (http://www.schoolslinkingnetwork.org.uk/PDF/Bradford%20Schools%20Linking%20Evaluation%202005-06.pdf dowloaded 22 April 2011

Ritchie, D. (2001), *Oldham Independent Review,* Oldham: Oldham Council

Robinson, G. (2004), 'Struggles against fascism in Bradford', unpublished talk given to Forum on Fascism conference, Programme for a Peaceful City, University of Bradford, February

Robinson, G. (2003), Bradford Rioters Research, private correspondence with research team, 8 July

Rhodes, D. (1997), 'Arts and Peace: The Bradford Festival', in Rank, C. (ed.), *City of Peace, Bradford's Story,* Bradford: Bradford Libraries, pp. 123-132

Samad, Y. (1992), 'Book Burning and Race Relations: Political Mobilisation of Bradford Muslims', *New Community,* Vol. 18, No. 4 July, pp. 507-520

Simpson, S. (1997), 'Demography and Ethnicity: Case Studies from Bradford', *New Community,* Vol. 23, No. 1 January, pp. 89-107

Simpson, L. (2003), 'Statistics of Racial Segregation: Measures, Evidence and Policy', *Urban Studies,* Vol. 41, No. 3, pp. 661-81

Simpson, L., Husband, C., Alam, Y. (2009), 'Comment: Recognising Complexity, Challenging Pessimism: The Case of Bradford's Urban Dynamics', *Urban Studies*, Vol. 46, pp. 1995-2001

Singh, Ramindar (2002), 'Race Relations Policies of the Bradford Metropolitan District Council', Notes of the presentation made at the Inaugural Conference of the Centre for Applied South Asian Studies, Manchester University, 18 March, mimeo

Taj, M. (1996), *A 'Can Do' City*, Supplementary Observations Comments and Recommendations to the Bradford Commission Report Bradford: Bradford Congress

Thomson, B. (1997), 'The Pioneering Work of the Interfaith Education Centre', in Rank, C. (ed.), *City of Peace, Bradford's Story,* Bradford: Bradford Libraries, pp. 105-110